MW00809746

Bridging the High School–College Gap

Bridging the
High School–College Gap

The Role of
Concurrent Enrollment Programs

Edited by
Gerald S. Edmonds and Tiffany M. Squires

Syracuse University Press

Materials contained in this volume, where noted, are reprinted with the permission of individual copyright holders. All rights reserved. No part of this book may be used or reproduced in any manner whatsoever without the written permission of the publisher. For information, contact Syracuse University Project Advance, 400 Ostrom Ave., Syracuse, NY 13244-3250.

Copyright © 2016 by Syracuse University Project Advance ®
Syracuse University Project Advance, 400 Ostrom Avenue, Syracuse, NY 13244-3520

All Rights Reserved

First Edition 2016
16 17 18 19 20 21   6 5 4 3 2 1

Published by:
Syracuse University Press, 621 Skytop Road, Suite 110, Syracuse, NY 13244-5290

∞ The paper used in this publication meets the minimum requirements of the American National Standard for Information Sciences—Permanence of Paper for Printed Library Materials, ANSI Z39.48-1992.

For a listing of books published and distributed by Syracuse University Press, visit www.SyracuseUniversityPress.syr.edu.

ISBN: 978-0-8156-3451-5 (cloth)   978-0-8156-3432-4 (paperback)
978-0-8156-5354-7 (e-book)

Library of Congress Cataloging-in-Publication Data
Names: Edmonds, Gerald S., editor. | Squires, Tiffany M., editor.
Title: Bridging the high school–college gap : the role of concurrent enrollment programs / edited by Gerald S. Edmonds and Tiffany M. Squires.
Description: Syracuse, NY : Syracuse University Press, [2016] | Includes bibliographical references and index.
Identifiers: LCCN 2016011787| ISBN 9780815634515 (cloth : alk. paper) | ISBN 9780815634324 (pbk. : alk. paper) | ISBN 9780815653547 (e-book)
Subjects: LCSH: Dual enrollment—United States. | High school students—Education (Higher)—United States.
Classification: LCC LC146.54 .B75 2016 | DDC 373.12/19–dc23 LC record available at https://lccn.loc.gov/2016011787

Manufactured in the United States of America

Contents

Figures, Tables, and Appendixes

Figures

Tables

Appendixes

Acknowledgments

The editors acknowledge Dr. Rob S. Pusch, whose significant technical and intellectual contributions made this manuscript possible. We sincerely thank Rob for his time and assistance.

Special appreciation goes to William R. Newell and Dr. Christina Parish, who reviewed information from the manuscript, provided thoughts and feedback, and helped to develop and improve our ideas.

We gratefully acknowledge permission to reprint from the National Association of Concurrent Enrollment Partnerships and the *Electronic Journal of Inclusive Education.*

We would also like to thank Sari Signorelli and Martin Walls for their review and edits.

Additionally, we appreciate the outside reviewers who provided suggestions and comments on the chapters.

Finally, we wish to thank the numerous faculty, teachers, and staff across the country who support concurrent enrollment programs.

PART ONE | **Definitions and Foundation**

1

Defining Concurrent Enrollment

GERALD S. EDMONDS

In 1972, six high school districts in the Syracuse, New York, area approached Syracuse University seeking help in challenging high school seniors who had met most of their high school graduation requirements (Diamond and Holloway 1975). The school districts expressed concern that some high school seniors had completed "nearly all the basic requirements for graduation before their senior year; and as a result, feel [*sic*] bored and frustrated because they see themselves as mostly 'marking time' during most of the senior year" (Diamond and Holloway 1975, 2). The high schools were uncertain of the best alternatives to keep students engaged and to prepare them for the transition from high school to college.

Syracuse University examined four alternative designs that were in place to offer high school students the opportunity to enroll in advance course options: (1) Advanced Placement programs, (2) college courses taught within the school by college faculty, (3) split-day programs, and (4) early graduation. Each of these programs had limitations that in some cases outweighed the benefits the programs offered:

1. *Advanced Placement*. Student assessments relied on a single examination.

2. *College courses taught within the school by college faculty*. A limited number of faculty were able and/or willing to teach in a high school. Potential union problems between high school teacher unions and college faculty unions could affect the course offerings.

3. *Split-day programs*. These programs, in which high school students spent a portion of their day on the high school campus and a portion of

their day on the college or university campus, faced limitations related to tuition, scheduling, and geography (e.g., rural high schools that are not proximate to the college).

4. *Early graduation*. While some students were academically ready to begin college courses, they may not have had the social or psychological maturity for matriculating full time into a college or university. Additionally, the senior year of high school was usually a highly involved experience for students (Diamond and Holloway 1975).

It was from an examination of the alternative programs and their limitations that the idea of Project Advance was born. Project Advance's central tenet was to offer Syracuse University courses as part of the regular high school day, taught by selected and trained high school teachers. The SU courses offered through Project Advance would fit into a high school student's schedule in those instances in which students had exhausted the high school course offerings or had met their subject-specific graduation requirements. In this way, Project Advance offered something new and different from other models of *dual enrollment*, which occur alongside or in addition to a student's typical high school schedule and also involve instruction provided by college level instructors.

In 1972 Project Advance became one of the first programs systematically to offer high school students the opportunity to earn university credit while still in high school. Over time, Project Advance would set the standard for what was to become known as *concurrent enrollment*, or, as noted above, opportunities that allow students to take college-credit bearing courses taught by high school instructors inside their familiar high school environment during the typical high school day (NACEP 2016).

Project Advance has never been a replacement for high school or a vehicle for high school students to simply rack up postsecondary credits before matriculating full-time at college. The core idea has always been to offer high school students the opportunity to begin postsecondary coursework in those subject areas where students had completed high school coursework. As such, Syracuse University offers a *concurrent enrollment program*, Project Advance, which serves as the unit that oversees and operationalizes the university's courses within participating high schools.

Fundamental to the establishment of such a program is the development of the *concurrent enrollment partnership*, or the relationship between the institute of higher education and the school or school district. Since Project Advance's creation in 1972, high school–college partnerships have increased, although an exact number is difficult to determine (see Wilbur and Lambert 1991 for the last known census of high school–college partnerships). In 1999, twenty institutions formed the National Alliance of Concurrent Enrollment Partnerships (NACEP)—sixteen four-year schools and four community colleges. Since NACEP's founding, the organization has grown to represent 322 institutions (NACEP 2016).

As the number of institutions implementing high school–college programs has increased, so has the confusion over the terminology used to describe the programs. Programs are variously described as *dual enrollment, concurrent enrollment, joint enrollment, dual credit, early college high school*, and *advanced placement*.

In this book, Project Advance is used as a basis for comparing these various programs because its consistency of mission and purpose, its long history of research and evaluation, its continuity in administration, and the substantial input it has received from university faculty have prompted other institutions to model their programs on Syracuse University's program. These institutions include Indiana University, University of Pittsburgh, University of Wisconsin–Oshkosh, and University of Minnesota.

Concurrent Enrollment Components

The means of delivering college courses to high school students differ between types of high school–college partnerships, but their main goal is in many respects the same—to allow high school students the opportunity to earn postsecondary credit while still in school. However, there can be key differences in several aspects of these partnerships:

• *Purpose.* Whether to provide juniors and seniors with additional coursework after they have met their high school graduation requirements or to provide any student the opportunity to earn college credits while simultaneously satisfying high school requirements.

• *Student level.* Should the program include seniors, juniors, or any student in any grade level?

• *Teacher selection and training.* What is the duration of the training process? Is there continuing professional development?

• *Oversight.* How vigorous is college/university oversight of courses offered to high school students? Are faculty thoroughly engaged and involved in the program?

The varying terminology used to describe high school–college partnership programs leads to confusion not only among practitioners but also research groups, media outlets, and policy developers. To bring a measure

TABLE 1.1

High School–College Partnership Programs Terminology

Defining Elements	Key Questions
Course Origin	• Is the course a regularly cataloged course of the sponsoring college or university? • Did the course originate at the high school? • Is the sponsoring college awarding college credit for the course?
Instructional Site	• Are the college courses offered to the high school students as part of the regular high school day? • Are the college courses offered to the high school students on the college campus?
High School Students	• Are the students enrolled as nonmatriculated students of the college or university (e.g., not degree seeking)? • Are the students enrolled as degree-seeking students of the sponsoring college?
Instructor	• Is the high school teacher the instructor of record? • Do college faculty offer the courses in the high school?
Credit Use	• Are the credits earned being used to satisfy high school graduation requirements? • Are the credits being earned part of a degree program?
Pre-/Post-graduation Requirements	• Are the college courses offered for both high school and college credit? • Are the college courses offered post–high school/post-graduation? (I.e., have the high school students met their high school graduation requirements in specific disciplines?)

of clarity to the survey of definitions offered by experts in the field, some of the common elements that comprise the definitions of high school–college partnership programs are presented in Table 1.1.

Survey of Existing Definitions

The awarding of credit and whether the college courses are counted as high school credit or toward high school graduation requirements is a defining premise in separating *concurrent enrollment* and *dual enrollment* programs, but these terms have been applied in ways that blur this distinction. For example, Greenberg (1998) stated, "Concurrent enrollment is the term used to describe programs that permit high school students to enroll in college-level courses prior to graduation and to receive credit for their diploma while simultaneously receiving college credit. Such programs sometimes are called joint- or dual-enrollment programs" (7). Greenberg (1989) also labeled the College Board's Advanced Placement (AP) as one of these programs. While AP offers college-level courses, there is a distinction between college-level and college courses. The AP program is a well-established testing program, but a postsecondary institution does not administer it, and therefore courses taught under the AP umbrella are not college courses. The AP does not award college credit—a student's college or university, upon the receipt of his or her AP test scores, administers the awarding of postsecondary credit.

Puyear (1998) noted that the Phoenix Union High School District, Phoenix Think Tank, and the Maricopa County Community College District defined concurrent enrollment as "high school students taking college courses" for ". . . college credit for the course, but not high school credit" (4). Andrews (2001) defined "concurrent enrolled students" as "high school students enrolled in college courses for credit while continuing to be enrolled as high school students" (5).

In concurrent enrollment the sponsoring postsecondary institution only awards the credit, whereas in a dual enrollment program the postsecondary courses also count as high school credit and are used to satisfy (or replace) high school graduation requirements. Syracuse University established its concurrent enrollment high school–college partnership program to serve students who, in a specific discipline, had met their high school graduation requirements or who had exhausted the advance courses the high school had to offer.

While preceding definitions of concurrent enrollment focused on the how and when credit is awarded, the National Alliance of Concurrent Enrollment Partnerships added to the established definitions by including the instructors' role. NACEP noted that "concurrent enrollment partnerships differ from other pre-college credit programs because high school instructors teach the college courses during the normal school day. Such programs provide a direct connection between secondary and postsecondary institutions and an opportunity for collegial collaboration. . . . Concurrent enrollment courses are taught, in the high school, during the regular school day by high school teachers" (NACEP 2011a).

However, NACEP does not identify the type of students who should enroll in the classes or where the college courses should be offered in terms of high school graduation requirements.

Nevertheless, NACEP has defined the parameters of concurrent enrollment further through its accreditation standards (NACEP 2011b), which focus on curriculum, faculty, students, assessment, and program evaluation. NACEP noted that these standards ensure the following conditions are met:

• Concurrent enrollment courses offered in the high school are the same as the courses offered on-campus at the sponsoring college or university.

• Students enrolled in concurrent enrollment courses are held to the same standards of achievement as students in on-campus courses.

• Instructors teaching college or university courses through the concurrent enrollment program meet the academic requirements for faculty and instructors teaching in the sponsoring postsecondary institution. (NACEP 2011b)

In defining high school–college partnerships, Andrews (2001) characterized dual credit students as "secondary school students enrolled in college credit classes who receive both college credit and credit toward meeting secondary school requirements for graduation. Some courses are used to replace required courses for high school graduation and others are used as electives toward the same graduation" (12).

Hughes (2010) made the following distinction between dual *enrollment* and dual *credit*: "In dual enrollment, high school students are permitted to take college courses and, if they pass them, earn college credit. Sometimes, as in the case of dual credit, students earn both high school and college credit for the same course" (1).

"Often dual enrollment and concurrent enrollment are considered together," explained Lerner and Brand (2006), "but there is an important distinction between the two. Dual enrollment describes courses from which students receive both high school and college credit simultaneously. Concurrent enrollment represents college courses for which students only receive college credit and are ineligible for credit from their high school" (7).

Lerner and Brand (2006) then offer this definition of concurrent enrollment in their glossary: "An arrangement that allows high school students to enroll in postsecondary courses, for postsecondary credit, but usually not for high school credit. Generally students are taught by college faculty, either at the college or high school, or through distance education" (149).

In defining dual enrollment for their glossary, Lerner and Brand (2006) cite Karp, Bailey, Hughes, and Fermin's characterization of it as a program that "allows high school students to enroll in college courses and earn college and high school credits simultaneously, thereby exposing them to the academic and social demands of postsecondary education" (150).

Finally, it should be noted that a newcomer high school–college partnership model is the *early college high school* movement, which has been defined as the blending of "high school and college in a rigorous yet supportive program, compressing the time it takes to complete a high school diploma and the first two years of college" (Early College High School Initiative 2011).

Conclusion

Having surveyed existing characterizations of concurrent enrollment programs and distinctions drawn between this type of high school–college partnership and others—and returning to the defining elements presented in Table 1.1—we offer the following definition for the purposes of this book:

• *Course origin.* Concurrent enrollment courses originate in the regular course catalog of the sponsoring college or university. In essence, the same courses are offered to high school students as are offered to matriculated college students.

• *Instructional site.* Concurrent enrollment courses are taught in high schools during regular school hours.

• *High school students.* Students prequalify for concurrent enrollment classes by having passed all prior course requirements and having a satisfactory average grade, usually B or better. Some courses have specific requirements (e.g., calculus).

• *Instructor.* Concurrent enrollment classes are taught by high school teachers who have been trained as adjunct college instructors. Teachers must have the same qualifications and experience expected of adjuncts working on the college or university campus. There is ongoing professional development for teacher-adjuncts.

• *Credit use.* The sponsoring college or university awards credit for a concurrent enrollment course. It is postsecondary credit only. Whether the course is used to satisfy high school requirements is at the discretion of the high school.

• *Pre-/post-graduation requirements.* Concurrent enrollment students have already completed their requirements for high school graduation and are enrolled as part-time, nonmatriculated undergraduates in the sponsoring college or university. The credits they earn can be used to fulfill postsecondary degree requirements.

Within this framework there exists a range of program styles. In this book, we concentrate on concurrent enrollment programs offered by both private and public colleges and universities. The remaining chapters in Part One profile concurrent enrollment programs from three different institutions: Syracuse University, a four-year private research university; the University of Minnesota–Twin Cities, a four-year public institution; and Rio Salado, a two-year community college.

Parts Two, Three, and Four of the book focus on various subject matter related to concurrent enrollment programs. Part Two focuses on concurrent enrollment program components such as professional development and advising. Part Three examines specific state policies related to concurrent enrollment. Part Four presents selected research and evaluation studies. Taken together, these chapters provide insights from various experts in the field of concurrent enrollment pertaining to best practices and necessary elements for building and sustaining such programs that contribute to student success in higher education. As a whole, the book provides research-based evidence of the benefits of high school–college partnerships and serves as a vital tool for all educators considering adopting a concurrent enrollment program.

References

Andrews, Hans A. 2001. *The Dual-Credit Phenomenon! Challenging Secondary School Students Across 50 States*. Stillwater, OK: New Forums Press.

Diamond, Richard M., and Richard E. Holloway. 1975. "Project Advance: An Alternative to High School–College Articulation." In *Our Courses: Your Classroom*, edited by Gerald S. Edmonds and Sari Z. Signorelli, 1–51. Syracuse, NY: Project Advance Press.

Early College High School Initiative. 2011. "Welcome to Early College High School." Accessed Dec. 15. http://www.earlycollege.org.

Greenberg, Arthur R. 1989. *Concurrent Enrollment Programs: College Credit for High School Students*. Bloomington, IN: Phi Delta Kappa Educational Foundation.

Hughes, Katherine L. 2010. "Dual Enrollment: Postsecondary/Secondary Partnerships to Prepare Students." *Journal of College Science Teaching* 39(6): 12–13.

Lerner, Jennifer Brown, and Betsy Brand. 2006. *The College Ladder: Linking Secondary and Postsecondary Education for Success for All Students*. Washington, DC: American Youth Policy Forum.

National Alliance of Concurrent Enrollment Partnerships (NACEP). 2016. "NACEP History." Accessed Feb. 16. http://www.nacep.org/about-nacep/history/.

———. 2011a. "Concurrent Enrollment FAQs." Accessed Dec. 15. http://nacep .org/about/what-is-concurrent-enrollment.

———. 2011b. "Standards." Accessed Dec. 15. http://nacep.org/standards/.

Puyear, Don. 1998. *Concurrent Enrollment of High School Students in Arizona Community Colleges: A Status Report*. Arizona: Arizona State Board of Directors for Community Colleges. ERIC ED423930.

Wilbur, Frank P., and Leo Lambert. 1991. *Linking America's Schools and Colleges: Guide to Partnerships and National Directory*. Washington, DC: American Association for Higher Education.

2

Syracuse University Project Advance

Credit with Credibility

GERALD S. EDMONDS

Enrolling more than twenty thousand main campus students annually, Syracuse University (SU) was founded in 1870 as an institution that transcends traditional education boundaries through a combination of innovative thinking, daring choices, and entrepreneurial attitude. Building on that foundation, SU continues to create opportunities for students and faculty to push limits, build pathways, and make connections that lead to new discoveries and transformational change. This made for a natural environment in which to create Syracuse University Project Advance (SUPA).

In 1972, six Central New York high schools approached SU about developing a program to offer college courses to qualified high school seniors. Project Advance began as an attempt to address "senioritis," the tendency for seniors who have completed their graduation requirements to relax rather than prepare for the transition from high school to college.

Enhancing Concurrent Enrollment

To solve the problem presented by the school superintendents, SU administrators explored ways in which carefully designed and controlled concurrent enrollment (sometimes called "dual enrollment") courses could be taught for credit within the high school as part of the regular academic program. A committee of deans, academic chairmen, and faculty discussed multiple solutions before proposing a college readiness program that would be self-sufficient and capable of implementation and expansion, without creating a financial burden for the university or an instructional overload for cooperating faculty.

The SUPA model was designed to best utilize existing resources. The college courses would be taught by trained high school teachers as part of their regular teaching load, and taught during the regular school day so as to not negatively impact students' schedules. After field-testing the program in nine schools, SUPA launched in 1974 with more than forty high schools offering SU courses taught by 180 teachers from Long Island to Buffalo, New York, with an enrollment of more than two thousand students.

Today, Project Advance offers forty-four SU courses from twenty-six academic disciplines, with new courses added annually. SUPA serves more than two hundred high schools in New York, New Jersey, Maine, Massachusetts, Michigan, and Rhode Island, with the largest concentration in New York State. Approximately ten thousand students enroll annually in SU courses through SUPA, and more than nine hundred high school faculty members—with SU adjunct instructor appointments—teach them.

Project Advance is expanding rapidly as educators realize the importance of a rigorous transition from high school to college. Every year, more SU courses are fed through SUPA's developmental pipeline and field-tested for potential inclusion in a high school curriculum. Project Advance is one of just a few "enhanced concurrent enrollment" programs offered through a four-year private university (as opposed to concurrent enrollment programs offered by institutions offering two-year degrees). And SUPA is the only program affiliated with a private research university in the Northeast accredited by the National Alliance of Concurrent Enrollment Partnerships (NACEP). In fact, the program is a founding member of NACEP, which serves as a national accrediting body and supports all members by providing standards of excellence, research, communication, and advocacy.

Legacy of Excellence

The program's sustainability over forty years can be attributed to the fact that all funds coming in go directly back into the program to serve students. While some programs may be dependent on government funding,

SUPA can function no matter what leadership changes occur at the state level. This financial model allows the program to have a dedicated, multiperson administrative staff to handle communication with school partners, customer service, registration, financial aid, student accounts, marketing, material requests, and coordination of campus visits and professional development trainings.

Due to its innovation in creating such an outstanding concurrent enrollment program, Project Advance has served as a model for similar programs at institutions such as Indiana University, the University of North Carolina–Greensboro, the University of Pittsburgh, the University of Wisconsin–Oshkosh, and the University of Minnesota. SUPA has been honored by the American Association for Higher Education, the Carnegie Foundation for the Advancement of Teaching, the National Commission on Excellence in Education, the National Institute of Education, and the New York State Assembly.

Project Advance continually improves the concurrent enrollment courses it offers, and the program as a whole, through feedback from students and staff. Not only do students help to improve the courses with feedback while they are enrolled, but they also receive surveys one year and four years out of the program about the impact SUPA has made in their future endeavors. SUPA also surveys teachers, guidance counselors, and building administrators at each site. This feedback ensures that SUPA provides the very best in enhanced concurrent enrollment programs.

Project Advance partners with schools and works with administration and staff to change the culture of a school to one that sets high expectations—and students are ready and willing to meet those expectations. To facilitate this culture change, SUPA offers Strategic Learning Workshops to teachers from grades 7 through 10 who have a SUPA program either in their high school or within their district. Providing professional development to all teachers—not just the ones involved directly with SUPA—allows for the whole school community to be involved in the success of their students.

Administration personnel in high schools report that offering SUPA provides their staff with opportunities to learn new teaching methods and theories, as well as the chance to put those innovative techniques into practice. Through professional development, instructors report feeling more confident teaching in their subject area, and they incorporate the pedagogies they learn teaching SU courses into other high school courses they teach. They also report finding their jobs more challenging and having a sense of increased job satisfaction.

Professional Development

Prospective SUPA instructors must have both undergraduate and graduate degrees, as well as five years of teaching experience in the academic discipline they would like to teach. They also must meet departmental requirements specific to their subject area. Once they have applied and been approved, instructors attend mandatory summer training. Each content area runs a workshop planned and conducted by SU professors who teach the particular course at the university and supervise the course in high schools. The workshops emphasize mastering course content and adapting the university-designed courses to high school schedules and settings.

After teachers complete their summer training, SUPA offers several opportunities for professional development including one-day seminars, special topic workshops, and the chance to work on course development. All instructors are required to attend annual professional development seminars to keep their SU adjunct faculty appointments. SU faculty members offer continuing communication and support to the instructors at the high school sites. Information is shared through e-mail, electronic mailing lists, blogs, and social media—a system of support provided not only by SU faculty members but also high school peers across all SUPA sites.

Furthermore, extensive ongoing research and evaluation provides for systemic improvement of concurrent enrollment instruction. This research and evaluation help to keep SU's concurrent enrollment courses on the cutting edge of each academic discipline.

Student Expectations

Project Advance offers SU courses to high school seniors who have a grade average of B or better overall and in their selected subject area. SU courses are normally restricted to high school seniors, and exceptions to this policy require prior approval from the appropriate SUPA administrator and/or university faculty coordinator.

In addition to meeting the grade requirements, any student interested in taking an SU course through Project Advance must be selected for their capabilities and potential. The high school administration and guidance counselors make the final decision on which students will be allowed into the program.

Studies show that SU concurrent enrollment courses offered through SUPA provide a unique opportunity for college-bound seniors to see how well they will transition from high school to college and to gauge their ability to do typical first-year college work.

Project Advance students are held to the same high standards as students on the main campus. They earn high school credit and are graded according to the systems set up by their high schools; at the same time, they are given a grade point average according to the grading standards of SU. Because the courses are the same as those taught on the SU campus, the coursework is more demanding than high school coursework, and students are expected conceptualize and draw conclusions from reading and research.

Principals, instructors, and guidance counselors report that students enrolled in SUPA manage time more effectively and have a positive gain on their preparation for college. As a result, SUPA graduates tend to be more adaptable, self-actuated, reflective, and innovative.

Project Advance has an excellent track record of credit recognition. More than 90% of SUPA graduates who sent an official SU transcript or attended SU received college recognition—credit, placement, and/or exemption—for completed SU coursework.

Along with receiving recognition, SUPA successfully exposes students to the requirements and standards of higher education, which enables them to be successful in their post-graduation endeavors. Throughout their four years of college, 80% of students who have graduated SUPA report maintaining an average grade of B or better in their courses.

Project Advance continues to be a leader in high quality and innovative concurrent enrollment programs. The program's leaders pledge

to conduct extensive ongoing research and evaluation in support of sys-
temically improving instruction and smoothing the transition from high
school to postsecondary education.

Currently, SUPA is furthering its global partnerships with international sites to extend the benefits of enhanced concurrent enrollment to
the world.

3

College in the Schools

University of Minnesota–Twin Cities

SUSAN HENDERSON AND BARBARA D. HODNE

Three broad goals have energized College in the Schools (CIS) at the University of Minnesota–Twin Cities (UMTC) since its launch in 1986: increasing access to college learning, supporting excellence in high school teaching, and strengthening high school–university connections.

In its earliest years, College in the Schools offered UMTC's Freshman Composition course and an English literature course. Ten high schools participated. During the 2010–11 academic year, CIS offered thirty-six courses from seventeen academic departments in four colleges, worked with 118 schools, and received nearly ten thousand course registrations. College in the Schools

• gives students firsthand experience with the high academic standards and increased workload typical of college education, as well as the personal responsibility required to be successful in college study

• provides teachers with ongoing, university-based professional development workshops that are directly related to the content, pedagogy, and assessment of the University of Minnesota courses they teach through CIS

• strengthens curricular, instructional, and professional ties between high schools and the university.

CIS Foundational Facts

CIS began in the 1986–87 academic year under Minnesota's 1985 Postsecondary Enrollment Options Act (PSEOA). This statute was intended to "promote rigorous academic pursuits and to provide a wider variety of options to high school pupils by encouraging and enabling secondary pupils to enroll

18

full time or part time in nonsectarian courses or programs in eligible post-secondary institutions" (Minnesota Statutes 1985, section 124D.09, https://www.revisor.mn.gov/statutes/?id=124D.09).

This legislation focused primarily on the option of high school students taking classes on postsecondary campuses. It also authorized concurrent enrollment courses. Under PSEOA, such course offerings could be provided "according to an agreement between a public school board and the governing body of an eligible public postsecondary system or an eligible private postsecondary institution, as defined in subdivision 3." Courses offered "by agreement" may be taught at the high school by a secondary teacher or a postsecondary faculty member. In recent years, the greatest growth under PSEOA has been in concurrent enrollment.

The Minnesota Department of Education requires schools and districts to pay the cost of concurrent enrollment courses; neither the postsecondary institution nor the high schools are allowed to bill students. Since 2007, the state has provided (very) partial reimbursement to high schools for the costs of offering a concurrent enrollment course.

CIS offers what many call a cafeteria-style program: schools may choose which course(s) they offer (provided a teacher is approved by CIS), and students can choose which course(s) they wish to take (provided they meet student eligibility requirements). No high school offers all the UMTC courses available through CIS. Many students take only one course through CIS, but some students take enough courses to enter college with significant advanced standing.

CIS resides within the credit unit of UMTC's College of Continuing Education (CCE). CIS has 4.8 full-time equivalent (FTE) staff and receives the services of approximately another 1.5 FTE staff located in CCE's Enrollment Services. Biannual meetings of all UMTC-CIS faculty coordinators and biannual meetings of the CIS advisory board play critical roles supporting program excellence. A sophisticated program database helps staff manage events, track processes, gather data, and more.

CIS Participation Characteristics

Originally CIS partnered primarily with high schools in the Twin Cities metropolitan area. However, in the past ten years, new partner schools have come primarily from rural areas in Minnesota, and CIS partner high schools now extend nearly to the North Dakota, Iowa, and Wisconsin borders—a few schools are actually in Wisconsin.

In the 2010–11 academic year, 36% of participating schools were located well beyond the metro area, many in small towns. During CIS's twenty-five years of operation, suburban schools have experienced major changes in the demographics of their student bodies, becoming much more racially and ethnically diverse and serving many more English-language learners (ELLs) and students living in poverty.

CIS does not have an open admissions policy. Student qualification requirements are set for each course by the UMTC academic department to which the course belongs. Currently, fifteen CIS cohorts use class rank as an admissions requirement (some use the 80th percentile, some the 70th, and a few the 50th percentile); two cohorts use placement exams; and five cohorts use a course-specific requirement, such as having earned an A or A– in a previous course in the same discipline. Until 2009, CIS served almost exclusively students who had already demonstrated high academic achievement as reflected in their grade point averages and class rank.

Many—if not most—high schools that partner with CIS offer students other opportunities to earn college credit. In fact, CIS coexists in most schools with Advanced Placement (AP) courses, the International Baccalaureate (IB) program, and courses from other Minnesota concurrent enrollment programs.

Professional Development and Ongoing Support for Teachers

UMTC-CIS is well known in Minnesota for the high quality professional development it provides to CIS teachers. The program requires teachers to participate in discipline-specific and even course-specific workshops for as long as they teach for the university through CIS. (Neither schools nor teachers are charged for these workshops.)

The CIS faculty coordinators—university faculty who oversee those teaching CIS university course(s)—lead the workshops. Because of the requirement to participate in workshops on an ongoing basis, teachers in the cohorts develop strong professional bonds with each other and with the university CIS faculty coordinator leading the cohort; they also develop a deep understanding of the content, pedagogy, and assessment of the course(s) they teach.

A high level of collegiality characterizes the work and learning in the cohorts. High school teachers and university faculty coordinators respect the work each does, and all happily give and take materials and ideas. Workshop presentations and discussions are led by teachers themselves, the faculty coordinators, other university faculty and staff, and by experts from the community.

The faculty coordinator for each cohort provides teachers with ongoing support in multiple ways: workshops are held in the fall, spring, and summer; CIS provides electronic mailing lists for each cohort; faculty coordinators observe classroom teaching; and many of the cohorts have Moodle sites where resources and ideas are shared. The minimum number of workshop days per cohort is three, although most of the twenty-two discipline cohorts meet for four to five days a year.

Although CIS encourages districts to pay teachers for the time spent in summer workshops, at least half of CIS teachers receive no pay for this time (neither the school nor the university pays CIS teachers beyond their regular salary for instruction). Schools are required, however, to release teachers for the academic year workshops and to provide substitute teachers to cover classes while teachers attend the CIS workshops and any required on-campus student field days.

University Campus Experience for Students

CIS hosts on-campus student field days for each cohort. Lasting three to six hours, these events allow students to experience the university campus and engage in activities that support the curricular goals of the university course they are taking through CIS.

Activities vary from cohort to cohort. Students may hear traditional lectures, participate in breakout discussions with peers from other high schools, explore the cultural and academic resources available to university students, watch student-made videos related to course content, or sit in on other university classes.

Students Served by CIS

One of the most significant developments in CIS was the launching of a
new initiative in fall 2009—the Entry Point Project (EPP)—to expand the
academic and demographic range of students served. (Historically, CIS
has served primarily students in the top 70th to 80th percentile of their
high school class.)

EPP comprises three regular UMTC credit-bearing courses that
employ Universal Instructional Design, a pedagogy that accommodates
a wide range of learning styles, uses multiple forms of assessment, and
embeds skill-building into content-area study. (Chapter 9 focuses on the
CIS Entry Point Project.)

State and National Contexts

Minnesota policy makers have a long history of supporting Advanced
Placement and, more recently, the International Baccalaureate program.
The state legislature has, for years, allocated funds to pay AP and IB
teacher training costs and to subsidize exam fees, especially for students
who qualify for free and reduced lunches. Not until 2007, however, did
the legislature provide any financial support to concurrent enrollment.
The legislature has continued to allocate significantly more state funds
for AP and IB than for concurrent enrollment programs (in a ratio of
almost two to one).

Nearly thirty Minnesota postsecondary institutions offer concurrent enrollment courses, including three of the five University of Minnesota campuses. Given this abundance of providers, students in almost
every region of Minnesota can access college courses through concurrent
enrollment.

In 2004, UMTC-CIS helped to spearhead creation of the Minnesota
Concurrent Enrollment Partnership (MnCEP), an informal organization
of concurrent enrollment administrators. MnCEP members meet twice a
year to share best practices and identify common interests. CIS played a
significant role in MnCEP's effort (with the Minnesota School Boards Association) to pass the 2007 legislation that provides partial reimbursement

to high schools for the cost of offering concurrent enrollment courses. CIS staff members also have been active in the National Alliance of Concurrent Enrollment Partnerships, with three staff members serving on the Board of Directors in the past ten years.

4

Rio Salado College Dual Enrollment

Twenty-Three Years of Collaboration and Student Success

E. J. ANDERSON

Rio Salado College, a founding member of the National Alliance of Concurrent Enrollment Partnerships (NACEP), has the largest dual enrollment program in Arizona and one of the largest in the country, with nearly seven thousand students.

A member of the Maricopa County Community College District (MCCCD), Rio Salado was established in 1978 with a focus on serving the nontraditional student throughout the entire county. Rio Salado is a regionally accredited community college that serves more than 51,000 students annually, delivering access, flexibility, and affordability. Rio Salado maintains a national reputation for quality online excellence and is recognized in the community for its innovative and collaborative partnership programs, such as the dual enrollment program.

Dual enrollment is a collaborative effort between colleges and high schools that allows high school students to earn high school and college credit simultaneously. These programs provide students with a challenging academic experience and the opportunity to earn college credit while still in high school.

Pioneering Dual Enrollment

Rio Salado College began its dual enrollment program in 1987, partnering with Xavier College Preparatory in Phoenix, Arizona, a private high school known for its high academic standards. In 1993, Rio Salado expanded its dual enrollment program into the public school system at the request of several high school teachers already working as adjunct faculty in the community college system. The instructors saw a parallel in curriculum between their advanced high school classes and their college course competencies.

Rio Salado's first public school dual course offerings were mathematics classes at five high schools from the same district. The win-win possibilities of these partnerships were quickly recognized, and rapid growth in the program followed. As of the year 2015, more than 58 high schools offered more than 141 dual enrollment courses and 2.161 sections for students with Rio Salado.

As a national leader, Rio Salado pioneered Arizona's dual enrollment program, lobbying state legislators to enact legislation to allow colleges to offer dual enrollment courses for students. As more colleges in the Maricopa District and across Arizona entered into dual enrollment partnerships with high schools in their communities, variations in these programs developed. A desire for common standards led to discussions with the State Board of Directors for Community Colleges of Arizona, a group appointed by the governor to oversee community colleges across the state. Rio Salado's original dual enrollment guidelines (crafted by faculty and addressing the purpose of the program, faculty and student selection and participation, course selection, delivery, and evaluation) served as a basis for establishing statewide standards and reporting requirements. In April 2001, the State Board approved a final draft of this policy—R7-1-709—and forwarded it to the Office of the Attorney General, who certified it on October 10, 2001, thus creating guiding standards for all dual enrollment programs at all Arizona community colleges.

Rigorous and Quality-Driven

In addition to meeting statewide standards, Rio Salado also follows the strict MCCCD requirements for dual enrollment programs that include an intergovernmental agreement that outlines the roles of the high school district and the community college district.

NACEP was formed in large part to ensure rigorous and quality-driven concurrent and dual enrollment programs. The first Arizona community college to seek NACEP accreditation, Rio Salado passed the stringent accreditation review in 2003. In 2010, Rio Salado was one of the first colleges to be reaccredited under NACEP's new measurable quality standards. A growing number of states now require NACEP accreditation for colleges seeking approval to offer dual enrollment classes for high school students.

Rio Salado's dual enrollment program focuses on able and ambitious students. Dual classes maintain the same rigor and academic standards as the traditional college class, and instructors carry the same certification. Dual enrollment high school partners agree to teach the college curriculum and adhere to the same standards and course elements adopted by MCCCD. The goal is for participating students to apply their dual enrollment credits toward college degrees. Rio Salado's program focuses on career pathways, including the Arizona General Education Curriculum, which comprises thirty-five to thirty-eight transferable credits and the associate degree. In May 2015, thirty-eight students graduated with their AA degree. A dual enrollment success coach helps students stay on track for completion. Many students earn enough credits to start a semester or two ahead in college.

Professional Development and Support

Rio Salado provides a number of professional development opportunities for dual enrollment instructors to meet NACEP and statutory requirements. Dual enrollment instructors are invited to attend Rio Salado's semiannual all-faculty meeting with breakout sessions for individual disciplines. In addition to the all-faculty meeting, an annual conference is held exclusively for dual enrollment instructors providing sessions to enhance instruction. Conference sessions include discipline-specific breakout sessions and general sessions for best practices and recruitment strategies.

High school teachers new to dual enrollment meet with their discipline-specific faculty chair or their representative for orientation prior to teaching. During orientation a variety of topics are discussed, including curriculum, textbooks, assessment, and grading. The faculty chair must approve dual enrollment textbooks and a syllabus for each course.

To facilitate syllabus approval, Rio Salado created and implemented new software called Syllabus Builder that allows dual enrollment instructors to create their dual enrollment syllabi online. Syllabus Builder allows instructors to create a uniform, professional document and allows faculty chairs a common, web-based approval and archival system.

Rio Salado is committed to providing an exemplary dual enrollment program across the college. Consistent with other programs it offers, Rio Salado College takes a systems approach that relies on multiple departments collaborating together in efficient support of the program. College faculty drive the program by providing academic leadership and direction, overseeing the curriculum and course competences, and approving instructors' credentials to teach dual enrollment classes for the college at the high school.

A dedicated dual enrollment team is responsible for many operational components of the program, including communication with school partners, customer service, coordinating course offerings, registration, and promotion of the program. In addition, a Rio Salado College site coordinator is assigned to each high school to facilitate operational issues. The college's testing department, admissions and records office, and faculty services also have staff assigned to work on dual enrollment issues.

Dual enrollment is also a highly collaborative effort with the high school partners. These partners are committed to the program, often seeking an instructor with the necessary college credentials to teach dual enrollment classes in the hiring process and encouraging teachers to become qualified to teach dual enrollment. Each high school also has a dual enrollment liaison who works with students to ensure they meet admissions standards and have the qualifying test scores. High schools also assist with the promotion and registration of dual enrollment classes, realizing the value these classes offer students.

Student Performance

Dual enrollment students at Rio Salado are held to the same standards of achievement as those expected of all students at the college. Just like their counterparts, dual enrollment students are required to have passing scores on placement tests before enrolling in English and math classes.

Furthermore, dual enrollment students also participate in the following college wide assessments: writing, reading, critical thinking, problem solving, and information literacy. Dual enrollment students also are encouraged to participate in the yearly Academic Profile skills assessment of college writing, reading, critical thinking, humanities, social sciences, natural sciences, and mathematics.

Participation of dual enrollment students in the nationally standardized Academic Profile helps ensure that the college instruments are valid and reliable, and it helps confirm—with other multiple measures—that dual enrollment students as a group are performing as well as or better than comparable college level students. In a recent Measurement of Academic Proficiency and Progress (MAPP), dual enrollment students scored extremely high compared to the national average.

Rio Salado's dual enrollment program is effectively preparing students for the rigors of college. According to a survey of dual enrollment students one year after high school, 98% were currently attending college, with 80% attending a four-year college or university. For students five years out of the program, two-thirds have graduated college, with one-third attending graduate school. Over half of the respondents had a 3.5 grade point average or higher. The most significant accolade given to Rio Salado's dual enrollment program is that 98.91% of the respondents indicate that the dual enrollment program was beneficial and that they would recommend it to current high school students. According to high school instructors, principals, and guidance counselors, dual enrollment offers students exposure to college-level expectations, increased preparation for academic rigor, the ability to earn college credits while in high school, savings of time and money, increased motivation, and the acquisition of study skills important for success in college.

Dual enrollment offers benefits for instructors by providing them with opportunities to teach a higher level of content and expand their knowledge of the curriculum. High schools also find that dual enrollment raises standards for student success, motivates students to succeed in college, provides extra funding, and creates a better culture for motivated students.

Rio Salado's commitment to quality, collaborative partnering, and a supportive, college-wide systems approach are what make its dual enrollment program so successful. Known for innovation in learning, Rio Salado is currently investigating further application of online technology and collaborative partnering to reach beyond current markets. The college is proud of its more than twenty-year tradition of dual enrollment excellence and is actively engaged in working with communities to take the program to new heights in decades to come.

PART TWO | **Program Components**

5

Professional Development

Does It Matter?

THOMAS E. LEAHEY

In light of current trends in education to advance opportunities for students to begin their college experience before leaving high school, it is imperative that all such opportunities come with a guarantee to students, parents, and various educational entities that such programs merit transcripted college credit.

As is the experience with many academic programs when they become recognized and embraced at the state and federal level by academic departments and other agencies, it is vitally important that there is oversight of the courses and content offered through dual credit programs. Maintaining the quality and merit has become the task of sponsoring colleges and universities that embark on these endeavors with partnering high schools. The best way to achieve that oversight and control is for the providing institutions to initially have in place a model for training. This model introduces rigor and pedagogy for course delivery in order to meet institutional standards and student needs. The program must provide solid training and ongoing professional development for the teachers who will deliver such courses to high school students, so that these teachers remain current and can make adjustments in the course as it evolves on the campus. Once a teacher is trained, follow-up by the institutions is one of the best ways to ensure quality. Having these safeguards in place guarantees program integrity, ensures delivery of quality courses to students, and serves as a check and balance of the providing institution.

The most important phase of the process is to begin with teachers who meet the basic criteria of the providing colleges and universities. These high school teachers must be selected by the sponsoring institution and meet the same expectations as if they were to teach the course on the college campus. Once these teachers are identified, a lifelong plan for preparation and ongoing professional development must begin. Teachers submit credentials that are forwarded to a liaison for each content course offered. In the Advance College Project (ACP) at Indiana University, the teacher application is reviewed, and teachers are accepted, denied, or listed as pending. Accepted teachers are scheduled for summer training; those denied or pending may be accepted at a later date if, for example, they take additional courses or acquire more teaching experience of upper level courses. A denied teacher who is unacceptable because of credentials or outside recommendations generally does not reapply. Those who require additional training may take courses (approved by the liaison) from any institution that is convenient to the teacher.

It becomes the college or university's responsibility to provide personnel to make all of this happen. An effective university liaison is the key to a successful program. This is the person who reviews candidates, creates a training model, provides materials, sets the parameters for training, and works directly with the concurrent enrollment program director/coordinator to prepare the high school teacher to offer college courses. This is where solid professional development begins. By carefully planning and articulating a training program, an institution immediately invites high school teachers into the academic conversation. A clearly defined method of instruction creates an environment of trust and respect among the trainees. Clearly, high school teachers have the ability, with good instruction, to make the shift to the expectations of a college course. Here are the words of Gail, a concurrent enrollment teacher of biology:

> Some important aspects of the training session for us were the great atmosphere provided by meeting on the IUB campus with university professors and professionals. The approach taken in the training was that students should begin integrating prior and new knowledge with experiences to make connections and develop ideas and analysis rather than stress memorization. This gave me much

food for thought. The time allowed for participants to share ideas and techniques was also very valuable. (Gail, Jan. 14, 2010)

Everyone wants to "take home" something concrete. Providing the teachers adequate time and materials to create a level of competence and confidence has a big payoff for the teacher, the students, and the university. Maintaining the integrity of the college course is tantamount, because the university's reputation is on the line for each course it sponsors in a local high school. Additionally, teachers and students must experience quality courses in order for this partnership to be a win-win situation. If a course does not meet these expectations, the university and the high school should abandon it. Consequently, the question of quality rests with the providing institution.

Making this happen takes time and preparation at all levels of the partnership. Each liaison has to determine the length of time required to accommodate content, pedagogy, practices, and implementation. Looking at text materials, lab manuals, and student products helps the trainee make the transition to the college level of expectation. So what should a trainee "take home"? Many programs provide texts, syllabi, training notebooks/discs, and all paperwork that students, parents, and schools will distribute. Depending on budgets, often the university brings authors of texts, researchers in the field, and other university faculty to assist in the trainings. Getting into classrooms, labs, and other facilities encourages the trainees to feel they are part of that larger community. Depending on program budget, teachers may receive stipends for attending the summer trainings. The following comments from trainees illustrate the value of implementing quality instruction and follow-up:

Professional development is not something one can accomplish in an hour or two. To do it right, professional development needs to provide not only the tools but also the time to be successful. A student isn't expected to comprehend Shakespeare or even the structure of a complex sentence in a day. It takes discussion, practice, repetition, application, and days upon days of instruction for some to grasp the concept. Why should professional development for teachers be any different?

All in all, IU has it right. I left my (written composition) and (literature) trainings with confidence because of your ability to not only tell us what needed to be covered but also how to cover it. You made us do the work that our students would do, which has now allowed me to better answer my students' questions in the classroom, having done the work myself. Moreover, the skills I received through the training were skills I could apply to any classroom setting, not just ACP. I felt better equipped as a teacher preparing students for college. You gave me a greater understanding of what skills students need for the next level of learning that I felt I was too old to know, having graduated from college in '91. You tuned me in to colleges today and what lies ahead for my students and I think that's awesome. (Jennifer, Jan. 11, 2010)

The initial three-four day training sessions that I participated in for teaching [history] and [political science] provided me with a very good understanding of what is expected of an ACP instructor, as well as what the ACP program is all about. The materials that were distributed, the discussions that were held, and the information given by the speakers were invaluable. This experience helped me to put myself on the next level when it came to teaching. Even today whatever I do in the way of preparation and instruction for my ACP classes, I always consider if what I am doing is at a college level. (Dick, Jan. 15, 2010)

ACP seminars have been some of the best professional development I receive. Not only do we receive information about cutting edge research, we are exposed to expectations at the college level, so we maintain our rigor and cover the appropriate curriculum with emphasis on the correct topics. In addition, we develop important relationships with our university support-subject liaison and ACP staff, and we also make important connections with our peers. The summer workshop where experienced ACP teachers were invited for a refresher was absolutely wonderful. Our liaison had changed and the topics emphasized had changed with the "new" 1:2:1 in chemistry at IU. I felt refreshed and more up to date. Perhaps most importantly, I developed relationships with teachers new to ACP and have been able to support them this year. (Cheryl, Jan. 28, 2010)

Jennifer is a novice, but Cheryl and Dick have been with the concurrent enrollment program for ten years. Though these teachers represent different content areas and trained in different decades, all sense that acquiring current pedagogy and having the ongoing support are clearly valuable components of professional development. Keep in mind, all of this is not without cost to the providing institution, but the investment has a significant return in quality of teachers and students. For the yearly required seminars, teachers at distances greater than fifty miles are housed overnight, and mileage is reimbursed for all attendees. At the seminars, often, departments absorb the cost for visiting professors, book authors, and researchers to participate in the seminars.

In the fall of 2007 the ACP was faced with several teachers who would reach retirement in the next five years. A concern for ACP was how the program would retain quality instructors who held masters in the content area when faced with a replacement population, many of whom did not hold masters in the content. Most new applicants held master's degrees in education or related fields without further study in the content. In order to add teachers who met the university's expectation, a new plan had to be developed. The model that evolved out of these concerns merits consideration for institutions facing a similar problem. ACP offers to applicants a tuition scholarship for courses offered by approved institutions that are close to the applicant's home. Current teachers in the program also are offered the opportunity to take up to three courses to further content knowledge with the tuition cost covered by the university.

Once a teacher submits an application and is reviewed by the liaison, a recommendation is made for specific courses the liaison deems necessary in order for the applicant to be considered as an instructor for the college course. If applicants want to pursue the opportunity to take coursework at minimal cost (the program covers tuition only), they submit a request that includes information on the providing institution, the course description, and a syllabus for the course. This request is directed to the liaison for approval or recommendation. Once a course is approved, the teacher registers and sends the bill to ACP for payment to the providing institution for tuition costs. In the following response, Doug references this opportunity:

> *The ACP Program through I.U. Bloomington offers a professional development meeting every fall in Bloomington. This meeting typically involves going over*

current issues in teaching I.U.'s version of a first-year college chemistry course,
as well as the status of research currently going on at I.U. We also spend time
designing the final exam for the ACP Chemistry course taught in high schools.
I.U. also offers other professional development opportunities for high school
teachers, usually in the summer, and provides ACP Chemistry teachers gradu-
ate credits and tuition remission. (Doug, Feb. 10, 2010)

An initiative at the university has encouraged departments/colleges
to offer summer courses at the graduate level specifically to give teachers
the opportunity to take courses. As a result, the ACP program will pay
the tuition for any of its accredited teachers to take courses in chemistry and math. Courses are synchronous and asynchronous as well as at
main campus, making them very accessible to teachers without incurring
additional costs (e.g., for residence). Other departments have started a
similar process.

But it is not just about the college. Teachers see great benefit in being
able to speak with one another. Commonly, each training, each seminar,
and each site visit results in an exchange that often does not happen at
the local level. Why not? Because high school teachers are caught up in
the day-to-day expectations of their schools. Coming together in a collegial environment without the daily pressures frees teachers to actually
examine not only their own pedagogy but also the practices of other high
school teachers and the college faculty. Notice in the next two reflections
how Maria and Josh critique their teaching as a result of the seminars:

Most helpful is learning some of the instructional techniques and strategies that
college level professors and instructors are currently using. I really benefitted
from the seminar that the [authors of our college text] provided recently. They
modeled some really terrific techniques . . . all to birth and develop some key
ideas that may later be explored. That experience is much more powerful than
any [instructor's manual]; subtleties that a text can never really capture that a
refresher seminar can. Just like our students need, I believe we ACP teachers
benefit from seeing others model the techniques that really lead to successful
analytical thought, work, and writing—be it in literature or the other content
areas. (Josh, Jan. 28, 2010)

I think it's easy for teachers to get involved in the busy-ness of teaching and get locked into their own little world and way of doing things . . . I value the opportunity I have had with ACP seminars to communicate with other teachers and hear what they are doing and the frustrations and successes we share. It is also nice to get refreshed and to be reminded of the direction we should be heading. Some of what we do in these classes also is useful in teaching other classes as well, so the training and seminars for this program have been helpful in other courses. (Maria, Jan. 15, 2010)

Maria and Josh clearly refer to the shared experience, but in her final sentence, Maria keys in on yet another value to not only the teacher, but also to students and the school system itself. Repeatedly in annual surveys of teachers, a pervasive comment speaks to the application and improvement of their teaching approach in *all* of their classes. This does not imply a deficiency in the teaching of high school courses; rather, it indicates that borrowing from the training can enhance the traditional high school class and elevate the level of instruction not only for the students but also for the school. In a visit with one of our larger schools, Ed, the chair of the English department at a local high school, spoke with me of the department's plan to realign the English curriculum for grades 9 through 12 to incorporate many of the skills necessary for success in not just college writing but all writing. Though he will most likely never teach ACP courses, Ed took training for the two CE English courses to have a better understanding of the course expectation. Ed's case is a good example of how professional development extends beyond the classroom intended for the college course. Here's what other teachers say:

Since I've been trained for ACP, I have been able to incorporate "good writing" skills in my other English classes. I am so sick of these "new" ideas on teaching writing . . . write about how we feel *. . . what we're* thinking *as we read . . . it's elementary and we need to prepare students for their future, whether it's in college classes or in the work force.* (Jennifer, Jan. 11, 2010)

For me, the ACP professional development coursework and seminars provide better footing as I try to instruct higher-achieving students with support from

*IU and fellow teachers. I have been able to adapt the format for regular stu-
dents as well—giving them a better chance for success beyond high school, too.
More important, this is a realistic tool to enable impactful results, which is not
especially true for recycled ideologies or techniques found in most professional
development venues.* (Julie, Jan. 13, 2010)

Equal opportunity is what ACP administrators consider to be the
major strength of offering these classes to high school students. The bottom line is this: Whether teachers and their students are situated in one of
the largest participating high schools (more than two thousand students)
in a metropolitan district or in a small school (five hundred students or
less) nearby a cornfield, there is a level playing field.

*I just wanted to say that my (writing) class and I visited the IU library today, and
once again it was pleasant and productive. Of course the kids always get spoiled
by seeing the big campus, and they seem to become even more eager to complete
high school and get out into the big college world.* (Donna, Nov. 22, 2004)

All teachers and students receive identical benefits. The same training, course, and professional development opportunity is there, regardless of location, for all stakeholders. Site visitors report seeing daily the
value of ongoing professional development. Because professional development has always been a benchmark of ACP, it is easy to say—anecdot-
ally, at least—that professional development speaks for itself.

6

A Quality Concurrent Enrollment Program

Five Considerations

DENNIS R. WALLER

Recently I was talking to a colleague at my university who tends to support concurrent enrollment. During our dialogue this supporter raised an important question asked by many: "How do we maintain a quality concurrent enrollment program at our institution?" It is this question, and my response, that form the central core of this chapter.

In this chapter, terms describing programs are defined and used in the following ways. First, the use of the term *concurrent enrollment program* is intended to encompass all similar programs no matter the name used (i.e., dual enrollment, dual credit, concurrent enrollment, concurrent credit). Second, references to institutions of higher education are noted by the term *college* as a means to define all such institutions that might have a concurrent enrollment program, whether in a two-year or four-year, public or private, college or university.

In addition, to help the reader understand my comments in this chapter I will provide a brief description of the concurrent enrollment program at my college. Northwest Nazarene University (NNU) is a private, Christian university located in southwest Idaho. Our concurrent enrollment program began in 1999, was accredited by National Alliance of Concurrent Enrollment Partnerships[1] (NACEP) in 2006, and was reaccredited in 2013.

---

1. NACEP is the only organization that currently provides accreditation specifically for Concurrent Enrollment Programs. Information about NACEP can be found at the website, www.nacep.org.

The program has grown consistently and had an unduplicated enrollment of more than two thousand students in the 2013–14 academic year.

This chapter addresses five considerations that are important to any staff or college administration in the process of beginning, evaluating, or maintaining a concurrent enrollment program.

1. Aligning the program with the college mission and priorities
2. Developing and maintaining a credible program
3. Determining and working with the stakeholders
4. Working with competitors
5. Creating and maintaining an administrative structure

My intent is to contribute to the dialogue involving concurrent enrollment. I do not pretend to be an expert; rather I see myself and the college I serve as being on an interesting journey in the land of concurrent enrollment, and my hope is to share insights that will be valuable to readers who are on a similar journey.

Aligning the Program with the College Mission and Priorities

No doubt other chapters in this book define what a concurrent enrollment program might look like organizationally. However, the following discussion will look at the concurrent enrollment program as a part of the academic community within the college.

Of importance would be thinking about the goals of the concurrent enrollment program at the college. It is possible that a program might regard these goals as components of the college's vision and/or mission. I do believe it is very important to link the goals of the concurrent enrollment program to the college's vision and mission, but the goals of the program should not be confused with the vision or mission of the college as a whole. The concurrent enrollment program at NNU has four simple goals:

1. *Provide high school students with an early opportunity to experience college.* This is probably the simplest goal and speaks to the underlying focus of any concurrent enrollment program. In short, this is what we do.

2. *Maintain the rigor of college courses.* This goal may be the most difficult and important, as academic departments within the college work to serve students taking courses through an individual major or minor with an eye toward rigor. Generally, the academic department tends to focus

on the regular, or "traditional," on-campus student rather than the "non-traditional" student off-campus at a partnering high school. This means the concurrent enrollment program staff must help the academic department remember to think about the nontraditional students when policies are made that impact all students taking courses from the college. The NACEP standards[2] help to provide guidance toward the academic parts necessary to fulfill this goal; however, the application occurs within the academic department and is facilitated by the concurrent enrollment program at the college.

3. *Provide a service-oriented program.* Another difficult goal for a concurrent enrollment program to reach is "service," and different audiences inside and outside the college may interpret the quality of service in many ways. Even the seemingly simple task of enrolling students in a series of the program's courses may become complicated. For example, we find it complex to manage enrollment procedures when nearly sixty partner high schools want to enroll their students at the same time. Therefore, staffing and time involved will impact the amount of service given and the perceived quality of that service. Although quality service is the goal, it must be tempered with reality (i.e., we always do the best we possibly can, given a limited amount of time and staff).

4. *Support the college recruitment endeavors.* The concurrent enrollment program at Northwest Nazarene University is not part of the recruitment area or office; we receive no funding from this source, nor are we actual recruiters. However, the program's staff does strive to work with the recruitment office and provide a ready target audience of prospective students for the college. In my view, one benefit of supporting recruitment efforts is the ability to track the progress of concurrent enrollment students who later matriculate and attend the college, reporting on their positive progress to support the program's existence.

2. The NACEP standards cover five areas: Student, Curriculum, Faculty, Assessment, and Evaluation. The standards form a measurement tool for evaluating the program quality of any concurrent enrollment program. However, a beginning program could use the standards as a helpful framework for development and ongoing evaluation.

A concurrent enrollment program may have wonderful goals, but these goals must fit in with the college and its vision and/or mission. Of course, regional accreditation organizations would look for this link between the concurrent enrollment program and the college, thus much more discussion here is probably not necessary. However, I would encourage those concurrent enrollment programs that have not thought about this to do so.

Academic alignment within the academic departments at the college is very important to the longevity of a quality concurrent enrollment program. The NACEP standards provide important guidelines in this area, especially in linking concurrent enrollment courses to catalog courses at the college, and in oversight by the department faculty. For example, at Northwest Nazarene University, the concurrent enrollment program offers courses that have been approved by an academic department and that fulfill general education requirements, or in a few cases, fulfill elective requirements. Additionally, in a few rare cases a special topics course might be developed for a specific program, such as a study tour, but even in this rare case the course would still require approval by an academic department for it to be offered for credit.

Another area for consideration may involve organizational alignment, or the placement of the concurrent enrollment program in an academic unit (department, division or school) within the larger college. Although some might argue otherwise, there is clearly no single best organizational model here. I would suggest that a concurrent enrollment program in a college is best served in a neutral location from which a variety of academic departments respond to the facilitation and guidance function of the program, rather than under the control of a single academic unit (department, division, or school). For example, the NNU concurrent enrollment program is located organizationally within the unit of Extended University Services (i.e., continuing studies); this allows courses from all academic departments to link to the program without any one academic department controlling it. In our case the concurrent enrollment program staff facilitates operations and communication across all academic departments, working impartially with all. Again, I would stress that there is no single best model; rather the key is finding the best place for your concurrent enrollment program within the organizational structure of your college.

Developing and Maintaining a Credible Program

Certainly every concurrent enrollment program wants to be perceived as credible; that is, perceived by all audiences (on or off campus) as a quality program. For most concurrent enrollment programs, this credibility stems from the development and maintenance of rigorous college courses about which the concurrent enrollment program is able to say "this is the same course," whether taught on-campus or off-campus at the local high school. Basically, the institution is certifying the equivalence of the course by offering a college transcript that could be used at the providing college or perhaps transferred to hundreds of other colleges. Therefore, credibility is tied not only to the course being offered, but to the entire academic integrity of the college offering concurrent enrollment courses.

It bears repeating that the NACEP standards provide important guidelines for developing and maintaining a quality concurrent enrollment program. Certainly a new or developing program would want to use the NACEP standards to help form its structure (i.e., organization, course processes, faculty policies, assessment, and evaluation). An existing program would use the NACEP standards to evaluate for change and ongoing improvement. Although I would suggest that all concurrent enrollment programs strive for NACEP accreditation, my practical side says that this may not happen for every college; however, this does not negate the value of employing NACEP standards as significant targets for any concurrent enrollment program.

No matter your interest in NACEP, it is important that your concurrent enrollment program maintain its quality through the use of academic courses. Academic courses may be broadly defined, at least for this chapter, to include those that might have various labels; i.e., general education, elective, or even technical preparation. Therefore, depending upon the purposes of the college, any academic course may have programmatic implications.

So, how does a concurrent enrollment program ensure academic courses have rigor and integrity? The easy answer is through NACEP standards. The hard answer is that the NACEP standards are only guide-lines for a concurrent enrollment program to follow. The truth is that the concurrent enrollment program and college are responsible. Some issues to think about regarding course rigor and integrity are noted below:

• Seek out other quality concurrent enrollment programs from which to take lessons for your own program. The NACEP website provides easy access to colleges throughout the United States that have concurrent enrollment programs. The annual NACEP conference provides an excel-lent meeting place to make personal connections with other concurrent enrollment staff, directors, and college administrators, as well as a vari-ety of presentations on issues facing beginning and ongoing concurrent enrollment programs.

• It is important to develop and maintain academic policies that cover the concurrent enrollment program, even if the policy-making process is unpopular. Meeting with and listening to the academic department fac-ulty and college leadership as academic policy is discussed is an impor-tant function of the concurrent enrollment program director.

• Exceptions to your college policy that are specific to the concur-rent enrollment program should be clearly noted. For example, general student policy exceptions should be listed as publicly (website and/or in print) as possible. In addition, the rare student policy exception would follow the same general academic petition process that is available to all students.

• Establish and follow a consistent process for authorizing concurrent enrollment program faculty and courses through the various academic departments at the college. By following a clear approval process, the pro-gram maintains an important level of academic credibility.

• Create a workable but rigorous evaluation system. Components of this system may include, for example, pre-/post-tests for students; instruc-tor and course evaluations; site visits by program staff and academic department mentors; and evaluation procedures for mentors.

• Develop an ongoing professional development process for concur-rent enrollment program high school faculty, including, for example, workshops and seminars on varied topics, content courses in the subject area, and short conferences and programs.

All of us would like to think that developing and maintaining course rigor and integrity is easy within each college that has a concurrent enrollment program, but it is not. No college would willingly develop a poor academic program, regardless of whether it was related to a concurrent enrollment program. Thus, guaranteeing rigor and integrity is the business of each one of us.

Determining and Working with the Stakeholders

Of concern to every concurrent enrollment program should be the individuals, and groups they comprise, that the program may impact and be impacted by. Some stakeholders (individuals or groups) are obvious while others are less so. Taking time to identify your stakeholders and assigning them a primary or secondary status, in terms of impact on your concurrent enrollment program, will help you more effectively respond to the needs inherent to each.

Part of the point in determining primary or secondary status involves your time. Not every stakeholder can be primary. For example, two phone messages need response from two different administrators. While one message is from a high school administrator the other message is from a college administrator. Although both messages are important, I have previously placed primary status on communication with high school administrators and would respond to that message first.

Following are some of the more common stakeholders that impact the concurrent enrollment program at Northwest Nazarene University. It is likely those stakeholders I might identify as primary might actually be secondary for you; thus, thinking about their impact on your specific concurrent enrollment program is key.

First on my list are the high school students and their parents, with both groups enjoying a primary status. Although separate stakeholders, students and parents are tightly linked, as both have similar course-specific concerns. We can say all we want about poor communication between these two groups, but I generally find that when it comes to educational issues involving the concurrent enrollment program and the future of their education, both students and parents tend to be fairly united in seeking the same information.

I find it beneficial to meet with students in the classroom and parents during a parent meeting. Both groups seem to respond better to a live person telling them about the concurrent enrollment program, describing its benefits, and explaining the registration processes. Further, both groups tend to be more willing to ask questions in person than when receiving a brochure or viewing a website with the very same information. Of course, a great deal of information, including FAQs (frequently asked questions), is available at the program website; do not ignore the power of the written word and technology to spread the word about your program. Although the issues important to high school students and parents are many and varied, two commonly concern both:

1. *Cost.* Concurrent enrollment programs take a wide variety of approaches to addressing the cost of courses to students, including tuition and/or fees. Involvement in NACEP and discussions with program staff from other colleges across the country opened my eyes to the range of approaches. Depending upon the state, school, or school district, the concurrent enrollment program course cost may range from nothing to a minimal tuition fee (usually a fraction of the tuition paid at the college for the same course). Scholarships may be available to defray even a minimal tuition or fee; however, they are usually based upon a temporary federal or state grant or offered through a local/regional foundation or service club, and so should not be confused with the normal scholarship processes of the college. Should a concurrent enrollment program charge a minimal tuition fee, the collection of payment requires its own set of policies and procedures that may raise questions from students or parents unfamiliar with tuition or educational fees.

2. *Benefits.* The benefits of concurrent enrollment program courses may seem logical to those of us in colleges that offer these programs. However, the logic is often lost on students and parents who have never attended college. They may not understand the academic concepts of credit acceptance, transferability, moving ahead on general education or elective courses, tuition discounts, or future tuition savings. Thus, explanation becomes very important to these students and parents.

Helping the student and parent understand how paying for concurrent enrollment program credit for a course now can mean later savings upon entering college can be difficult. Basically, each course offered through a concurrent enrollment program and transferable for general education or elective equivalency can save the student hundreds of dollars in tuition. For example, one story I love to tell involves a parent who called me one September and reported that his daughter had all of her concurrent enrollment program credits accepted at an out-of-state private college, which gave her sophomore standing and saved him more than $20,000 in tuition. Similar stories recur every year.

Next on my priority list of stakeholders are the high school teachers and administrators, who also enjoy primary status in my book. Teachers and administrators are tightly linked, but they seem to have slightly differing concerns associated with the concurrent enrollment program.

Teachers seem to be most concerned about the students and opportunities offered to them by taking a concurrent enrollment program course. Thus, course rigor is important only because it is ultimately important to the student in receiving credit for the course. Benefits for involvement as a concurrent enrollment program faculty member tend to be of limited personal interest, except for direct benefits received through professional development opportunities that may result in educational credit, which may in turn help move teachers up the school district salary scale. The use of monetary compensation paid to the concurrent enrollment program faculty member for participation is mixed across the United States, but when allowed it does provide an additional incentive for faculty participation. The option of offering monetary compensation can be limited by state, district, or teacher union policies. In addition, it may increase the competition between different colleges, as some qualified faculty may "shop around" and even offer their services to the highest bidder. The offering of teacher benefits is not a simple issue and should be thought through carefully, as it will likely have direct budget implications for the program and college. NACEP standards require that professional development be provided for concurrent enrollment program faculty; however, nothing is specified as to other benefits or incentives that might be provided or offered. At the very least, a new program would want to find out what benefits are being offered to concurrent enrollment program faculty in the area. At the same time, a continuing program might need to revise its benefits based upon what competitive programs offer.

Administrators in the high school tend to be concerned with course rigor and professional development opportunities for their teachers. Course rigor is important in as much as it is reflected in graduation rates, college preparation, and credit transfer. Of equal importance for administrators are the public relations benefits gained by offering advanced opportunities to students. To the administrator, concurrent enrollment offered through the college program is simply another advanced opportunity in the same category as Advanced Placement (AP), Gifted and Talented Programs (GTP), or International Baccalaureate (IB). In some instances, the high school administrator may have an inherent bias in favor of an advanced opportunity other than concurrent enrollment, or concurrent enrollment may be an unknown. Either instance will require that the program staff spend additional time explaining the intent and educational value of concurrent enrollment. Never push your program onto an unwilling recipient; rather, step back and allow other pressures (usually parent or state related) to open the eyes of the administrator to the opportunity that is being offered. High school administrators have a variety of concerns; advanced opportunities, including concurrent enrollment, is only one. The concurrent enrollment program staff should understand what advanced opportunities are offered by the high schools they work with and how each category might impact administrator support toward the concurrent enrollment program. The development and maintenance of positive relations with high school administrators is an ongoing task of the concurrent enrollment program staff.

The secondary stakeholders for a concurrent enrollment program are a collection of local and state education organizations. These organizations may be representative of other equally important organizations you will come in contact with through your concurrent enrollment program. The point is, become aware of those organizations that might impact your program now and in the future.

• *Local educational organizations.* The local school district would be the most common educational organization after the high school itself. Most school district administration members (superintendents or area/content coordinators) are interested in the same issues as the high school adminis-trator. It is likely that the school district will be even more concerned than the high school administrator about the concurrent enrollment program as an advanced opportunity as well as the public relations situation with parents and the community. Generally, the size of the school district will determine the amount of oversight placed upon the program in the high school. For example, one school district may allow the individual high school administrator to handle all concurrent enrollment program issues within their school; another district may assign a district administrator to coordinate all concurrent enrollment program issues with all high schools in that district. The point is that administrative oversight from the high school and/or school district may become complicated, which requires the program staff to be somewhat flexible in process. Such flexibility may require the concurrent enrollment program staff to spend more time com-municating with district and school administrators so that policies related to oversight of the program are clear to all involved.

• *State educational organizations.* Most states have some form of depart-ment of education, or staff, that oversees educational policies in that state. Becoming aware of how the state's education department might impact your concurrent enrollment program is very important; for example, not-ing state policies on all advanced opportunities (i.e., AP, concurrent enroll-ment, GTP, IB), professional development for teachers, and grant options. The concurrent enrollment program staff should actively communicate with state-level staff and be available to participate on committees when asked. Do not ignore the value of public relations opportunities with state educational organizations.

• *State legislature and committees.* Depending upon the state, the legis-lature may have a great deal of impact on the concurrent enrollment pro-gram. At the very least, the assignment of money for education through the legislature may be of interest to program administrators and staff. Being aware of the legislative education committee(s), assigned represen-tatives, and potential actions will at least allow you to communicate your views as a state citizen. Being prepared with information, or even being available to testify before a legislative committee, may be important to your concurrent enrollment program and college.

Working with local and state organizations, and the individual administrators involved with each, requires concurrent enrollment staff to spend extra time creating relationships, communicating opportunities, and carrying out basic public relations efforts with these stakeholders. However, the payoff in doing so is important to the longevity of your concurrent enrollment program.

Working with Competitors

Colleges are not immune from competition from other colleges. We know that colleges, public or private, compete through the process of recruitment to bring students to their individual campuses. The concurrent enrollment program can be an effective part of a college recruitment effort by providing rigorous college courses. A quality program strengthens the college's name brand in the eyes of high schools, students, and parents, so that the college is considered seriously when students are ready to apply. At this point we know that no college wants to be on the "not interested" list from the start.

Since competition does exist, it is important for concurrent enrollment programs to work with each other. Working with competitors does not mean that the playing field is level; it does mean keeping the lines of communication open and agreeing to disagree. Do not forget that competition is two-way.

Before you can work with your competitors you need to determine who they are and what courses they offer. This is especially important for a new or developing concurrent enrollment program. To prepare your competition list you may need to broaden your perspective and look at local, state, and regional competitors.

• Local competitors are the most logical to be aware of and may be the easiest to identify. What colleges are located in your community and recruit students from the local high schools? Identification may be as simple as asking the local high school administrators, or doing a web-based search. Once identified, the competing college's website is an easy way to determine whether a concurrent enrollment program exists and what it offers, and to find program staff contact information. Also, remember that the college may not use "concurrent enrollment" for identification, but another term (dual enrollment, dual credit, concurrent credit).

• State competitors may be easy to identify, but may seem less important than a direct local competitor. However, if these competitors do recruit students from the local high schools, then it is important to be aware of them. The same process for locating local competitors will work for identifying competitors elsewhere in the state. Of interest here would be branch campuses of in-state academic colleges that might offer concurrent enrollment program courses by traditional face-to-face delivery or through e-technology (online, live-connect broadcasts).

• Regional or out-of-state competitors may be harder to identify or may seem less important. Yet, if they do recruit students from the local high schools that you might work with then they are important to consider. Asking local high school administrators may be the best way to identify them. Once these competitors have been identified, a website analysis will be important to you. Of continuing interest will be the use of branch campuses and e-technology course options by the regional competitor.

Now that you have identified your competitors, it is important to establish and maintain communication with them individually. At the very least contact each competitor and identify yourself, with the intent of opening an ongoing dialogue. Find out if your state has formed a group of concurrent enrollment program directors from the competing colleges, ask when that group meets, and attend the next meeting. If your state does not have such a group (formal or informal), the state education department might be interested in helping to create such a group for discussion purposes.

The entire concept of competition is not an easy one to think about, especially in the academic setting of the college. Yet competition is real and important to address by any concurrent enrollment program staff because of its close ties to recruitment issues. The point is to address competition positively through identification and ongoing communication.

Creating and Maintaining an Administrative Structure

A concurrent enrollment program is really only as good as its administrative structure. There are almost as many different administrative structures as there are concurrent enrollment programs, and each model seems to work well. Some common aspects of a program's structure are its administrative team, budget, evaluation, and accreditation.

The program's administrative team facilitates all of its associated parts for the college. Granted, the program falls under an organizational structure and may be one of many programs reporting to an academic officer at the college. But an effective concurrent enrollment program seems to need a director and staff that work as a team.

The director should serve as the coordinator of policies for the program. This may mean interpreting existing policies, academic and nonacademic, as well as creation of policy that may be specific to the concurrent enrollment program. The director serves as the primary contact for academic and other issues, from all stakeholders inside and outside of the college, and must be seen as an academic professional deserving of the position.

Staff members support the director and keep the program going. It is the staff that serves on the front line and keeps the wheels on the tracks. There is no magic number of staff members; however, the program should have enough staff to make sure all of the parts are covered, i.e., registration, coordination of courses, support of faculty, evaluation, research, etc. Rarely does a concurrent enrollment program have too many staff members; rather the concern is not having enough people to do what needs to be done.

Budgeting is another one of those multiple model situations, depending upon the college. The process of budgeting may be impacted by whether the college is public and receives state support or private and receives no state support; location of the college in relation to its high school partners; whether the concurrent enrollment program charges a tuition fee; and whether the program pays or does not pay high school partners. Though budget models may differ, there are some common factors that will likely impact every beginning or continuing concurrent enrollment program:

1. *Concurrent enrollment program administrative staff.* Of course, the administrative team (director and staff) must be paid. These individuals

might be paid out of a program line item or an organizational staff budget within the college.

2. *High school faculty partners.* Some colleges "pay" the high school faculty partner, while others do not, depending upon the state or other restrictions. Those that do not pay the faculty partner may instead provide an honorarium or instructional allocation for offering a concurrent enrollment program course and/or attending an academic department workshop during the year or summer.

3. *College mentors or coordinators from each academic department.* Models differ in terms of budgeting for the role of the college's academic department: some programs pay a flat fee per course, an adjunct fee based upon a series of courses and/or instructors monitored, or a fee per visit to the high school.

4. *Office supplies.* Program supplies may include registration forms, evaluation forms, postage, copying, and business cards. Even using the college print shop, if one is available, will likely have a cost, as will the use of copy machines, printers, computers, and even phone systems that are on contractual agreements held through the college. Costs may also be associated with promotional items carrying the program's name and college logo, such as pens, paper pads, coffee cups, and bags provided to students and teachers each year.

5. *Research processes.* The NACEP standards include a requirement for, at minimum, the survey study of students (one-year and five-year) and high school partners (multiyear). Various means for cost control may exist; for example, shifting from hard copy to a web-based survey, sending a postcard rather than a letter in an envelope, using the college research office staff rather than concurrent enrollment program staff, or outsourcing to some off-campus group. No matter the procedures used in collecting data, there is still a cost associated with the research process, as staff time must be factored in for maintaining and evaluating the research.

6. *Travel expenses.* Depending upon the location of the college with respect to the high school partners, travel expenses may be a major factor in the program budget. Many programs serve rural school districts that

are hundreds of miles from the college, so travel can become a significant part of the budget.

7. *NACEP Costs.* Membership fees are based upon a concurrent enrollment program's membership category within NACEP. Attending the yearly NACEP conference has an expense associated with it, too.

8. *Program-sponsored workshops and academic department conferences.* Hosting a workshop for several hours or days may involve costs that should be anticipated in budget planning. Some colleges digest the cost of having a conference as part of the academic process; others charge a conference rate for rooms, furnishings, setup, food, and other expenses.

9. *Miscellaneous.* Every budget should include a catch-all category for the unknown or unexpected costs that seem to surprise us. Even public relations, which may have no direct monetary benefit attached to it, still have a cost in staff time.

Evaluating the high school faculty partners is essential to maintaining a quality concurrent enrollment program. The emphasis on evaluation should be supportive and proactive, not punitive. Two forms of evaluation are common: (1) classroom evaluation by the department mentor and/ or program staff, and (2) course evaluation by students at the end of the course.

1. *Classroom evaluation by the department mentor and/or program staff.* These opportunities to get into the high school classroom and watch the high school faculty partner teach can be a very rewarding experience when approached in a supportive way. Most of my college academic department mentors find the process as much a learning experience for them as for the high school faculty partner, as ideas are exchanged both ways.

When preparing to visit high school faculty partners, be sure to contact them ahead of time to find a mutually agreeable date. Also, notify the high school administrator, who might be interested in a quick visit, and always check in at the high school office before wandering off to the classroom. There is nothing to be gained by dropping in unannounced at the high school, as that only gives the appearance of potential punishment, and it may disrupt the educational process in the classroom. Assure the high school partner that the visit is intended as one of support, a check on academic content, and an opportunity to dialogue about the course. When possible, try to stay for the faculty partner's preparation time so that you can discuss the visit. Of course, a short written report should be given to the concurrent enrollment program staff for review.

In the rare cases in which there are issues of concern, or when corrective action must be taken, be sure to deal with all parties with sensitivity and in a spirit of learning and development. Since the academic department at the college does control the curriculum, the views of the department mentor are very important to the concurrent enrollment program and its ongoing quality.

2. *Course evaluation by students at the end of the course.* This form of evaluation is usually required of academic courses taught by the college and its various faculty, including high school faculty partners. Some colleges use a hard copy evaluation form while others have a website for completing evaluations by the students. The same process used by the college to collect data on campus should be used by the concurrent enrollment program in the various high school sites whenever possible. The evaluation process may require some adaptation in which forms may need to be sent to each instructor for distribution, given and collected appropriately in the classroom, and returned to the program office. Since every college follows a different evaluation process, it is important that the program staff adapt the evaluation process to make it as legitimate, workable, and trustworthy as possible.

Many colleges send their course evaluations to an outside agency for tabulation and summary. Although cost effective, the information may be somewhat dated by the time it is returned to the concurrent enrollment program staff, then sent on to the high school faculty and college department mentor for discussion and collaboration purposes. Although immediacy may be lost, a great deal of information can be gleaned from an ongoing course evaluation procedure.

NACEP standards provide additional guidance and comparison tools that can be very helpful in evaluating concurrent enrollment programs. The NACEP website provides information, resources, and contacts to use.

It is not my assumption that the components noted in this chapter are all of the considerations involving concurrent enrollment programs. Nor is there a belief that my comments are definitive in any way. Rather, my hope is that you have received a "taste" of the issues that should begin or inform the dialogue concerning concurrent enrollment at your college. Please feel free to agree or disagree with anything written here, but think about each consideration as you begin or continue your journey in the land of concurrent enrollment.

My colleague asked, "How do we maintain a quality concurrent enrollment program at our institution?" I believe the answer may vary, but for me the ultimate answer is: We focus above all on the students and their future, and we maintain quality through the efforts of dedicated concurrent enrollment program staff, a supportive college, and academic departments that are committed to making the program work.

7

Changing the Future

Rigor and High School Mathematics Courses

ANGELA L. KREMERS AND AMANDA L. NOLEN

The Path Less Traveled

Somewhere between co-author Angela Kremers's undergraduate degree in occupational therapy from St. Louis, Missouri, and an eventual teaching position in her local public school district in Arkansas, her path crossed by chance with concurrent enrollment. After leaving the field of occupational therapy practice to teach as a medical academy instructor in a rural Arkansas high school, she quickly found herself disheartened by the lack of rigor and involvement in today's high school classroom. The career academy concept, as part of the High Schools that Work initiative and Workforce Education movements, brought wonderful stories of success. It was easy to see a tangible difference in the excitement of students and involvement in coursework that interested them. The college-level courses were somehow different. The courses challenged students to push harder, utilizing better study habits with fewer excuses for lack of achievement in coursework.

Kremers spoke with a classmate and colleague in higher education who talked about concurrent enrollment at the University of Central Arkansas (UCA) and how it related to Kremers's interest in the achievement gap between secondary and postsecondary education. Her questions at the time were simple and straightforward regarding how UCA's concurrent enrollment program addressed this issue. The classmate shared information about UCA's program and its growing pains and difficulty with university buy-in and support. Their concurrent enrollment program would soon become a steppingstone to discovering more about the gap Kremers saw firsthand in the lack of preparedness among today's high school students. Kremers was hired as a consultant with UCA's concurrent enrollment program to assist with the mass of research, including legislative issues affecting the state and UCA's and other concurrent enrollment programs.

One of the watershed moments of UCA's program was Kremers's discovery of the National Alliance for Concurrent Enrollment Partnerships (NACEP). The university's program joined as a provisional member and began to network with other programs across the country. Kremers was offered a full-time position with the university in 2007 to assist with coordination of concurrent enrollment for UCA. The staff attended NACEP conferences seeking best practices from other concurrent enrollment programs across the country. The university was pleasantly surprised to find that the program was off to a good start; the administration and staff just needed to focus more on the political, policy, and procedural challenges facing the program to continue to improve its quality.

The university was drawn into a larger turmoil over concurrent enrollment in the state during 2009, with legislators and faculty working to establish greater oversight of the programs with clearer boundaries for them. Some of the political and institutional challenges being weighed at the time are reflected in the Arkansas Department of Higher Education's 2007 concurrent enrollment revised policy document, which states:

> The concurrent enrollment policy was first approved by the Arkansas Higher Education Coordinating Board (AHECB) in October 1998 and revised in July 1999. During the past several years, greater emphasis has been placed upon concurrent enrollment as a means of providing curricular options to high school students and the opportunity for students to begin earning college credit while still attending high school. Act 102 of the Second Extraordinary Session of 2003 raised the issue of high schools offering both Advanced Placement and concurrent enrollment classes to their students. Act 936 of 2007 has set in place a pilot program of endorsed concurrent enrollment courses at Rich Mountain Community

College during the 2007–9 biennium. As a result of the interest raised by these legislative acts, concurrent enrollment courses have come under heightened review concerning the quality and efficacy of these courses. (Arkansas Department of Higher Education 2007, 5.16.1)

Through endless campus meetings, specially formed faculty and administrative committees, and state legislative discussions of concurrent enrollment practices and policy, the UCA program emerged stronger and better defined. Despite turnover of organizational leadership at the university's highest level and uncertainty of future support for the program, staff persevered. The concurrent enrollment program prevailed, albeit with some battle wounds. UCA was accredited by NACEP in 2012 and continues to evolve into a higher quality, clearly defined program.

Several questions were raised under scrutiny: Is the program making a difference? Was the turmoil and hard work for a good cause? Would students perform better in college if they participated in this program? For Kremers, these questions informed her dissertation topic, involving concurrent enrollment and Advanced Placement (AP) and its effect on postsecondary math achievement. In this chapter, Kremers and Nolen share the conclusions of that dissertation study and discuss implications for practitioners involved with concurrent enrollment programs. The study illustrates findings in areas of outcome achievement and concurrent enrollment, and its goal is to influence development of programming that changes the future for today's high school student and future college graduate.

Closing the Gap: The Issue

Reports covering two decades of literature suggest a lack of student preparedness for college in the education of American youth, revealing a serious gap in rigorous and effective curriculum pathways (National Commission on the High School Senior Year 2001). The global knowledge-based economy requires educated workers with a college degree and math acumen. The need for American workers who possess college-level knowledge and skills is a significant issue for higher education, which must address academically unprepared students who complete minimal core secondary requirements before transitioning to college. Unprepared college students affect all Americans. The implications of poor academic performance can be seen in a variety of critical state and national indicators, all of which have an impact on bridging the gap between high school preparedness and postsecondary success.

There is a growing emphasis on the need for more advanced math skill accumulation, which stems from a decades-long effort by stakeholders across the United States to counter global competition from countries such as China and India. These countries have been successful in improving technical skills within their labor forces while keeping wages much lower than in the United States. There continues to be a shortage of U.S. citizens trained for high-tech science, technology, engineering, and mathematics (STEM) careers. Experts in the field of education are more unanimously identifying where the United States is making a serious error in our approach to education—the mile-wide, inch-deep phenomenon, as described by William Schmidt, an expert on math education from Michigan State University (Schmidt, Geary, and Henion 2013). The phenomenon is characterized by educational efforts to cover too many topics, all with little to no depth. The consequence is that students fail to achieve mastery of either basic or advanced concepts. Other countries far more advanced in math education, such as Japan, use applied math and scenario teaching in short lessons with longer discussions to allow ample time for connections and relationships among learning concepts to emerge. Why does the United States lag behind? Is it a question of pedagogy, curriculum, teacher qualification, or poor assessment and measure? Is it a combination of these?

Even with effective curricular pathways and effective teachers, all too often the importance of the culture of a high school is overlooked. Administrators are beginning to embrace a stronger college-going culture found in many of the new charter school models emerging across the nation. These schools instill the belief in students and families that going to college is not only possible, but also critical. Teachers also embrace the belief that students should go to college. The teacher's responsibility includes presenting a curriculum to prepare students for college. Enhancing mathematics instruction in Career and Technical Education programs can significantly improve math ability (Stone, Alfeld, and Pearson 2008). The pieces of the systemic puzzle remain disjointed. Key pieces are taking the shape of reform to improve college preparedness; however, postsecondary math achievement and college preparedness have not been fully addressed by curricular pathways alone.

By examining the outcome of current curricular pathways into college preparation, decisions can be better made as to where critical and limited dollars should be focused for both secondary and postsecondary institutions. Bailey and Karp (2003) stated that concurrent enrollment is an effective pathway for rigor and achievement. They concluded that students who participated concurrent enrollment programs "experienced less drops in GPA during their freshman year as compared to students who did not participate" (Bailey and Karp 2003, 23). Taking more advanced-level mathematics courses in the 11th and 12th grades provides a positive effect on academic success. High- and low-achieving students can benefit from taking more advanced math coursework in middle school and high school (Pyzdrowski et al. 2011).

Additionally, policy and further analysis of existing pathways could help identify best practices. Given the issues of need for increased academic rigor, difficulty in transitioning to college, and concern for the

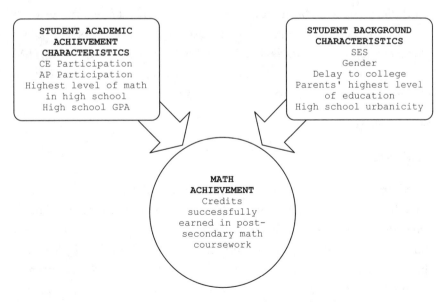

Figure 7.1. Conceptual Framework for Postsecondary Math Achievement

efficacy of curricular pathway trends such as concurrent enrollment and Advanced Placement, the purpose of the current study was to examine the effect of AP and concurrent enrollment on postsecondary math achievement. The conceptual model for the study examined the student's academic achievement characteristics and background characteristics to determine outcome (see Figure 7.1).

Closing the Gap: Outcome Evidence

Though there has been an enormous amount of descriptive research on concurrent enrollment and Advanced Placement, little of this research has examined outcomes. Current literature describes programs and students participating, but it does not indicate the effect of the classes on student outcomes in postsecondary education. In this study, using postsecondary math achievement as the study variable offered a unique perspective to focus more narrowly on a curricular area that requires a developmental skill set rather than an intuitive one. Math aptitude is also a known predictor of college preparedness, as well as a common key component of standardized testing for benchmarking and entrance screening for institutions (Bressoud 2005). Participating in mathematics requires a different vocabulary and level of thinking and higher-order skills that brings critical thinking into the forefront. As our nation works to compete in today's global economy, more students will need to be better prepared for STEM careers, something that can be realized only through curricular pathways that ensure college preparedness and degree attainment.

Methodology

Theoretical Model

Based upon the literature review, the purpose of the study was to understand how curriculum pathways for high school students influenced math achievement in postsecondary education. To achieve this goal, Tinto's model (1996) was used as the guiding theoretical framework. Tinto stated that a student transitions through life stages based upon certain environmental and contextual factors that influence the decision to persist in particular pathways throughout the life span. Other models, such as

Swanson (2008), also reflect Tinto's transition process in studying concurrent enrollment based on his theory. Academic struggles comprise 30% to 35% of all student departures (Tinto 1996). Many students lack the academic competence and study skills needed to be successful. Among even the most academically sound students there have been transitory difficulties associated with the move from secondary to postsecondary environments. As Tinto noted, "college is a sometimes 'foreign' experience, the transition to it, difficult" (1996, 2).

Research Design

To examine the quantitative differences among high school graduates' math achievement in postsecondary education, the study included two groups of variables. The main independent variables in group one, measuring student academic achievement, included concurrent enrollment participation, AP participation, highest level of math taken on the high school transcript, and grade point average (GPA) for all academic courses taken on the high school transcript. The main independent variables in group two, measuring student background characteristics, included socioeconomic status (SES), gender, delay to start college, parents' highest level of education, and high school urbanicity. The dependent variable measure was student academic achievement evidenced by earning math credit in postsecondary education. Stepwise linear regression was utilized in which at each step, the independent variable not in the equation that had the smallest probability of F was entered, if that probability was sufficiently small. Variables already in the regression equation were removed if their probability of F became sufficiently large. The method terminated when no more variables were eligible for inclusion or removal.

Instrument

The National Education Longitudinal Study (NELS) is a nationally representative sample of 8th graders who were first surveyed in the spring of 1988. In the base year of the study, known as NELS:88, schools were selected from a universe file of approximately forty thousand public and private 8th-grade schools across the United States. For the approximately one thousand public and private schools with 8th graders that were sampled and agreed to participate in NELS:88, complete 8th-grade rosters were produced for each school. From this roster, approximately twenty-four students were randomly selected. Samples of these respondents were resurveyed through four follow-ups in 1990, 1992, 1994, and 2000. The remaining students on the roster were then grouped by race and ethnicity.

To prepare for the first follow-up, approximately 90% of the students moved from a K–8/junior high school/middle school setting to high school. Because of these transitions, students had to be traced to their new schools. In addition, school dropouts needed to be identified, contacted, and convinced to participate in the follow-ups. New (updated) students needed to be added to the sample so that the first follow-up data would be representative of high school sophomores. Without these updated students, the file would not be representative of 10th-grade students who did not have the opportunity to participate during the base year (e.g., students who were out of the country in 1988, or who were 9th graders in 1990 but not in 8th grade during spring term 1988). Also, 8th graders who had been considered ineligible (e.g., students with physical or mental disabilities or limited English proficiency) during the base year but whose eligibility status had since changed were added in. These base-year ineligible students were given the opportunity to participate during the 10th grade. Because of the wide dispersal of students, the base-year 8th-grade cohort was subsampled.

For the second follow-up, students needed to be traced. Many stayed in the same high school in which they were surveyed as 10th graders. Others transferred to new high schools, graduated early, or dropped out of high school. It was also necessary to update the sample with 12th graders who did not have the opportunity to be surveyed in prior waves. While no students were subsampled out of the 1992 round, some components (full contextual data from school, transcripts, parent) are based on subsamples.

Prior to data collection for the third follow-up, the decision was made to subsample the NELS:88 respondent population to 14,000 respondents. Selected groups were selected with certainty, meaning all were selected.

For the fourth follow-up, both respondents and nonrespondents for the third follow-up sample were selected for the 2000 survey. Subsampling was then performed upon sample members who had proved difficult to interview, producing an overall sample of 15,237 members of the NELS:88 population at the start of data collection.

On the questionnaire, students reported on a range of topics including school, work, and home experiences; educational resources and support; the role in education of their parents and peers; neighborhood characteristics; educational and occupational aspirations; and other student perceptions. Additional topics included self-report on smoking, alcohol and drug use, and extracurricular activities. For the three in-school waves of data collection (when most were 8th graders, sophomores, or seniors), achievement tests in reading, social studies, mathematics, and science were administered in addition to the student questionnaire. The base year of the National Education Longitudinal Study of 1988 (NELS:88) represents the first stage of this major longitudinal effort designed to provide trend data about critical transitions experienced by students as they leave middle or junior high school, and progress through high school and into postsecondary institutions or the work force.

The first follow-up in 1990 constitutes the first opportunity for longitudinal measurements from the 1988 baseline. It also provides a comparison point to high school sophomores ten years before. The dataset captures the population of early dropouts (those who leave school prior to the end of 10th grade), while monitoring the transition of the student population into secondary schooling.

The second follow-up took place in early 1992, when most sample members were in the second term of their senior year. It provides a culminating measurement of learning in the course of secondary school, and captures information that facilitates investigation of the transition into the labor force and postsecondary education after high school. Because the NELS:88 sample was freshened to represent the high school class of 1992, trend comparisons can be made to the high school classes of 1972 and 1980 that were studied in NLS-72. The NELS:88 second follow-up returned to students who were identified as dropouts in 1990, and identified and surveyed additional students who had left school since the prior wave.

The third follow-up took place in 1994, when most sample members had completed high school. The primary goals of the 1994 round were (1) to provide data for trend comparisons with NLS-72; (2) to address issues of employment and postsecondary access and choice; and (3) to ascertain how many dropouts had returned to school and by what route.

Data from the fourth follow-up interview in 2000 permitted researchers to examine what this cohort had accomplished twelve years after the 8th-grade baseline survey. The 2000 data were collected at a key stage of life transitions for members of the 8th-grade class of 1988, most of whom had been out of high school for nearly eight years. Many had already completed postsecondary education, started or even changed careers, and started to form families. To further enrich the data, students' teachers, parents, and school administrators were also surveyed in 2000. Coursework and grades from students' high school and postsecondary transcripts were also available in the restricted use NELS:88 dataset, although some composite variables have been made available in the public use file. The NELS:88 data can be used for policy-relevant research about educational processes and outcomes; for example, student learning; early and late predictors of dropping out; and school effects on students' access to programs and equal opportunity to learn.

Finally, the dataset utilized for this study to identify the specific independent and dependent variables included use of restricted access to the NELS Postsecondary Education Transcript Study (PETS). PETS postsecondary transcript data was collected as part of NELS:88, in which PETS summary data is presented on postsecondary attainment, attendance, curriculum, and performance of the NELS:88 sample members who attended postsecondary institutions. Postsecondary attainment was broken down by race/ethnicity, sex, and socioeconomic status for different categories of student attendance (based on number of credits and institutional type). Postsecondary attendance was examined through the number of institutions students attended, the number of states in which students attended institutions, types of institutions attended (such as community colleges), and credits taken during the summer term. College course-taking patterns were broken down by high school courses taken and by college major.

Finally, postsecondary performance was examined through undergraduate GPA, remedial courses, and number of postsecondary credits.

Variables

In order to define the variables in this study, the following specific variables in NELS:88/2000 were chosen.

Student academic achievement. The dependent variable of student academic achievement was defined as the number of advanced math credits earned prior to fall 2000. Advance math credits were defined as credits in calculus, differential equations, post-calculus topics, advanced math statistics, engineering math/statistics, numerical methods/analysis in computer science, and physics with calculus. This definition was chosen for four reasons. First, receiving credit was chosen over grade in coursework because neither the NELS:88/2000 nor the PETS dataset contains transcript data such as GPA in the first semester of postsecondary curriculum. Second, quantifying achievement with grades, such as the difference between an A and a D, embeds subjectivity, whereas defining achievement as credit earned incorporates objectivity. Third, if the student had successfully earned credit within their concurrent enrollment or AP curriculum, entry freshmen college math classes would have already been completed. Finally, availability of variables on this limited dataset to examine outcome were very restricted.

The definition of student academic achievement reflected the global need for more college math coursework for STEM education professions that require education beyond what is available through concurrent enrollment and AP classes. The NELS:88/2000 variable that measures postsecondary math achievement (MTHCRD3) was defined as the number of undergraduate credits in calculus and advanced math as defined above on the college transcript prior to fall 2000.

Concurrent enrollment participation. For the purposes of the study, concurrent enrollment and dual credit were used interchangeably. Due to the omission of concurrent enrollment flagging of students in the NELS:88/2000 dataset, concurrent enrollment students are identified by the presence of college credit on the high school transcript prior to high school graduation. Swanson (2008) worked closely with the National Center for Education Statistics (NCES) to assist with identification of students who participated in concurrent enrollment. The resulting variable (TCREDD) in the PETS dataset defines concurrent enrollment participation as having a college credit on the student's high school transcript (Adelman, Daniel, and Berkovits 2003).

Advanced Placement participation. AP participation (F2S13E) was defined by the answer to question 13, part e, on the NELS:88/94 questionnaire (first follow-up), "Have you ever been in any of the following kinds or courses or programs in high school? . . . e. advanced placement programs" (Adelman, Daniel, and Berkovits 2003).

Highest level of math taken on the high school transcript. The NELS:88/2000 variable HIGHMATH measured the highest level of math a student took in college. The highest classes were coded: (1) Calculus, (2) Pre-calculus, (3) Trigonometry, (4) Algebra 2, (5) Geometry, (6) Algebra 1, (7) lower math such as pre-algebra and general mathematics (Adelman, Daniel, and Berkovits 2003).

GPA for all academic courses taken on the high school transcript. The high school GPA was measured by the NELS:88/2000 variable HSGPAV. HSGPAV was a continuous variable standardizing the student's GPA to a 4-point range and multiplying by 100 (Adelman, Daniel, and Berkovits 2003).

Socioeconomic status (SES). SESQUINT was a conversion of the percentile presentation of socioeconomic status of the student's parents from the NELS:88 second follow-up (1992). Included in the original scale are parents' education levels, parents' occupations, and family income.

Gender. COMSEX was a variable to describe gender of the student and was coded male = 1, female = 2.

Delay to start college. The NELS:88/2000 variable DELAY was a continuous variable from the NELS:2000 transcript file that measured the extent of delay between high school graduation and postsecondary entry (Adelman, Daniel, and Berkovits 2003).

Parents' highest level of education. F2PARED was a categorical variable that characterized the level of education attained by either of the parents of the student. It was constructed using parent questionnaire data (BYP30 and BYP31). Student data (BYS34A and BYS34B) were used whenever parent data were either missing or not available. If both parent and student data were missing, BYPARED was assigned a value of missing.

High school urbanicity. G12URBN3 was a categorical variable that trichotomized the urbanicity of the area in which the sample member's second follow-up school was located. The metropolitan status was defined by QED for public school districts, for Catholic dioceses, or in some cases for the county in which the school is located. Dropouts who did not complete a questionnaire or who did not indicate their last school attended were coded as missing.

Weights

Weights included variables put onto the data file to compensate for unequal probabilities of selection and to adjust for the effects of nonresponse. Using weights allowed the researcher to make generalizations to the national populations represented by NELS:88. On the NELS:88 student files for the base year through second follow-up studies (N2P/N2R), there were twelve different analysis weights, each of which were specific for a given population. A panel weight was used to generalize with the individual weights having positive values (>0) for respondents who were members of the designated group and zero (0) for all others.

Participants

Students were selected from the NELS national data set according to fit with selected variables. Students selected were narrowed based upon student background characteristics and academic characteristics. Advanced Placement students were identified as those who were flagged as ever having participated in an AP program, and concurrent enrollment students were identified as those who had college credit on their high school transcript prior to graduation from high school.

The following descriptive statistics indicate the identity of participants in this study: $N = 4,131$ students with dual enrollment credits, $N = 3,804$ students who had ever been in an AP program. Only students who graduated from high school by 1994 were included in the study, and the sample was weighted with adjustments made for design effect.

Multiple linear regression (MLR) allowed the researcher to ask the general question of what were the best sets of predictors for a particular research question. For example, educational researchers might want to learn what the best predictors of success in high school are.

The regression coefficient, b, is the average amount the dependent variable increases when a single independent variable increases one unit while other independents are held constant. Put another way, the b coefficient is the slope of the regression line: the larger the b, the steeper the slope, the more the dependent changes for each unit change in the independent. The b coefficient is the unstandardized simple regression coefficient for the case of one independent.

F test

The F test is used to test the significance of R, which is the same as testing the significance of R^2, which is the same as testing the significance of the regression model as a whole. If $p < .05$, then the model is considered significantly better than would be expected by chance and we reject the null hypothesis of no linear relationship of y to the independents. F is a function of R^2, the number of independents, and the number of cases. F is computed with k and $(n - k - 1)$ degrees of freedom, where k = number of terms in the equation not counting the constant $F = [R^2/k]/[(1 - R^2)/(n - k - 1)]$.

When considering the use of any statistical methodology, the researcher must first be aware of statistical assumptions that must be met. For multiple linear regression these assumptions include (1) correct specification of the model, (2) normality, (3) independence of exogenous variables, (4) sufficiently large sample size, and (5) no systematic missing data. In addition to meeting the assumptions, researchers using data that is hierarchical or has a complex sample design must decide how the data are to be treated. The following section on conceptual framework describes both how the assumptions were met and the considerations for complex sample design. Additionally, the advantage of the MLR analysis was its ability to predict if even violations have occurred due to its robust and flexible nature.

Conceptual Framework

The conceptual framework used in this study aligns with the theoretical model in Figure 7.1, which represents two major constructs based on the grouping of variables and relationships among them. The first construct was student background characteristics based upon socioeconomic status, gender, delay to start college, parents' highest level of education, and high school urbanicity. The second construct was student academic characteristics based upon concurrent enrollment participation, AP participation, highest level of math course taken on the high school transcript, and GPA for all academic courses on the high school transcript. It was theorized these constructs would guide in understanding what predicts postsecondary math achievement.

Limitations

Although various school factors were examined in this study, other potentially important school characteristics were not covered. Additionally, the measures in this study may not quantify what matters most about a school. This could be nearing a subjective component of consideration of this gap between concept and measurement. The labeling in the NELS database made identification of concurrent enrollment and AP students a matter of process of elimination rather than clear identification; additionally, transcript data for the freshmen year in college in follow-up data was not readily available.

Results

The results of the study indicate that participation in Advanced Placement and concurrent enrollment programs per se does not have a significant effect on postsecondary math achievement. Specifically, a multiple linear regression analysis was conducted to evaluate how well each of the independent variables, including AP and concurrent enrollment, predicted postsecondary math achievement. The adjusted R^2 (Table 7.1) indicated that 12% of the variation in postsecondary math achievement was explained by differences in highest level of math taken in high school.

TABLE 7.1

Model Summary Predictors of Postsecondary Math Achievement Change Statistics

Model	R	R^2	R^2 Change	SE	F Change	p
1	.35(a)	.12	.04(a)	5.03	64.75	.01
2	.36(b)	.13	.02(b)	5.02	70.99	.01
3	.37(c)	.14	.02(c)	4.98	55.32	.01
4	.38(d)	.14	.00(d)	4.98	7.99	.01

An additional 2% was added by high school GPA, gender, and parents' highest level of education, and no other variable tested was a significant predictor of math achievement at $p < .05$.

Only 12% of the variance in college math achievement was explained by the research; the second model explained only an additional 1% of the variance in math achievement, and the third and fourth models explained only another 1% of the variance in college math achievement (Table 7.1). Neither concurrent enrollment nor AP course participation predicted postsecondary math achievement; however, there was a correlation between concurrent enrollment and three of the four variables that did predict achievement. The correlation between gender and the remaining independent variables did not result in a significant finding.

Factors such as parental level of education, high school GPA, and highest level of math taken in high school did have a significant effect; conversely, participation in AP or concurrent enrollment alone did not have an effect on outcome. These findings suggest there is a serious gap between rigorous and effective curriculum pathways and instruction.

The growing demand for a national mathematics standard to improve academic outcomes for all American students exists regardless of race, ethnicity, socioeconomic status, or other diversities (Schmidt 2008). According to Nomi and Allensworth (2013), improvements are needed in math instruction for increased rigor to be realized. They piloted an approach that included increased hours learning algebra, with an integration of algebraic concepts into coursework throughout the day: "By integrating math into CTE programs, students were able to grasp math concepts better than their counterparts who did not have math integrated. The theory is that, by seeing math in an applied setting, students will be more interested and more comfortable with mathematical concepts they see in a more traditional math environment" (114).

Setting and aligning clear standards, policy, practice, and assessment at the local, state, and national levels will benefit the field of education. Standards and specific components of programs and program design are more important than mere student participation. Nomi and Allenworth's findings (2013) are consistent with Conley (2005), who also found that merely taking college-prep classes and maintaining a required GPA for college admission was not enough to guarantee success in college. Research has been consistent in defining factors that play a significant role in college achievement. The 2004 ACT Policy report defined these factors as both academic (ACT score, high school GPA, parents' educational attainment) and nonacademic (motivation, self-confidence, goals, social support) (Lotkowski, Robbins, and Noeth 2004). Likewise, Swanson (2008) concluded that concurrent enrollment participation alone did not improve chances for a student to graduate from postsecondary education or attain a degree, as compared to nonconcurrent enrollment participants.

Based on this study, concurrent enrollment and Advanced Placement were not significant predictors of postsecondary math achievement; however, previous studies have shown a positive impact related to social and psychological metrics (Swanson 2008). This study indicates participation alone will not help the student to be successful in undergraduate math coursework and credit earning.

Standardization of both concurrent enrollment and AP programs continues to be an issue, as are variations in professional development of faculty who teach within the programs, which may lead to inconsistent rigor in coursework. The findings of this study highlight the significant need for standardized coursework that includes higher levels of math in high school and better-prepared faculty. If the high school course is to be equivalent to college-level coursework, the faculty within the high school must transition in philosophy and practice to expect the same rigor and academic demand found in the freshman math course. Common best practices for programs include professional development that supports collaboration of both the K–12 systems and higher education institutions. Collaboration includes observations with feedback from higher education peers; networking; utilizing pre- and post-test data to examine course effectiveness; use of postsecondary tests in the high school to ensure similar knowledge is tested and graded; and the philosophy of increasing student independence to utilize resources that include higher-level thinking. Additional lab hours and library research and reading are also common best practices for more rigorous programs.

Closing the Gap: Next Steps

Implications and Recommendations for K–12 Curriculum Specialists

When a commitment is made to participate in concurrent enrollment programs, full examination of quality and scope should be mandated. To address assessment of programs, K–12 curriculum specialists should observe and consider teacher preparation. Specifically, minimum degree and hours earned in the subject area should be equal to that of the college faculty member. Some states, such as Arkansas, are requiring a master's degree plus eighteen additional credit hours in the subject area being taught by the high school faculty member. However, even with these qualifications, rigor is still an issue. High schools allow concurrent enrollment students to follow high school rules, forgiving missed due dates and assignments and even waiving students from taking final exams based on good attendance or other high school philosophy and policy. Students need to be challenged, with teachers targeting higher levels of Bloom's taxonomy, critical thinking, and problem solving to assure adequate rigor and quality.

The focus of academic advising should turn from taking minimal coursework to graduate and toward genuine guidance on pursuing challenging and more rigorous math courses and other demanding, rigorous curricula. As Bressoud (2005) suggested, curriculum specialists need to consider the student in the equation when designing curriculum pathways. Specifically, mathematical sciences curricula must take into account student strengths, weaknesses, career plans and goals, how those goals align with the courses and programs being offered, and how effectively those courses are helping students achieve their career goals. Schools must monitor and adjust their academic offerings and counseling by strengthening course offerings to better align with the needs of the student and must follow up by assessing the outcome of those efforts.

Educators in the K–12 system need to connect mathematics and science across the K–12 spectrum by emphasizing inquiry, presentation of key science and math concepts, and connection across grade levels. Rather than continuing the same long-standing focus on pedagogy, a paradigm shift to change how teachers think about mathematics and science education needs to occur. This is currently being pursued in New Jersey through an innovative consortium that includes thirteen public school districts, three colleges and universities, and the National Staff Development Council. According to the Education Development Center, research data from this approach are showing initial significant results (Lord 2010).

Implications and Recommendations for
Postsecondary and K–12 Partnerships

Administrators with oversight of concurrent enrollment programs should evaluate whether those courses on their schedule truly parallel the college equivalent course. If the course does not fully challenge students to push harder than their regular academic courses, then they are no better prepared for college, risking matriculation failure. It benefits everyone to raise the bar on these programs and not rely on research that shows superficial benefits or findings. Stakeholders in education reform need to move the needle toward outcome-focused studies while continuing to examine the quality of current programming. What good does it do to perpetuate programs utilizing limited funds without critically examining precisely what is working and what is not? This study suggests it is necessary to consider the long-term impact of college preparedness. Although these programs are entrenched and expanding nationwide with funding provided by federal and private dollars, a paradigm shift must occur that embeds evaluation of outcome achievement and results. At minimum, efforts to focus on professional development of concurrent enrollment teachers are critical, as is the constant monitoring and evaluation of coursework rigor and benchmarking against college-level work.

Recommendations include better collaboration and training between secondary and postsecondary faculty to assure the rigor and academic quality of these courses are maintained. Examples of professional development opportunities could encompass summer workshops held on the college campus for high school faculty, common tests between the high school and college, and peer review and observation. The implication for administrators is to assess the quality of the faculty and of the program, and to ensure the program incorporates critical coursework that literature suggests improves the chances for academic postsecondary success.

Pipeline initiatives such as STEM education are gaining more support from recent research. However, Lowell, Salzman, Bernstein, and Henderson (2009) reported that the numbers of brighter students are decreasing in STEM education pathways. The decreased number of students choosing to pipeline in STEM coursework is critical in light of the findings of this study; the findings suggest that to have success in freshman math achievement, students should enroll in more STEM coursework or stronger math-emphasized courses. A lack of STEM-prepared future workers could create long-term consequence. Teachers, parents, counselors, and programs must engage and recruit students into higher-level math coursework and advocate for quality, rigorous math instruction.

Implications and Recommendations for Policy Makers

Until policy begins to push practice in this area, students will continue to have the freedom to meet minimal requirements, which ultimately affects everyone through eventual job barriers based on degree attainment level required. The ability of a high school student to graduate without taking math higher than Algebra 1, or without taking any math at all in the final senior year of high school, could be a devastating blow to our nation's capacity to continue to compete and survive globally for generations to come. Policy makers should seriously examine the current trend to fund the expansion of these programs without further expectation for quality assurance. To provide funding based upon descriptive research without the balance of outcome research is a disservice to taxpayers and educators who demand a better prepared student able to function in a global workforce. Policy must support rigorous math requirements in high school that aligns with quality math instruction.

Future Research

Future suggested research could include using different metrics to indicate achievement, such as transcript data. By examining GPA and transcript data, achievement could be defined by grade earned versus credit earned. This approach would answer further questions of how achievement is defined and measured beyond the interpretation taken in this study. Additionally, suggested research includes examining other curricular disciplines to see if similar findings are discovered; replication of this study examining differing variables; and state- or region-specific research to locate pockets of programs that may be showing more success, rather than looking at national data to find model programs to emulate. Future research to examine other disciplines' curricula may yield useful information on whether this study's findings can be generalized across multiple curriculum areas or are unique to mathematics. The examination of different variables provides numerous options to look at other factors that could potentially affect outcomes, such as GPA in the specific subject areas, number of courses taken in the subject area pipeline, private versus public school, etc. Finally, research could focus on a particular state's data for a localized examination versus use of the national database of information to yield a localized set of data.

Closing the Gap: Final Thoughts

If educators are truly committed to closing the gap between high school and college preparedness for successful postsecondary math achievement, programs and pathways need to be reevaluated to assure inclusion of rigorous math coursework in both quality and quantity. Although some states, such as Arkansas, are requiring teachers to have a master's degree and additional hours of training in the subject area they are teaching, recent research is showing that the degree and training in the subject area are not the key factors for student academic success (Zehr 2009).

By realizing the potential larger scope of the results of this study, a social justice issue is indicated where policy change may be necessary.

Educators in the United States continue to track students into AP, concurrent enrollment, and other specialized pathways. The implications of this study show that tracking into such programs does not have significant effect on postsecondary math achievement. General math courses, including higher-level advanced math coursework, are available to all students without a need for special placement or pathways. Students can access general higher-level math coursework regardless of ability to meet specific requirements, which in turn affords them access to tracking into AP or concurrent enrollment pathways.

Rather than the secondary education concurrent enrollment math teacher having the knowledge to share with the students, it is the actual ability of the teacher to be able to translate that knowledge into learning for the student that counts. Possessing the knowledge and being able to teach that knowledge to others in a meaningful way are two completely distinct skill sets. Pedagogy then becomes just as important if not more important than degree background in the subject area being taught. Finally, it is necessary to link this skilled pedagogy with a philosophy of a true college-going atmosphere, one in which students are considered capable. Ralph Waldo Emerson once stated that the secret in education lies in respecting the student; how profoundly true his statement is.

We are not suggesting that concurrent enrollment programs be eliminated or given less emphasis in national and state discussions; rather, this study suggests that academic programs have room for quality improvements in level of rigor, choice of courses offered, consistency and standardization, teacher preparation, and accessibility. Although tracking students into programs offers opportunity to further advance students who excel, subpopulations of greater need are often excluded from such tracking into advanced curriculum.

The results of this study emphasize the need for better guidance of students into higher-level and a greater number of math courses in high school. With this approach, theoretically a far greater number of students would have access and opportunity to be better prepared to succeed at the postsecondary level. The assumption that being in a transition program alone will provide the student better outcome is in error. As stressed by Bressoud (2009), advanced curriculum pathway students are able to opt in or out of courses throughout their high school years, and thereby have the option to bypass the higher-level advanced math courses that better prepare them for postsecondary success. And even with completion of secondary higher-level math courses, such as AP Calculus with an AP exam score of 3 or higher, postsecondary preparedness is still not assured. Of the 575,000 estimated high school students, including AP and concurrent enrollment students, who take a calculus course offered at the secondary level, approximately 40% think they have completed at least half of an academic year of postsecondary level work. However, based upon a growing body of research, there is no evidence that AP and concurrent programs are significant predictors for postsecondary math achievement and progression into higher-level advanced math coursework, such as Calculus II (Bressoud 2009).

Even with AP students who earn a 3 or higher on the AP Calculus exam, advancement into higher-level math can be counterproductive to achievement. Students may be eligible to advance based upon their AP exam score; however, they are likely to remain unprepared to do so. Bressoud (2009) cites a study by Theresa Laurent at the St. Louis College of Pharmacy which revealed that students who came into their program with concurrent enrollment credit in calculus performed no differently from students who had no credit, even when the research controlled for ACT scores. In fact, Bressoud concludes that taking calculus in high school is of little benefit unless the student learns it well enough to eliminate the need to take an introductory calculus course once the student begins postsecondary education. Again, quality instruction is critical to prepare students in math for success in college.

Concurrent enrollment programs are doing good things. Research is extensive in the benefits of transition programs. But since much of the research has been qualitative or descriptive, it is evident that quantitative outcome studies are needed. Participation in concurrent enrollment had tangible benefits such as motivational and aspirational effects, consistent with data from past researchers such as Paulsen (1990) and Garg, Kauppi, Lewko, and Urajnik (2002), who found that participation was an important predictor of educational aspirations, even more so than grades or parents' highest level of education, which were significant predictors in this study.

With the increase in national and state policy dialogue surrounding the issue, it benefits all stakeholders to move forward cautiously in funding, policy, and implementation. New national initiatives, such as Race to the Top, an education initiative funded through the American Recovery and Reinvestment Act of 2009 (ARRA), encourage academic improvement with math and science initiatives strongly embedded. Expanding concurrent enrollment programming as part of this initiative should be weighed against requirements to increase the number and quality of math courses with no opt out. Initiatives to improve teacher development and training in math and science are encouraging, and could address the inconsistencies between programs and outcomes nationwide.

A final question to consider: Would math-taking patterns in postsecondary education be changed if students were encouraged to take an increased number of advanced math courses in high school? Further examination could explore the effect of such a change on STEM education and its role in feeding an education pipeline of globally prepared students who are poised for postsecondary success and degree attainment. Ultimately, an increasing need for STEM-prepared workers could continue to highlight the gap between underprepared high school students and college freshmen who struggle to complete coursework and matriculate through to earn a degree.

It is critical that education reformers and policy makers begin to reconsider the current path of promoting and funding initiatives to expand concurrent enrollment programs without establishing standards of academic quality and rigor beyond those currently in place. U.S. students must be better prepared for postsecondary education in order to acquire the skills to succeed in a global workforce. Stakeholders should move forward by taking best practices and model programs to the forefront and leaving the status quo behind.

Great teaching is the ability to bring interest and higher expectations into students' academic experience through an iterative process of knowledge building. Parents generally trust academia's ability to make the right choices on their behalf. The next step belongs to educators, administrators, and policy makers to shape concurrent enrollment to change the future. We must all commit to the path less traveled.

References

Adelman, C., B. Daniel, and I. Berkovits. 2003. *Postsecondary Attainment, Attendance, Curriculum, and Performance: Selected Results from the NELS:88/2000 Postsecondary Education Transcript Study (PETS), 2000.* E.D. Tabs. Washington, DC: National Center for Educational Statistics, U.S. Department of Education. Accessed Feb. 2010. https://nces.ed.gov/dasol/index.asp.

Arkansas Department of Higher Education. 2007. *Arkansas Higher Education Coordinating Board Policies.* Accessed Nov. 17, 2011. http://www.arkleg.state.ar.us /education/HigherEd/AHECB/Board%20Policy%20May%202010.pdf.

Bailey, Thomas, and Melinda Mechur Karp. 2003. "Promoting College Access and Success: A Review of Credit-Based Transition Programs." Office of Vocational and Adult Education, U.S. Department of Education. Accessed Nov. 11 2013. http://ccrc.tc.columbia.edu/publications/access-success-credit-based-transi tion.html.

Bressoud, D. M. 2005. "Launchings from the CUPM Curriculum Guide: Who Are We Teaching?" Mathematical Association of America website. Accessed Feb. 4, 2010. http://www.maa.org/external_archive/columns/launchings /launchings_03_05.html.

———. 2009. "AP Calculus: What We Know." Launchings. Mathematical Association of America website. Accessed Feb. 4, 2010. http://www.maa.org/external _archive/columns/launchings/launchings_06_09.html.

Conley, D. T. 2005. *College Knowledge: What It Really Takes for Students to Succeed and What We Can Do to Get Them Ready.* San Francisco: Jossey-Bass.

Garg, Rashmi, C. Kauppi, J. Lewko, and D. Urajnik. 2002. "A Structural Model of Educational Aspirations." *Journal of Career Development* 29(2): 87–108.

Lord, B. 2010. "Connecting Math and Science across Grades." *EDC Update* (Winter): 6.

Lotkowski, V. A., S. B. Robbins, and R. J. Noeth. 2004. *The Role of Academic and Non-Academic Factors in Improving College Retention: ACT Policy Report.* Iowa City, IA: ACT. Accessed Jan. 2014. www.act.org/research/policy/index .html.

Lowell, B. Lindsey, H. Salzman, H. Bernstein, and E. Henderson. 2009. "Steady as She Goes? Three Generations of Students through the Science and Engineering Pipeline." Institute for the Study of International Migration, Georgetown University, Heldrich Center for Workforce, Rutgers University, and The Urban Institute. Accessed Nov. 16. http://www.heldrich.rutgers.edu/sites /default/files/products/uploads/STEM_Paper_Final.pdf.

National Commission on the High School Senior Year. 2001. "The Lost Opportunity Of Senior Year: Finding A Better Way, Summary Of Findings." Princeton, NJ: Woodrow Wilson National Fellowship Foundation.

Nomi, Takako, and Elain M. Allensworth. 2013. "Sorting and Supporting: Why Double-Dose Algebra Led to Better Test Scores but More Course Failures." *American Education Research Journal* 50(4): 1–33, doi: 10.3102/0002831212469997.

Paulsen, Michael B. 1990. *College Choice: Understanding Student Enrollment Behavior* (ASHE-ERIC: Higher Education Report). Washington, DC: George Washington University.

Pyzdrowski, Laura J., Melanie B. Butler, Vennessa L. Walker, Anthony S. Pyzdrowski, and Michael E. Mays. 2011. "Exploring the Feasibility of Dual-Credit Mathematics Courses in High School via a Web-Enhanced, Blended Model." *Journal of General Education* 60(1): 43–60.

Schmidt, William H. 2008. "What's Missing from Math Standards? Focus, Rigor, and Coherence." *American Educator* (Spring). Accessed Jan. 10, 2014. http://dbweb01.aft.org/pdfs/americaneducator/spring2008/schmidt.pdf.

Schmidt, William H., Nicole Geary, and Andy Henion. 2013. "Lagging U.S. Students Need More Rigorous Math." *Michigan State University Today*. Accessed Dec. 23. http://msutoday.msu.edu/news/2013/lagging-us-students-need-more-rigorous-math/.

Stone, James R., Corinne Alfeld, and Donna Pearson. 2008. "Rigor and Relevance: Enhancing High School Students' Math Skills Through Career and Technical Education." *American Education Research Journal* 45(3): 767–95.

Swanson, Joni L. 2008. "An Analysis of the Impact of High School Dual Enrollment Course Participation on Postsecondary Academic Success, Persistence and Degree Completion." Doctoral diss., Univ. of Iowa.

Tinto, Vincent. 1996. "Restructuring the First Year of College." *Planning for Higher Education* 25: 1–6.

Zehr, Mary A. 2009 (Feb. 23). "Scores Unaffected by Teacher-Training Route." *Education Week* 28(22): 9. http://www.edweek.org/ew/articles/2009/02/25/22altcert.h28.html.

8

Transitional Advising in Concurrent Enrollment

BRENDA E. ABBOTT, TIFFANY M. SQUIRES,
AND JASON P. ALTERI

Imagine for a moment two high school seniors, both of whom will graduate soon, sitting at a table in front of the admissions counter at a community college. Both students attend the same high school and took the same concurrently enrolled (high school and college level) courses. One student holds a copy of a college transcript from those concurrently enrolled classes, already showing a full semester of college level credits. He is prepared to transfer these credits to this community college for the fall semester, starting him at an advantage over other incoming college freshman. The other student does not have a college transcript. Although this student potentially did the same work as the first (provided expectations were the same for registered and nonregistered students), the second student did not complete the paperwork to earn college credits. In this scenario, no one took the time to explain the advantages of earning college credit while attending high school; or if they had, the student had turned a deaf ear. This student, without a college transcript, is now at a great disadvantage compared to the other. Imagine now how different registration at this same community college will look for these two, otherwise similarly prepared, students.

Concurrent enrollment programs permit high school students to enroll in college-level courses, simultaneously earning college credit and credit for high school graduation (Greenberg 1989). In this way, concurrent enrollment programs not only accelerate student achievement, but they also provide students with a more comfortable transition to post-secondary education (Chapman 2001; Puyear, Thor, and Mills 2001). With college credits in hand, students have to pursue and master the challenging courses awaiting them in college (Greenberg 1989). Dual credit courses provided by concurrent enrollment programs offer valuable and challenging learning opportunities for advanced, average, and lower-level achieving students alike (Karp, Calcagno, Hughes, Jeong, and Bailey 2008). These programs lead to higher levels of persistence, especially for students from lower socioeconomic status levels, by helping them anticipate new routines and adjust to new norms, as well as develop their understanding of college-level work and expectations (Bailey, Hughes, and Karp 2002; Swanson 2008). Overall, concurrent enrollment programs offer high school students a chance to experience college in the familiar environment of their high schools, which essentially prepares students for the psychological and intellectual transformation they experience in their transition to college.

Although programs allowing secondary students to earn college credit before high school graduation are now widely available in various forms around the country (Chapman 2001), most programs do not have structured services in place to help students understand the program and use these credits effectively. These services that guide students toward a seamless transition from high school to postsecondary education are best delivered through a program for transitional advising integrated within a partnership between the concurrent enrollment program and high schools. Development of a program for advising provides students with "the opportunity to use information, to relate this information to themselves, and to begin the critical task of assessing themselves in relationship to their academic interests and abilities" (White et al. 1995, 27). Other factors that may deter a student from registering aside (lack of funding for example), the student without a transcript, described in the introductory scenario above, is an example of those students who fail to fully benefit from the college credit that may be obtained through the concurrent enrollment program due to lack of transitional advising.

Transitional advising is the individual guidance students need to maximize the benefits offered to them through their concurrent enrollment program, including college credit recognition, college level academic rigor and experience, and anticipatory socialization (Karp 2006; Swanson 2008) or the behaviors and attitudes that influence students' transition to the college environment. Even the student described in the opening scenario with completed transcript in hand, due to lack of a transitional advising program available to him, likely did not fully understand the significance of what he had accomplished. Without adequate transitional advising on an individual and consistent level, students miss out on the opportunity to employ a strategy regarding their college plan. Even worse, they fail to document and receive credits they have rightfully earned for college.

Belasco (2013) suggested advising programs provide for seamless transition to college through relationships with an advisor who encourages college aspirations (Holcomb-McCoy 2010) through varied and thorough efforts including aiding students' academic preparation (Brown and Trusty 2005), guiding students through the college application process (Bryan, Moore-Thomas, Day-Vines, and Holcomb-McCoy 2011), and informing parents and clarifying their role as advisors in college planning (Rowan-Kenyon, Perna, and Swan 2008). Students' transition to college is also improved within schools grounded by a shared vision focused on development of and dedication to a college mission (McDonough 1997).

Belasco (2013) noted that advisors play a significant role in an integrated program for transitional advising, in that they increase the likelihood that students of low socioeconomic status (SES) will attend college, increase acceptance into college for students who apply (by informing and supporting them through the process), and support students in the transition to college by aligning high school exit and college entrance requirements. In addition, by requiring accessibility of a college preparation program for all students, advisors even increase academic achievement for all students. In this way, the research provides powerful arguments for developing integrated programs for advisement. The role of the transitional advisor is a critical link for students to that transition and their readiness for college.

It is true that most districts have guidance counselors to advise students on academic matters and, in some cases, even help with the application to college. In many cases, however, these counselors may likely be overburdened with paperwork, multiple duties (beyond the scope of the job description), and additional requests from the equally overburdened school administrators (Murray 1995). As Murray noted, the general characteristics of the role of the school guidance counselor include developing instructional programs that teach students autonomy and responsibility, providing programs that promote self-esteem and self-efficacy, informing students on career planning, and providing individual support to students as needed. Guidance counselors, however, are typically employees of the school district in partnership with the concurrent enrollment program and not employees of the program itself.

Transitional advising involves duties beyond the scope of the average school counselor job description especially with regard to transfer credit recognition, strategic planning regarding concurrent enrollment courses specific to college and career, and college expectations especially relevant to levels of autonomy. Upon entering college, students struggle most with the transition to new behavioral norms and attitudes, college level goals and intentions, intellectual demands, and college socialization (Tinto 1987; Swanson 2008). Transitional advising serves to prepare students to anticipate these changes in ways that go beyond the scope of what a school guidance counselor may set out to do. Therefore, it is school guidance counselors who may be the best and most qualified individuals to partner with a transitional advisor in concurrent enrollment programs with relevant models for addressing transitional advising, or where interaction with students is facilitated through multiple advisors by a coordinator of transitional advising.

A transitional advisor is a resource for students, as well as an asset for the high school and concurrent enrollment program in partnership together on behalf of those students. Transitional advisors explain the program's mission to students and guide them toward a seamless transition to post-graduate study. They are knowledgeable about requirements for both high school graduation and college entrance. Transitional advisors help students understand their college placement test score, like the SAT or the ACT, and how it determines their placement in college courses. They also advise students on how to use their college credits in ways that are most relevant to their chosen college program. Transitional advisors are not counselors or coaches or academic advisors, although elements of those duties may exist within the role if desired or necessary. Transitional advisors are also not agents for college recruitment. Rather, a transitional advisor serves as an integral role within the transitional advising program for any high school or concurrent enrollment program for the benefit of the students.

Without integrated programs for transitional advising, students are placed in their first college-approved high school class with little understanding of how to complete or submit the college application form associated with that class. Some students may seek help from parents, but parents may not know the answers to students questions, or be privy to necessary information to educate students on college application and transition matters; and at this point it may be too late to ask for help. Once in place, a transitional advising program would communicate with parents long before the student enters the class, providing these parents with the information necessary to help their son/daughter(s) make decisions about and prepare for college. Without the support of transitional advising, younger or less motivated students may overlook the required paperwork and fail to receive the college credit they have earned.

This chapter discusses the importance of transitional advising programs for high school students planning for college. It explains the benefits of concurrent enrollment programs and argues that transitional advising is an important facet of such programs that helps students understand and maximize these benefits. The chapter describes concurrent enrollment programs at Laramie County Community College and Syracuse University Project Advance and considers ways transitional advising is addressed within them. It discusses implications for practitioners, including concurrent enrollment in the context of education reform, as well as for remediation and enrichment, credit recovery for high school graduation, and concurrent enrollment as a pathway to career. Finally the chapter provides conclusions regarding the implementation of integrated programs for transitional advising in high schools and colleges offering programs in concurrent enrollment.

Laramie County Community College:
A Transitional Advising Model

Laramie County Community College (LCCC) offers numerous opportunities for free college credit to all students in the LCCC service area. To ensure local high school juniors and seniors know about opportunities for free college credit available to them through concurrent enrollment with LCCC, the transitional advising staff developed a structured advising component to their concurrent enrollment program, which extended services to all high school students in the LCCC service area. The program provides one-on-one transitional advising sessions for all junior and senior high school students in the LCCC service area. It emphasizes the numerous opportunities available for free college credit and how best to use them to the student's advantage.

Transitional advising of high school students paves the way for the more focused on-campus academic advising that all college students receive while completing the requirements for a college degree. Academic advising differs from transitional advising in that the former is specific to the college program and happens during college, while the latter provides assistance to high school students during the shift from high school to college and helps students prepare for successful change between those phases. At LCCC the transitional advisor is a partner for the high school student taking concurrent enrollment courses and his or her parent(s). The role of the transitional advisor at LCCC is to provide information, answer questions, and advocate for the student's benefit throughout the entire early college registration and enrollment process.

In the infancy of concurrent enrollment at LCCC, when it was still offered only for a few high school classrooms, the loosely structured process of enrolling high school students in courses at LCCC was a public relations embarrassment. The task of organizing registration was given the status of "other duties as assigned" and fell to college staff members already busy with existing primary responsibilities. This created a problem meeting the needs of the LCCC community, especially those of incoming students at registration time. Students and their parents were sent from one office to another in hopes that they would stumble on someone who might know what to do with them. It became apparent that students concurrently enrolled in LCCC courses at their high schools were in need of specific advisement from an informed college staff member. This led to the designation of a part-time concurrent enrollment coordinator, which slowly led to greater improvements in all services provided to the high school population.

Over the next decade, the coordinator position was increased to full time as the need for direct services for high school students and their often-confused parents increased as well. High school students registering for dual credit classes through LCCC now make an advising appointment, as required by the program, with the coordinator before they are able to enroll. Meetings with program advisors are required for all concurrently enrolled students prior to registration for each new semester. In this way transitional advising provides students with the information necessary to navigate a complicated billing process, to meet requirements aligned with the specific memorandum of understanding from their service area district, and to determine their eligibility for free classes based upon correct information. The opportunity for advisement through concurrent enrollment further prepares students for the expectations awaiting them at the college level.

The LCCC Transitional Advising program is now being implemented in full cooperation with high schools in the local service area. A team of two transitional advisors spends one or two afternoons a month at each high school campus. High school students, especially juniors, are encouraged through televised morning announcements and/or in district newsletters to schedule an appointment with their transitional advisor from the college. Each advisor visits with one student for a twenty-minute session. The advising session is designed around a one-page checklist covering the basics of making a smooth transition from high school to college (see Figure 8.1). This checklist allows a transitional advisor to efficiently gather basic information, answer questions, and schedule a follow-up advising session at the college campus.

Communication with parents is important within the transitional advising program. Parents are invited to attend all advising sessions, including those preliminary sessions conducted at the high school. It is

Transitional Advising Checklist for Secondary Students

Student
Name _____ EMAIL _____

HS School: <u>Central/East/South High School</u>   Today's Date: _____

LCCC Transitional Advisor (TA):

      Student is on track for high school graduation.   **YES** List:

      Student has taken concurrent enrollment classes.   **NO**

      Current grade level _____

      Student is credit deficient at this time for high school graduation.

STOP - You must CONTACT your high school counselor for permission before registering for any LCCC college courses through which you hope to address credit deficiency for graduation. Credit ratio: 6 college credits = 1 high school credit.

_____ **Student attended ACT Prep sessions (online, at LCCC or high school) prior to testing.**

_____ **Student has taken the ACT or**   **Dates:**
      Compass Placement Test

_____ **Future ACT testing date(s) planned:**

_____ **Highest ACT scores to date: Composite**

      ENGLISH (18) _____ **MATH (21)** _____ **READING (21)** _____

_____ **(Senior's ACT or Compass test scores indicate need for remediation in at least one area of college readiness.**

         _____ **ENGLISH** _____ **MATH** _____ **READING**

      Completed KCPS assessments: 1. **Interests** 2. **Skills** 3. **Values)**

      Student has met with high school Career Counselor to interpret KCPS assessment(s).

_____ **Student has chosen a Career Cluster** _____ **Career Pathway** _____

_____ **Student is preparing for the Hathaway scholarship through high school course selections.**

_____ **Senior and parent have requested separate pin numbers for FAFSA (date)**

_____ **Student self-selected a college program of study (not KCPS based choice)**

_____ Student is aware of dual credit opportunities on the LCCC campus. (Provided in writing.)

_____ Student is aware drop/add policies in effect for dual credit classes at LCCC. (Provided in writing.)

_____ Student is aware of the steps necessary to acquire a student copy of his college transcript.

Concurrent enrollment credits are the bridges on your Career Pathway!

Student Signature _____

Varos/Transitional Advising   Revised: 11/20/13

Figure 8.1. Transitional Advising Checklist for Concurrent Enrollment Students

important for students and their parents to meet face to face with the transitional advisor to discuss necessary information and ensure that students can take advantage of concurrent enrollment benefits to which they are entitled, including, but not limited to, college credit and free or reduced tuition.

Laramie County Community College is an example of a concurrent enrollment program that is flourishing in large part due to its development of a transitional advising component. LCCC has direct knowledge of the advantages for students who seek out advising and the disadvantages of students who do not, as well as the advantages for high schools and colleges whose concurrent enrollment programs include an integrated transitional advising component. Although students benefit more, both in high school and when they move on to college, from concurrent enrollment programs that include formal advising specific to the college transition, some programs do manage to thrive even without an official transitional advising component. Syracuse University Project Advance is one such thriving program, and results of an ongoing study have prompted this program to revisit the transitional advising needs of enrolled students.

Syracuse University Project Advance: Post-graduate Survey Analysis

Transitional advising is a key factor in the success of students participating in concurrent enrollment programs. However, transitional advising is not required as a formal component of the development of a concurrent enrollment program, so the level at which important factors in transitional advising are addressed varies with each individual program. Syracuse University Project Advance (SUPA) provides concurrent enrollment opportunities that benefit many schools and teachers in the northeastern United States and in other parts of the world. Currently SUPA does not have a formal component for transitional advising built into their program, so the transitional needs of students are addressed in other ways within the program.

The mission of Project Advance is to provide challenging Syracuse University courses to qualified high school students as a means of promoting college readiness. Through SUPA, high school teachers, who must be qualified according to the university's standards as adjunct instructors, deliver instruction to students at their high schools. A Syracuse University faculty member, assigned by the department respective to each course, oversees delivery of instruction. This faculty liaison also provides initial training and regular professional development for participating high school instructors teaching courses offered through SUPA, reflecting the program's commitment to providing professional development and ongoing dialogue between university faculty and high school teachers.

In 1972, SUPA was created for high school seniors who had completed graduation requirements and needed a means of preparing for college. The program was founded for the very purpose of smoothing the transition for students from high school to college. That first year, five SU introductory courses were offered to more than four hundred students in nine different high schools. The program has grown to provide more than forty SU courses today for almost ten thousand students across seven states and three continents. SUPA strives to address more specific transitional needs for students in various ways embedded throughout the program.

Transfer credit advising, including how to apply to college and strategies for college program preparation, is provided directly to students through one-on-one communication with a SUPA administrator. A formal student guide is provided to all students with detailed instructions for how to seek and obtain transfer credit. Advisement for planning a college program and seeking transfer credit is informed by reports (generated and updated annually) that track the history of transfer results (attempts and successes) across various colleges to which students apply. Records are maintained to aid students with requests for transfer credit. Information for students and families is regularly updated on the program website, which includes college application steps, access to relevant forms, and guidance for fulfilling various college program requirements like general education courses and major or minor courses. Additionally, Syracuse University faculty make regular school visits to talk with students about what to expect when they go to college.

SUPA administrators also provide group presentations for schools in the form of parent student nights and regional information sessions for members of the school community. One such type of information session is provided specifically for high school guidance counselors. Guidance counselors may play an integral role in the development of advising services for students in transition to postsecondary education, whether in a formal transitional advising role as part of a concurrent enrollment program, or working as transitional advisors from their professional role in high schools. SUPA's annual information sessions for counselors from partner schools are designed to explain the program and support these guidance professionals' efforts to support their students. These sessions, in addition to support provided by SUPA as needed throughout the school year, allow guidance counselors to network and form support systems with each other. Albeit an indirect form of support for students in transition, this approach enables SUPA to facilitate the sharing of information necessary for guidance counselors to help students understand the program and transfer their earned college credits, and ultimately serves to meet the transitional needs of those students.

As part of its dedication to continual improvement, SUPA conducts an annual survey of its graduates. The Post-graduate Survey instrument was developed for the first cohort of graduates at the start of the program in 1975 and continues to be implemented today. The purpose of the survey is to measure impact of participation for SUPA students and monitor credit transfer for students at their respective colleges after they have enrolled, registered, and gone through the credit transfer process. The survey instrument is comprised of questions required by the National Alliance of Concurrent Enrollment Partnerships (NACEP) for the purpose of accreditation, and in fact, SUPA's questions were used as the model for determining those NACEP requirements. Results are analyzed each year and shared among staff and with stakeholders as one means of assessment for improvement of the program.

Data collected in May 2014 from high school seniors who had completed courses through SUPA in 2013 were analyzed to ascertain what, if any, type of credit students received for transferring their Syracuse University course credits into their programs at college. Surveys are disseminated at what would be the end of a student's freshman year of college to provide time for students to seek and obtain transfer credit. All high school seniors age eighteen or older, which is the age of consent, having completed a course(s) the previous school year are surveyed. For the purpose of the survey, all students receiving a survey are considered graduates. The survey is conducted to ascertain if and how students sought and or obtained transfer credit from their college for courses taken through Project Advance.

Disseminated electronically (e-mail) and via postal mail, the May 2014 Post-graduate Survey was sent to the target population of 8,426 graduates. Based on information compiled, 16% of SUPA graduates from 2013, or 1,339 graduates, participated in the survey.

A majority of respondents (90%) reported they were attending a four-year university other than Syracuse University at the time of the survey. Some of the remaining participants did attend SU; others, however, were either attending somewhere other than a four-year institution or were not in college at all at the time the survey was taken.

Overall, 80% of respondents reported they did not qualify for a Pell Grant, and 87% reported they did not qualify in high school for free and reduced lunch, indicating a majority of respondents may be from a higher socioeconomic status level. Additionally, diversity was lacking in this sample, as 1,014 (76%) of those responding to the survey identified themselves as European American or white. Other respondents consisted of 83 (6.2%) Hispanic/Latino, 46 (3.4%) two or more races, 73 (5.5%) Asian, 46 (3.4%) African or Black Americans, 5 (0.37%) American Indian/Alaska Native, 1 (0.075%) Non-Resident Alien, and 5 (0.15%) Native Hawaiians/Pacific Islanders. Additionally, 10 (0.75%) participants identified as being of unknown races, and 38 (2.8%) students left the question blank.

The data revealed that 1,163 of the 1,339 participants, or about 87%, did seek credit transfer for their Syracuse University courses. Of those 1,163 credit seekers, more than 80% received a decision for their request: almost 80% reported they received recognition for their Syracuse University courses with direct credit transfer; about 10% reported no recognition; and another 10% reported recognition without credit. Other forms of credit reported as received included the fulfillment of a general education or core distribution requirement, fulfillment of a prerequisite course that allowed admittance into a more advanced course, or fulfillment of a program requirement for an anticipated major or minor program. It can be seen from this data that students who attempt to seek credit from their colleges for concurrent enrollment courses do receive recognition in some form. In general, students who had completed concurrent enrollment course(s) entered college at an advantage in terms of preparation and placement, whether this took the form of direct transfer of three course credits, fulfillment of a program requirement, or placement in a more advanced level course.

What about the students who do not seek credit transfer? Of the 1,339 survey participants, 176 reported they did not attempt to transfer their college credits. A majority of those students, more than 75, reported they planned to transfer Syracuse University courses but had not done so yet. About 20 students decided repeating the course would benefit them in some way. Less than 10 reported their grades were too low to transfer. The remaining (±) 70 students reported they did not think their college would recognize their credits, they were unaware recognition was possible or they did not know how to obtain it, or some other form of difficulty transferring their credits. That means about 40% of students from this survey who did not seek credit did not do so under circumstances that may have been helped by more direct transitional advisement. It should be recognized, however, that those 70 participants who may have needed more direct advising make up only 5% of the participant population, a marginal representation overall.

Most important, what may be assumed from the data regarding students who did not seek credit transfer is that these students did not know it was necessary to send a transcript in order to obtain credit and/or recognition from their college. In some cases, students did not understand that a high school transcript differs from a college transcript, in that a college transcript obtained from Syracuse University is required in order to be awarded credit transfer and/or recognition. This lack of understanding amounts to a student's ability to understand and navigate college culture. First-generation college students, for example, may have more trouble with understanding and navigating college culture than students with parents who attended college themselves. Transitional advising is essential for these students and others who struggle to anticipate and/or grasp college culture. It is those students—the ones who need help transitioning to college culture, or who do not understand the importance of obtaining a college transcript upon completion of a course taken through SUPA—who prompted SUPA to consider how efforts to meet transitional needs of students might be further improved.

The SUPA program, operating for more than forty years, is thriving and continuing to grow and develop each year. It has served as a model for other successful concurrent enrollment programs and has set standards for criteria required by NACEP for all accredited concurrent enrollment programs nationwide. SUPA can credit its success in part to a strong foundation of challenging coursework developed at Syracuse University as well as high-caliber professional development and support for SUPA instructors from faculty and qualified administrative staff. What SUPA does not have, however, is a formal transitional advising component integrated into the program. Advising is addressed mainly via the designation of a SUPA associate director responsible for the coordination of programs for high school guidance counselors. However, this form of support is indirect, as it is subject not only to a third party but to the interpretations of various individuals serving in even more varied capacities and duties as guidance counselors at the high school level.

It may not be achievable to integrate a formal transitional advising component into programs the size and scope of SUPA, which serves a large population of students and families across the world. Future research may assess the impact and effectiveness of efforts already in place for programs like SUPA in more dispersed forms (e.g., information provided to guidance counselors via information sessions conducted by program administrators). Research may also consider, especially for larger programs conducted across great geographic distance, what types of transitional advising is necessary. Is service for credit transfer enough, or should students be provided more comprehensive forms of transitional advising like college/career planning guidance and designated advisors available for consultation. These questions may be difficult to conceptualize and answers even more difficult to ascertain. The solutions for large programs like SUPA may even exist within more intensive training for guidance counselors from partner schools. However, given the importance of transitional advising in the context of concurrent enrollment programs, these questions warrant consideration, time, and attention.

Advising students in their transition to college is important, and programs like SUPA stand to grow stronger from research and evaluation specific to the advising needs of students and, if possible, the development of integrated programs for transitional advising or transitional advising components within a larger concurrent enrollment program. As previously stated, the mission of SUPA includes a commitment to research and evaluation of programs, tools, and services that increase college readiness for students and smooth the transition from high school to college. Already impacting many schools in different states and even in other countries, SUPA provides students an experience in challenging college-level courses, increases motivation and gives students more reason to remain in school, and provides students the advantage upon entering college of course credit, advanced placement, and/or exemption. Students enrolled in concurrent enrollment programs benefit from transitional advising to help them understand these advantages available through the program.

For concurrent enrollment programs considering the development of transitional advising components, it is important to be informed about transitional advising as it relates to facets of education like enrichment and remediation, as well as the impact of transitional advising on college and career readiness. Implications of developing such components within concurrent enrollment programs for practitioners and partners are further discussed in the sections of this chapter that follow.

Transitional Advising to Address Educational Reform

The National Governors Association and the Council of Chief State School Officers introduced the Common Core State Standards in 2010 to provide guidelines for teaching and learning intended to better prepare students for college and career. These standards are designed to increase instructional rigor (Blackburn 2011) and further develop critical thinking and problem solving skills (Alberti 2013), goals that are also central to the development and implementation of a concurrent enrollment program. The standards contributed to a larger reform movement of education in the United States, a movement that benefits from efforts to bridge the gap between high school and college in its mission to better prepare students for college and career.

Education reform has a history of falling short of success (Newman and Wehlage 1995) due to the various factors that influence what is required for a successful change to take effect (Fullan 2006). Reform is change, and often the extent of influence from factors affecting change is too great to process in any definite way. Similarly, there are many facets to effectively preparing students for a successful transition to college. One critical factor is increasing rigor, relevance, and engagement of high school academics for all students (Tinto 1997; Karp et al. 2008; Swanson 2008; Hirsch 2010). Equally important is the development of awareness for what it takes to transition, persist, and succeed in college socially and academically (Swanson 2008; Hirsch 2010). Courses taught through concurrent enrollment programs offer a means of addressing the existing gap between high school and college and teach students to think and learn strategically by providing increasing rigor of academic coursework through firsthand experience with college-level courses. Transitional advising prepares students to think critically and plan strategically, and it works directly to prepare students for college, factors critical to successful reform called for by the Common Core State Standards.

Providing academic support through individual advising sessions with trained college personnel can help high school students see the value of concurrent enrollment courses in the much more focused and relevant picture of their own educational needs and goals. By allowing students of varied academic levels and grade point averages to enroll, concurrent enrollment programs offer an opportunity to address these areas where educational reform is needed, and thereby contribute to decreasing the need for remediation at the college level.

Reducing the Need for Remediation at the Postsecondary Level

In recent decades, the need for academic remediation at the college entrance level has become a topic of debate for secondary and postsecondary educators. Criteria to identify students in need of remediation at the postsecondary level are often determined by college faculty/staff members. At Laramie County Community College, for example, postsecondary educators experiencing an overwhelming need for remediation in their courses seek attention from secondary educators to better prepare students for college level work. Without knowledge of criteria used to determine the need for remediation, secondary-level educators are at a disadvantage, especially when remediation is implemented without their awareness. The two sides are left with a gap between high school preparation and college readiness, which ultimately leaves students unprepared and abandoned in a compromising position.

As Conley (2005) explains, the two systems of education in the United States, high school and college, evolved separately and were not designed to work together. Conley (2010) also suggests that this readiness gap is evidenced by large numbers of students who enroll in college only to drop out after a semester or two. Closing the gap requires educational collaboration and cooperation. Concurrent enrollment programs lend themselves to the development of partnerships between high schools and colleges. Such partnerships work to align core competencies required of graduating seniors, especially in math and English, with the competencies expected of incoming college freshmen.

Transitional advisors cultivate these partnerships by serving as a link between college level expectations and high school classrooms. Transitional advisors work directly with high schools and students. Not only are they are able to inform teachers and administrators about college level criteria for entrance and success, but they can also provide information specific to individual student performance, such as college entrance exams.

Students often take college entrance exams like the SAT or the ACT in their high school junior year. These exam scores are used to determine a student's readiness for college. Transitional advisors focused on individual academic scores can identify students who will not likely meet basic college-level competencies by the end of the 11th grade. Given a year to provide remediation, secondary schools may then address the problem and thereby ultimately better meet the needs of their students.

At LCCC the cooperative attitude that distinguishes local educational partnerships has fueled several efforts to help students get ready for college classes. Recently LCCC began sharing the actual curricula for their college remediation courses in English with their high school partners. The same outcomes expected in the remediation classes at the college are now being addressed in some service area senior high school classes. It should be noted these are not concurrent enrollment courses, because the credit is below college level (i.e., 1000 level). Theoretically, the students mastering these classes should be able to test into college-level freshman English 1010 the following year. For example, at two high schools local to the LCCC community (one an alternative school and the other a rural high school), the following college remedial course competencies (ENGL 0700—Fundamentals of English) are now incorporated into the basic senior level English classes at LCCC:

• Employ the writing process (pre-writing, drafting, revising, editing, writing final drafts).

• Write at least five essays that address various rhetorical situations involving example/illustration/description; comparison/contrast; cause-effect; process analysis; persuasion/argumentation; summary; and/or summary-response.

• Write focused, developed, unified, and coherent texts employing thesis statements, introductions, conclusions, and body paragraphs (minimum of two pages in length each).

• Write with an awareness of a defined audience and purpose in a formal academic style.

• Organize information.

• Synthesize information from resources into essays.

• Format texts to meet established guidelines.

• Write texts that maintain a consistent formal point of view.

• Write final texts that consistently produce correct sentences free of word-level errors and sentence-level errors.

A secondary/postsecondary team approach to transitioning students successfully from high school into college opens doors to many previously untapped resources. A transitional advisor, trained to watch both sides of the graduation divide, can help to facilitate practical strategies for students in need of remediation. The role of the transitional advisor is also important with regard to the development of high-achieving students.

Enrichment for Advancement of Students

By design, concurrent enrollment programs "increase the rigor of secondary education and strengthen the links between the secondary and postsecondary sectors" (Karp et al. 2008, 1) of education. Research continues to suggest participation in these programs is linked to college enrollment and persistence, and research also maintains that the increased rigor of engaging concurrent enrollment courses can lead students to greater success (Karp et al. 2008; Speroni 2011; Rodriguez, Hughes, and Belfield 2012). Concurrent enrollment programs are a challenging academic experience for advanced high school students (Rogers and Kimpston 1992; Bailey, Hughes, and Karp 2002), and as such, by design, are a form and means of achieving enrichment. These programs provide focus and direction for advanced students to accelerate their knowledge and skills in preparation for college. Participation in concurrent enrollment programs provides motivation for underperforming students who may be bored in class or missing a connection between high school coursework and their postsecondary plans (Bailey et al. 2002). Concurrent enrollment programs provide teachers with advanced knowledge and skills and enhance educational opportunities for students, which can potentially elevate whole schools. The role of the transitional advisor in informing students, guiding students through the process, and advocating for such programs in schools is critical to the success of concurrent enrollment programs and for students to maximize on their opportunities within such programs.

Syracuse University Project Advance is an example of a concurrent enrollment program designed and offered as a means of enrichment. It was initially created in response to what some call "senioritis" or the tendency for seniors at advanced levels of instruction and/or high grade point averages to grow bored and fail to take seriously their senior year due to lack of incentive. Research shows high school seniors frequently opt out of challenging coursework and/or find little relevance to their high school program with regard to their postsecondary work (Bailey et al. 2002). Courses offered through SUPA follow the same syllabi as SU coursed offered to students matriculated on campus. Generally these courses also utilize the same textbooks, materials, assignments, and tests. The academic rigor and expectations are the same as campus courses. By design, SUPA intellectually challenges students with college courses that require deep exploration and thorough interaction with university-level subject matter. Even though SUPA is not provided in every classroom of a given high school, SUPA instructors often pass on what they learn to other teachers in their school community. The school as a whole potentially begins to raise its academic standards and provide instruction at higher levels of rigor. Partnerships with concurrent enrollment programs like SUPA serve in this way to improve motivation and overall academic performance for all students.

Administrators and staff at SUPA, informed by regular research studies and assessment practices, have come to value the importance of advisement for students in order to maximize enrichment opportunities accessible to participants in the program. As noted previously in this chapter, there are various ways SUPA addresses the transitional advising needs of partner schools and participants, including the designation of SUPA administrators to various advisement roles and responsibilities throughout the regions served by the program. While visiting participating high schools throughout the school year, SUPA administrators meet and interact with teachers and administrators to understand and assess the evolving needs of students. In the information sessions provided for high school educators as well as parents and local community members, administrators help individuals understand how to maximize the opportunities available to students through SUPA. Additionally, SUPA has a designated administrator to act as a special liaison providing professional growth and information for guidance counselors to successfully advise students in their respective high schools. A SUPA administrator is also designated to direct research and evaluation to inform SUPA assessment practices and continually improve the advisement SUPA offers for the benefit of participating students. Another SUPA administrator, informed by regular analysis of college credit transfer statistics, individual college entrance requirements, and other forms of data, serves as a liaison for parents and students seeking individual counseling. Collectively, SUPA staff work together to meet the transitional needs of partner schools and the students they serve.

Transitional advising is an important factor in the success of students participating in concurrent enrollment programs like SUPA for the purpose of seeking enrichment. Transitional advisors, working directly with students, play an integral role of helping students maximize opportunities for enrichment offered through concurrent enrollment programs. Transitional advising also plays an important role in helping students plan their respective college programs according to requirements for a chosen career.

Concurrent Enrollment on a Career Pathway

Transitional advising as part of a concurrent enrollment program is especially useful in informing students and their parents regarding how these courses fit into career pathways. The unadvised student rarely knows how to seek out courses in high school that directly relate to his or her intended career. Even if a student is aware concurrent enrollment courses exist in their high school, these unadvised students may not know how to enroll or, even more important, how to achieve college credit for these courses. Concurrent enrollment courses form solid stepping stones along well-designed career pathways as students' transition from high school to postsecondary education. Transitional advisors help high school students identify courses aligned with a chosen career and guide them through the enrollment process. All educators, teachers, and administrators who facilitate these programs should have a working knowledge of career clusters, or ways occupations may be grouped according to basic commonalities, and the role of concurrent enrollment courses on a defined career pathway.

Transitional advisors create for students a seamless transition to a college program of study along the student's chosen career pathway. Transitional advisors, however, should also know which career pathways require or recommend locally approved concurrent enrollment courses as part of those pathways. Effective transitional advisors would be capable of explaining a career pathways template, roadmap, or other visual aid in simple terms, offering valid alternatives to recommended courses where needed to individualize the advising experience for each student.

Whether on a career pathway to finance, human services, hospitality and tourism, or another career cluster, students benefit from increased potential for a seamless transition to college and college-level work that is experienced through concurrent enrollment programs. Arbitrary grade point average or grade-level requirements sometimes prevent students who may benefit the most from being allowed to participate in a concurrent enrollment program. A transitional advisor will act as a liaison between the program and high schools to advocate for students. In such cases, a previously unmotivated or struggling student is allowed to experience what may be his or her first real success in school. Earning an A in a concurrent enrollment Auto Body or Health Care Careers class, and simultaneously starting a college transcript along a career pathway with that grade, could have a major impact on the educational future of such a student.

Conclusion

It is widely accepted that concurrent enrollment programs work to better prepare students for college, but someone must take on the role of helping the students themselves understand how it all works. Too many students lack information about what a concurrent enrollment program is and what it can do to help prepare for college and career. The primary goal of a concurrent enrollment program—to create a seamless transition to a college program of study along the student's chosen career pathway—is all too often not explained. A transitional advisor knowledgeable in high school graduation requirements as they relate to college readiness, application, and enrollment can serve as an important resource for high schools, concurrent enrollment programs, and students.

Meeting the transitional advising needs of students to help them maximize the dual credits they earn should be part of any quality concurrent enrollment program. Transitional advisors play an integral role in the explanation of these programs, provide guidance with processes to secure college credit, and serve as a resource for academic planning and college application. Transitional advisors help students understand their scores on college placement tests like the ACT or SAT. Even more important, the knowledgeable transitional advisor is able to recommend approved courses within a given high school that align with the individual student's career pathways, including the ability to recommend alternative options for courses when necessary. If the staff resources exist—either within a concurrent enrollment program or within the high school it serves—and the number of participating students warrants it, the best option is to integrate advising as a formal component of the program itself. In smaller districts, advising for concurrent enrollment students may fit under a broader range of services called "college prep" or "career pathways" advising; but by any name, it must take place.

Students who participate in concurrent enrollment programs enter college at an advantage, and students who are properly advised in their program are even better equipped to maximize these advantages. Transitional advising is especially important for low-income, rural, and urban students who may otherwise struggle with college access and opportunity (Karp 2006). If no one is designated to help students understand the value of a concurrent enrollment program, the value of a program is sharply diminished. Traditionally, random advising duties may fall to any or all of the educators with whom the student comes into contact: the high school teachers, the career counselors, the school counselors, the college admissions team, college testing personnel, and the entire college-based concurrent enrollment team. Students are better served by a designated transitional advisor, trained with knowledge of the program and local high school graduation requirements, than by varying or inconsistent opinions, suggestions, and knowledge of multiple educators.

A high quality concurrent enrollment program strives to offer a truly seamless transition to college, and formal integration of transitional advising is an important facet of that seamless experience. For those who are considering adding transitional advising to an existing program or are in process of developing and implementing a new program, a good place to start is to ensure all participating educators are well informed about how the process works and where their piece of the students' transitional process fits into the overall picture. In a concurrent enrollment program, where the primary goal is to guide students toward a seamless transition from high school to college, it is essential that a component for transitional advising be integrated within the program to provide explanation of that goal and guidance toward that transition.

References

Alberti, Sandra. 2013. "Making the Shifts." *Educational Leadership* 70(4): 24–27.

Bailey, Thomas R., Katherine L. Hughes, and Melinda Mechur Karp. 2002. "What Role Can Dual Enrollment Programs Play in Easing the Transition Between High School and Postsecondary Education?" Paper prepared for the U.S. Department of Education, Office of Vocational and Adult Education. New York: Community College Research Center and Institute on Education and the Economy, Teachers College, Columbia Univ.

Belasco, Andrew S. 2013. "Creating College Opportunity: School Counselors and Their Influence on Postsecondary Enrollment." *Research in Higher Education* 54(7): 781–804.

Blackburn, Barbara R. 2011. *Common Core State Standards . . . Only the Beginning!* Larchmont, NY: Eye on Education.

Brown, Duane, and Jerry Trusty. 2005. "School Counselors, Comprehensive School Counseling Programs, and Academic Achievement: Are School Counselors Promising More Than They Can Deliver?" *Professional School Counseling* 9(1): 1–8.

Bryan, Julia, Cheryl Moore-Thomas, Norma L. Day-Vines, and Cheryl Holcomb-McCoy. 2011. "School Counselors as Social Capital: The Effects of High School College Counseling on College Application Rates." *Journal of Counseling and Development* 89: 190–99.

Chapman, Brian. 2001. "A Model for Implementing a Concurrent Enrollment Program." *New Directions for Community Colleges*: 15–22. doi: 10.1002/cc.4.

Conley, David T. 2005. *College Knowledge: What It Really Takes for Students to Succeed and What We Can Do to Get Them Ready.* San Francisco, CA: Jossey-Bass.

———. 2010. *College and Career Ready: Helping All Students Succeed Beyond High School.* San Francisco, CA: Jossey-Bass.

Fullan, Michael. 2006. *Change Theory: A Force for School Improvement.* Seminar series paper no. 157, Centre for Strategic Education, Victoria, Australia. Retrieved Oct. 10, 2012. http://www.catalyst-chicago.org/sites/catalyst-chicago.org/files/michael_fullen_change_theory.pdf.

Greenburg, Arthur R. 1989. *Concurrent Enrollment Programs: College Credit for High School Students.* Bloomington, IN: Phi Delta Kappa Education Foundation.

Hirsch, Deborah. 2010 (June). "The High School to College Transition: Minding the Gap." *New England Journal of Higher Education.*

Holcomb-McCoy, Cheryl. 2010. "Involving Low-Income Parents of Color in College-Readiness Activities: An Exploratory Study." *Professional School Counseling* 14(1): 115–24.

Karp, Melinda Mechur. 2006. "Academics Aren't the Only Outcomes: Role and Identity Development Among College Now Students." Paper presented at the meeting of the Association for the Study of Higher Education, Anaheim, CA.

Karp, Melinda Mechur, Juan Carlos Calcagno, Katherine L. Hughes, Dong Wook Jeong, and Thomas R. Bailey. 2008. "Dual Enrollment Students in Florida and New York City: Postsecondary Outcomes." CCRC Brief No. 37. New York: Community College Research Center, Teachers College, Columbia Univ.

McDonough, Patricia P. 1997. *Choosing Colleges: How Social Class and Schools Structure Opportunity.* Albany, NY: State Univ. of New York Press.

Murray, Barbara A. 1995. "Validating the Role of the School Counselor." *School Counselor* 43: 5–9.

Newman, Fred M., and Gary G. Wehlage. 1995. *Successful School Restructuring: A Report to the Public and Educators by the Center on Organization and Restructuring of Schools.* Madison, WI: Center on Organization and Restructuring of Schools, Univ. of Wisconsin-Madison. ERIC ED ED387 925.

Puyear, Donald, Linda Thor, and Karen Mills. 2001. "Concurrent Enrollment in Arizona: Encouraging Success in High School." *New Directions for Community Colleges*: 33–42. doi: 10.1002/cc.6.

Rodriguez, Olga, Katherine L. Hughes, and Clive Belfield. 2012. "Bridging College and Careers: Using Dual Enrollment to Enhance Career and Technical Education Pathways." NCPR Working Paper. New York: National Center for Postsecondary Research, Teachers College, Columbia Univ. http://ccrc .tc.columbia.edu/media/k2/attachments/bridging-college-careers.pdf.

Rogers, Karen B., and Richard D. Kimpston. 1992. "Acceleration: What We Do vs. What We Know." *Educational Leadership* 50(2): 58–61.

Rowan-Kenyon, Heather, Laura W. Perna, and Amy K. Swan. 2008. "Contextual Influences on Parental Involvement in College Going: Variations by Socioeconomic Status." *Journal of Higher Education* 79(5): 564–86.

Speroni, Cecilia. 2011. "Determinants of Students' Success: The Role of Advanced Placement and Dual Enrollment Programs." NCPR Working Paper. New York: National Center for Postsecondary Research, Teachers College, Columbia Univ.

Swanson, Joni L. 2008. "An Analysis of the Impact of High School Dual Enrollment Course Participation on Postsecondary Academic Success, Persistence, and Degree Completion." Doctoral diss., Univ. of Iowa.

Tinto, Vincent. 1987. *Leaving College: Rethinking the Causes and Cures of Student Attrition*. Chicago: Univ. of Chicago Press.

———. 1997. "Colleges as Communities: Exploring the Educational Character of Student Persistence." *Journal of Higher Education* 68(6): 599–623.

White, Eric R., Judith J. Goetz, M. Stuart Hunter, and Betsey O. Barefoot. 1995. "Creating Successful Transitions through Academic Advising." In *First Year Academic Advising: Patterns in the Present, Pathways to the Future*, edited by M. L. Upcraft and G. L. Kramer, 25–34. Columbia, SC: National Resource Center for the Freshman Year Experience and Students in Transition, Univ. of South Carolina.

9

Concurrent Enrollment Program Prepares Academic Middle for College and Career

SUSAN HENDERSON, BARBARA D. HODNE,
AND JULIE WILLIAMS

Introduction

At its fall 2007 meeting, members of the advisory board of the University of Minnesota's Twin Cities College in the Schools program (UMTC-CIS) hijacked the agenda to make the case that CIS should serve a broader academic and demographic range of students. CIS staff, already inclined to agree with their arguments, took the message to heart and embraced the challenge. In 2009–10, CIS launched the Entry Point Project (EPP), a set of three University of Minnesota courses offered through CIS to serve students who have academic potential but have not demonstrated it in traditional ways. The goals of EPP are to (1) serve a broader academic range of students than CIS had previously served; (2) serve more students of color, students from low socioeconomic families, first-generation college-bound students, and English language learners (ELL); (3) improve these students' college readiness; and (4) increase their sense that when they get to college, they will belong there. This chapter articulates the context and process for the development of EPP, the project's goals and strategy, and evaluation results for EPP's first year.

Local and National Contexts

Achievement, Participation, and Completion Gaps in Minnesota

Like many states—if not most—Minnesota has an achievement gap between the academic performance of White and minority K–12 students.

112

Unlike most states, however, Minnesota's student achievement gap has been overlooked in the past because Minnesota students as a whole usually rank near the top of national achievement tests. For example, among states in which 70% or more of high school students take the ACT college entrance exam, the average score of Minnesota students is repeatedly among the highest in the country (ACT 2010a, 20). However, when the data are broken out by ethnicity and race, a very different picture is revealed: In 2010, while 38% of White students who took the ACT exam scored above the college-ready benchmark in all four subject areas, only 23% of Minnesota's Asian students, 17% of our Latino students, and 8% of African American students did so (ACT 2010b, 22). Another case in point: Minnesota's 8th graders in 2009 "had the second highest math scores in the nation on a widely used standardized test. But while the overall average was higher than most states, the gap between the scores of white students and both African American and Latino students was the seventh largest in the country" (Weber and Baran 2011). Minnesota Education Commissioner Brenda Cassellius is keenly aware that, despite small gains by all groups of Minnesota students, "significant gaps remain between the state's white students and students of color" (Weber and Baran 2011).

Graduation rates show similar disparities: In 2008–9, while 82% of White Minnesota students graduated from high school on time, only 44% of African American students and 45% of Latino students did so. In categories overlapping to some degree with these are other groups of students who have low on-time graduation rates: 46% of LEP (limited English proficiency) students graduated on time and 54% of students qualifying for free and reduced lunch graduated on time (Minnesota Department of Education 2011).

A variety of gaps permeate Minnesota's postsecondary education as well. Participation data broken out by race and ethnicity are telling. For example, fall 2009 data show Black, Hispanic, and American Indian students attended two-year institutions at rates higher than their White or Asian counterparts: 76% of Black students, 68% of American Indians, and 59% of Hispanics attended two-year institutions, either full time or part time. In contrast, 50% of White students and 52% of Asian students attended two-year colleges. Conversely, significantly greater percentages of White and Asian students—50% and 48%, respectively—attended four-year colleges either full time or part time; significantly lower percentages of Black students (24%), Hispanic students (41%), and American Indian (32%) students did so (Minnesota Office of Higher Education 2011).

Minnesota's postsecondary graduation rate, reported by Complete College America (2011), indicates that gaps among student groups are evident as well in on-time graduation rates:[1]

• White two-year college students graduate in three years at a significantly higher rate (33%) than do African Americans (11%), Hispanic (16%), and Asian/Pacific Islanders (20%).

• White four-year college students graduate in four years at a significantly higher rate (63%) than do African Americans (37%), Hispanic (51%), and Asian/Pacific Islanders (54%).

On a national scale, even the six-year completion rate data for students at four-year colleges reflect that differential in completion rates, based on race and ethnicity: "60% of white students who attend four-year colleges full time complete a bachelor's degree within six years, compared to 49% of Hispanic students and 42% of African American students" (Complete College America 2011, citing data from the U.S. Department of Education, National Center for Education Statistics, Integrated Postsecondary Education Data System [IPEDS] 2007). According to Amanda L. Ziebell-Finley of the Minnesota Minority Education Partnership and the Minnesota College Access Network, "Minnesota has one of the largest gaps in the nation between whites and persons of color when it comes to degrees awarded per 100 college students" (Espinosa and Ziebell-Finley 2010).

Not surprisingly, a significant disparity in concurrent enrollment participation among groups of Minnesota high school students exists. The Minnesota Department of Education's 2009–10 data show that

• White students participate in concurrent enrollment in disproportionately high numbers.

---

1. Rates are based on data aggregated by the National Center for Higher Education Management Systems (NCHEMS) from IPEDS 2007–9 Graduation Rate File.

TABLE 9.1

Minnesota Concurrent Enrollment Program Participation, 2009–10

	MN Concurrent enrollment program participation (public school students only)*		Total MN public school student population (grades 11–12)**	
White	19,143	91%	109,880	78%
Asian/Pacific Islander	850	4%	8,572	6%
Black	507	2%	13,310	9%
Hispanic	405	2%	6,789	5%
American Indian	230	1%	2,846	2%

Sources:

* Minnesota Department of Education. 2013. "Rigorous Course Taking: Advanced Placement, International Baccalaureate, Concurrent Enrollment and Postsecondary Enrollment Options Programs." *FY 2012 Report to the Legislature*, page 26, Minnesota Legislative Reference Library website. Accessed Feb. 2, 2016. http://www.leg.state.mn.us/lrl/lrl.

** Minnesota Department of Education. 2010. Data Reports and Analytics web page (Student Data, Enrollment, Ethnicity/Gender). Accessed Feb. 2, 2016. http://education.state .mn.us/MDE/Data/index.html.

• Students of color, broken out by race and ethnic groups, participate in disproportionately lower numbers. (See Table 9.1.)

University of Minnesota–Twin Cities Campus

The University of Minnesota is a large, Tier One research university with five campuses located throughout the state. The Twin Cities campus is the largest of the five, enrolling more than 50,000 of the university's nearly 65,000 students. In recent years, the Twin Cities campus has become more selective in its undergraduate admissions; in fall 2010, 18.8% of freshmen on the Twin Cities campus who submitted composite ACT scores had earned scores between 31 and 36. The campus is predominantly White, with Black students comprising only a bit over 4% of the student body, Hispanic students slightly over 2%, Asians over 8%, and American Indians comprising slightly over 1%. Nearly 10% of the student body (undergraduate and graduate) is composed of international students (University of Minnesota 2011).

College in the Schools

The university's concurrent enrollment program, College in the Schools, was founded in 1986, just as the university began its efforts to become more selective in its student admissions.[2] For years, about half of the courses offered through CIS courses required students to be in or above the 80th percentile of their class; the other half of courses required students to be in or above the 70th percentile of their class. CIS offered thirty-six university courses in 2009–10 and served nearly six thousand individual high school students. Two hundred fifty-nine teachers in 106 high schools taught UMTC courses through CIS.

When considering their response to the CIS advisory board's recommendation to broaden the academic and demographic profile of CIS students, CIS staff did not know if undertaking an initiative to serve a more diverse student population would be viewed positively by the larger university community, because the university was becoming more selective in its student admissions. We wondered if CIS might be viewed by university administrators as working in the "wrong direction" if we began serving a broader range of students. Already, critics of concurrent enrollment programs often questioned whether authentic, college-level rigor could be achieved off the postsecondary campus, in high school classrooms with high school teachers and high school students. To counter this long-standing skepticism, CIS, like many other concurrent enrollment programs, built its program by serving students with high test scores and high grade point averages (GPAs), believing they could best handle the faster pace, higher expectations, and greater personal responsibility required of postsecondary students. We also knew that these highly successful students would be easy to recruit—they would seek out advanced coursework. We did not know just how we would effectively, successfully reach and serve a broader range of students.

2. As the university president, Kenneth Keller led an initiative called "Commitment to Focus," which sought to strengthen graduate and undergraduate education and faculty research in order to enhance the university's national reputation. For more detail, see http://president.umn.edu/about/presidential-history/kenneth-h-keller.

National Trends in Dual Enrollment

While the Minnesota trends we have described provide important context for the Entry Point Project, CIS staff were also aware of national debates about employing dual enrollment as a strategy for preparing at-risk students for postsecondary study. In 2003, Bailey and Karp pointedly questioned whether the growing trend could be defended. After reviewing claims made in "45 published and unpublished articles, reports and books . . . about their ability to increase college access and success for a broad range of students," the researchers found most claims relied on the common sense belief that "transition courses" make sense; the authors' overall finding was that "experience and logic have fueled the continued development of the programs" rather than research-based evidence of their effectiveness (33). Four years later, Melinda Mechur Karp asked, "Why are policymakers and educators so enamored with dual enrollment programs?" and pointed out that "there is startlingly little evidence of their efficacy" (Karp 2007, 6). But she added that dual enrollment "intuitively addresses a variety of problems that reformers have identified," including worries that high school curricula do not sufficiently challenge students, that students have difficulty with the transition to college, and that too many students do not persist and graduate (Karp 2007).

As the trend toward employing dual enrollment as a strategy for preparing at-risk students for college continued, the Community College Research Center (CCRC) at Columbia Teachers College attempted to provide that research-based evidence of success. CCRC researchers, Bailey and Karp among them, have conducted multiple studies assessing the benefits of dual enrollment for a broader range of students than traditionally served in concurrent enrollment programs. Their work has included longitudinal measurement of the impact of dual enrollment on college enrollment, persistence, and success rates in Florida and New York (Karp, Calcagno, Hughes, Jeong, and Bailey 2007); a report on the benefits of participation in dual enrollment for career and technical education students in particular (Karp and Hughes 2008); and case studies measuring changes over time in dual enrollment students' conception of the skills and behaviors required of college students (Karp 2007). In

2007, CCRC researchers began managing a three-year initiative in which the James Irvine Foundation had funded eight partnerships between high schools and postsecondary institutions to implement "high-quality career-focused dual enrollment programs" for students in groups traditionally underrepresented in higher education (Golann and Hughes 2008). In fall 2010, Barnett and Hughes reported promising results: strong academic achievement, with 60% of the high school students earning an A or B in their college class; and high engagement, with 71% participating in outside-of-class supports (Barnett and Hughes 2010).

Minnesota is also seeing increased interest in using dual enrollment as a strategy for closing achievement gaps. Jessica Espinosa, representing the Minnesota Department of Education, has argued that "as a key component of an educational equity agenda, dual enrollment programs can help to both raise achievement levels of all students and close the achievement gap between members of different income and racial/ethnic groups" (Espinosa and Ziebell-Finley 2010). Citing a 2006 report by the Western Interstate Commission for Higher Education, she noted that "groups that may benefit from dual enrollment programs but do not now participate at proportionate rates include low-income students, students of color, first-generation college goers, English Language Learners, average students, and students in isolated high schools that cannot offer a wide variety of courses" (Espinosa and Ziebell-Finley 2010).

Launching the Entry Point Project

Buoyed by the passion of the CIS advisory board and supported by the university's College of Continuing Education, which administers CIS, we started working.

Guiding Principles

CIS staff started planning, based on these assumptions and within these parameters:

1. We did not believe simply admitting a broader range of students to the already-existing courses would serve students well; instead, we wanted courses that would intentionally help students scaffold their skills and knowledge.

2. We did not want to create a separate program that would be perceived as second class; instead we would design the Entry Point Project as an integral part of the CIS program and would publicize these new courses as part of the CIS course offerings.

3. The program would need to be started and maintained without short-lived, external funds; EPP needed to be economically sustainable from the revenue it generated, just as the CIS program had always been. We decided we would build on existing CIS practices and policies but would focus on finding collaborating partners who embraced our goals and courses that would support all students; we also knew we would have to develop criteria that would help us identify the "right" students—students in our target populations who would benefit and succeed.

Identifying University and External Partners

CIS identified two critically important partners within the university—an academic department and a university K–12 reform office that focuses on increasing the number and diversity of Minnesota students ready for postsecondary study.

University Partner: The Department of Postsecondary Teaching and Learning. Developing a partnership with the Department of Postsecondary Teaching and Learning (PSTL) made sense because its faculty are experts not only in traditional academic disciplines but also in teaching and learning; a primary focus of PSTL faculty research is discipline-based pedagogy. The department's mission is to "provide student-centered, multicultural, multidisciplinary learning opportunities for a diverse population of students, faculty, and staff; conduct research related to postsecondary pedagogy, student development, learning outcomes, access, and success; and develop engaged partnerships with communities, organizations, and programs so as to support access to and success in higher education" (PSTL website, http://www.cehd.umn.edu/PSTL /About/).

PSTL is home to the First Year Experience Program for the university's College of Education and Human Development. Teaching in learning communities, PSTL faculty regularly teach a First Year Inquiry course. Many of the same faculty teach courses for PSTL's post-baccalaureate certificate in Innovations in Undergraduate Multicultural Teaching and Learning, or the Master of Arts in Multicultural College Teaching and Learning. Informed by their research, PSTL faculty scaffold instruction and employ Universal Instructional Design (UID) to enable students from diverse backgrounds to reach the level of knowledge and skills required for rigorous postsecondary study.

PSTL faculty not only ask but also study whether college courses and college classrooms can engage and support students who do not thrive in traditional classrooms. They start from the assumption that college classes "can be structured to meet students at their present level and help them improve their ability to fulfill these demands" (Hsu 2005, 334). This is the basic premise of Universal Instructional Design. Originally developed in response to the needs of students with learning disabilities, UID offers guidelines for designing courses to accommodate a wide range of learning styles, to use multiple forms of assessment, and to embed skill-building into content-area study. Rather than relying on stand-alone courses in study skills and critical thinking to prepare students for traditionally taught courses, UID asks content-area teachers to redesign their courses and their teaching to accommodate the learning needs of all students.

While the original impetus was to address barriers for students with learning disabilities, the UID model has been found equally supportive for students who are nonnative speakers of English, as well as students who do not achieve high scores on standardized tests or sit silent in classrooms where lecture is the dominant mode of delivery. Commuter students or working students who have fewer opportunities to seek help outside of class also benefit from UID course design.

Fundamental UID components include

1. Integrating skill-building (e.g., critical thinking, problem-solving, written and verbal communication) with the acquisition of content knowledge

2. Communicating clear expectations and providing constructive feedback

3. Promoting interaction among and between teachers and students;

4. Using teaching methods that consider diverse learning styles, abilities, ways of knowing, previous experience, and background knowledge

5. Articulating a commitment to diversity and integrating multicultural perspectives into all aspects of the learning process.[3]

Because PSTL is a multidisciplinary department, CIS could find within one department potential courses and faculty in a range of fields: math, science, social science, and the humanities. In effect, we recruited a cohort of new faculty liaisons already united by a shared mission, philosophical orientation, and commitment to pedagogies consistent with the objectives and philosophy of the CIS Entry Point Project.

University Partner: College Readiness Consortium. Founded in 2006 at the University of Minnesota, the consortium pursues a comprehensive strategy for increasing "the number and diversity of Minnesota students who graduate from high school with the knowledge, skills, and habits for success in higher education" (College Readiness Consortium website, http://www.collegeready.umn.edu, Oct. 2013). Working both within and outside the university, the consortium seeks to facilitate collaboration among PreK–12 educators, the university, business communities, policy makers, business people, and families that focuses on issues of college readiness.

Ramp-Up to Readiness, a major initiative of the consortium, is closely allied with the mission of the Entry Point Project. Ramp-Up engages junior and senior high schools to create and implement a school-wide guidance program that leads students through a sequence of lessons, projects, and experiences that prepare them for postsecondary success. By partnering with the College Readiness Consortium, CIS expanded its professional networks and increased access to expertise regarding K–12 education reform and best practices. As of June 2011, the College Readiness Consortium showed that some high schools participate in both the Ramp-Up project and EPP, thereby intensifying their efforts on behalf of students.

---

3. This summary is created on the basis of Hodne's extensive teaching experience, participation in many workshops, and professional reading.

External Partners: Minnesota AVID coordinators and Association of Secondary Principals. The consortium connected CIS to two other crucial partners: district coordinators from Minneapolis–St. Paul area AVID programs (Achievement Via Individual Determination) and the Minnesota Association of Secondary School Principals (MASSP). AVID coordinators played a significant role by helping CIS identify appropriate student qualifications, the discipline areas from which to select courses, and options for academic support for CIS Entry Point Project students.

MASSP played an important role by inviting secondary school administrators to the first information meeting about EPP. This introduction was critical, because educators throughout Minnesota have equated College in the Schools with top-performing high school students, and CIS faced—and still faces—the challenge of "selling" a new "product" under an old "brand" (more on this at the end of the chapter).

External Partners: Thirteen Minnesota High Schools. A highly varied group of schools participated in EPP the first year: three charter, four urban, one first-ring, and five suburban. Schools ranged in size from small to very large. Demographics varied, too, but, as is happening across the country, each school had growing populations of students of color. (See Appendix 9.1 for demographic data about EPP schools.)

As required of all schools participating in CIS, these thirteen schools agreed to release teachers a minimum of three days each school year they could attend CIS teacher workshops and accompany their students to the university for a day of course-related on-campus activities. In addition to these requirements, the schools wanting to offer EPP courses agreed to comply with three more:

1. Select students on the basis of these requirements: students must be in the 50th to 80th percentile of their high school class; meet or exceed any course-specific qualifications; and be a junior or senior. Teachers could exercise their own professional discretion in order to enroll students who did not meet all of the student qualifications, but who nevertheless would be well-served by the University of Minnesota course. Teacher recommendations often helped identify students for EPP courses.

2. Reserve 60% of class seats for the target audience meeting the required student qualifications. Teachers and schools may also exercise discretion in targeting particular groups who are currently underserved in their schools, giving priority to students in those groups.

3. Provide academic support outside of the classroom to students enrolled in the University of Minnesota courses offered through EPP.

Entry Point Project Goals and Conceptual Frameworks

Working together, CIS and its partners articulated the goals of the Entry Point Project:

1. Serve a broader academic range of students than CIS had previously served.

2. Serve more students of color, students from low socioeconomic families, first-generation college-bound students, and English language learners.

3. Improve these students' college readiness.

4. Develop their sense that when they get to college, they will belong there.

Serving a Broader Academic Range and Broader Demographic

We recognized that the university's and CIS's status quo lacked some key element for easing access and supporting success. Our baseline assumptions parallel the thinking of Lani Guinier, a professor of law at Harvard University who has argued that, like miners who bring canaries into the mines to warn them of a "toxic atmosphere," we in academia should see the absence of students of color in university classrooms as reflecting the atmosphere there (Guinier 2002). In parallel fashion, we surmise that if 91% of students in dual enrollment courses in Minnesota are White (Espinosa 2010), then some aspect of dual enrollment programs needs rethinking in order to achieve successful student outcomes among all groups of students.

Improving College Readiness

The work of David Conley has helped us think more deeply about what it means to be college ready. Specifically, we have focused on his statements of the "Big Four" indicators of college readiness found in his 2009 report, *Creating College Readiness: Profiles of 38 Schools that Know How*:

1. *Key cognitive strategies* describe the ways of thinking that are necessary for college-level work. They include: problem solving, inquisitiveness, precision/accuracy, interpretation, reasoning, research, and intellectual openness.

2. *Key content knowledge* refers to the need for students to master writing skills, algebraic concepts, key foundational content, and "big ideas" from core subjects in order to be college ready.

3. *Academic behaviors* consist largely of study skills, and self-monitoring. Examples include time management, awareness of one's current level of mastery, and the selection of the learning strategies.

4. *Contextual skills and awareness*, or "college knowledge," refers to the understanding of college admissions processes, college culture, tuition and financial aid, and college-level academic expectations. (Conley 2009, 4)

Increasing college readiness has always been the hallmark of College in the Schools' work. But Conley's work helped us articulate all the areas that need to be explicitly addressed in order to serve students well. Conley (2007) eloquently describes the shock that most first-time college students experience and consistently argues that their transition can be eased by college-prep programs that intentionally focus on these areas. We would add that college classes can do more to ease the transition. Many high school and college teachers incorrectly assume that the college-ready student is one who readily comprehends textbooks and lectures, completes homework assignments independently, understands what an assignment sheet is asking for, and knows both how and when to ask clarifying questions. They assume that students arrive with a basic understanding of disciplinary concepts and are able to apply thinking skills appropriate to the discipline. But even among students not identified as underprepared, "research shows that a significant number of students do not and are not, and that this lack of understanding and proficiency impedes their learning" (Hsu 2005, 338). From this perspective, the problem is not that classes—even on college campuses—fail to enroll the right students, but that college classes are not designed to serve the students they do enroll.

For us, increasing students' college readiness means intentionally building critical thinking skills, content knowledge, and academic behaviors.

Sense of Belonging and Mattering

Our fourth goal focuses on students' perceptions of themselves as college material. Since the early 1990s, scholars who focus on students' adjustment to college have looked to Vincent Tinto's research on student engagement and persistence. Karp, Hughes, and O'Gara (2010) summarize the lessons from Tinto's research in this way: "Students who do not feel at home in an institution or do not believe that an institution can help them meet their goals are unlikely to persist. Likewise, students who are isolated, or who do not engage in social interactions within the college, are less likely to persist in the institution" (3). Tinto's insights into academic integration and social integration as key predictors of persistence in college have informed conversations about college retention ever since. Dissenting voices counter that students are not solely responsible for integrating into institutions of higher education, that we must consider not only the student's ability to fit in but also the institution's ability to be a good fit for traditionally underrepresented students (Johnson et al. 2007).

In their study of 2,967 first-year students on thirty-four college campuses in twenty-four states, Johnson et al. (2007) found that "students from all racial/ethnic backgrounds who experienced a smooth academic and social transition to college are also likely to perceive a strong sense of belonging to their campuses" (534). When students reported that their transitions to college had been smooth, they cited comfortable contacts with instructors outside of class, access to academic supports such as tutoring, and participation in study groups outside of class. Also important were indications of a "positive racial climate," which they saw in "frequent transracial interaction, friendship, trust, and respect" (537). Such interactions can occur or be encouraged within courses designed to support collaborative learning.

A related construct frames the discussion around "mattering." In their study *Do I Belong Here?* Michael Stebleton and colleagues summarize the scholarship on how this feeling develops, citing five contributing factors identified in the literature: (1) The sense that others are interested in and notice us; (2) the sense that others "care about what we want, think, and do"; (3) the sense that others "will be proud of our accomplishments or saddened by our failures"; (4) a sense of depending on others; and (5) "the feeling that an individual's efforts are valued" (Stebleton, Huesman, and Kuzhabekova 2010, 3). To believe that we have a place in academia and could possibly play a significant role there, we have to believe that someone might be listening, watching, rooting for us, and even influencing us.

Our approach is informed by these discussions of students' sense of belonging; we believe that if concurrent enrollment programs hope to enroll and retain a more diverse student demographic, the concurrent enrollment classrooms will have to be welcoming spaces. Before navigating university campuses and commuting or dorm life, EPP students can learn that they are capable of college work, that their ideas are valuable, and that college classes are actually a good fit for them. In other words, they can develop a sense that when they get to college, they will belong there.

Pedagogy as Strategy

CIS staff knew from the start that a supportive pedagogy would be key to any CIS initiative to serve a broader academic and demographic range of students. For this reason, we were drawn to the Department of Postsecondary Teaching and Learning, which consistently and comprehensively employs UID in its courses. PSTL's pedagogical commitment rests on the assumption that the gaps we have discussed in this chapter—the achievement gap, the participation gap, and the completion gap—all indicate that something is not working in the world of education.

CIS staff and our planning partners identified three courses taught by PSTL faculty—one course already in the CIS portfolio and two courses that were not—to be appropriate for EPP: Writing Studio; Mathematical Modeling and Prediction; and Physics by Inquiry. All three courses support students' transition to the faster pace, higher expectations, and greater personal responsibility of college work by implementing Universal Instructional Design in the following ways:

1. *Interactive pedagogy*: These courses draw on what students already know or care about, with the aim of tapping into knowledge and abilities often masked in courses taught using traditional methods and traditional content. Coaching students in cooperative group learning further encourages them to recognize and use. experiences, insights, and abilities they bring to the classroom.

2. *Practice and feedback*: The courses incorporate regular cycles of practice, individual feedback from the teacher, and opportunities to use that feedback; as the semester progresses, students apply what they've learned to more challenging questions and assignments.

3. *Critical thinking and reflection on learning*: Activities and assignments not only promote learning, but guide students to reflect on their learning and to recognize factors that enhance or impede their learning.

The Importance of Course Design and Pedagogy

Why are interactiveness, practice and feedback, and critical reflection on learning key for promoting access and supporting success? Why emphasize these particular supports? The answer is that these pedagogical strategies support both academic and social integration. Classroom climate matters, and these pedagogies can set up a climate that eases the adjustment to college-level work. We see this in the results of Karp, Hughes, and O'Gara's study of integration among community college students, which found that a sense of at-homeness in college, the experience of interaction as opposed to isolation, can trace back to course design (2010). All students would benefit from supportive individual attention and coaching— practice coupled with feedback—but at-risk students are more likely to be missing other sources of support for creating pathways to integration.

Entry Point Project Course Profiles

Writing Studies 1201: Writing Studio

Writing Studio is an introductory writing course that carries University of Minnesota regular graduation credit and focuses on developing strong foundational writing skills (focus, developing ideas, writing with sources).[4] The EPP faculty coordinator for the course, Barbara Hodne, explains that the practice and regular constructive feedback from the instructor helps students gain confidence and competence in responding to college-level assignments. Students write both in class and outside of class, discuss assigned readings, respond to each other's writing, and engage in various activities designed to coach them through generating ideas and drafting, revising, and editing their work.

Required readings include an extended autobiographical narrative that is engaging and accessible, that deals with educational growth, and that represents the experiences of an underrepresented ethnic group. (Recent classes have read *The Color of Water*, by James McBride; *Lucky Child*, by Loung Ung; and *Holler If You Hear Me: The Education of a Teacher and His Students*, by Gregory Michie.) Also required are expository readings that raise questions, suggest new perspectives, and invite reflection on the topic of education (recent classes have read articles in *Rethinking Schools: An Agenda for Reform*, edited by David Levine).

This course is designed to serve highly motivated students who do not qualify for admission to WRIT 1301: University Writing, also available through CIS. Writing Studio students must show potential as thinkers and motivation to improve their writing abilities. To be accepted into Writing Studio, students must (1) have passed the state basic standards writing exam; (2) have a 3.0 minimum GPA; (3) submit a writing sample in response to a reading provided by the University of Minnesota faculty coordinator; (4) be recommended by high school teacher(s), and (5) be a junior or senior in the academic middle, between the 50th and 80th percentile of their class.

Writing Studio pedagogy incorporates the key elements of Universal Instructional Design. First, it is interactive. The overarching theme of

----

4. WRIT 1201 prepares students for WRIT 1301: University Writing. On campus, students with low ACT English scores and/or low high school English grades are placed in 1201; they fulfill their freshman composition requirement only after completing WRIT 1301, which assumes such foundational skills and focuses on writing with research, developing flexibility as a writer, learning to use varied registers and write for varied purposes, and writing with a wider and more academic vocabulary.

the reading and writing in this class is the topic of education. Students enter the class with years of experience in the American education system, experience whose lessons have largely been internalized without critical inquiry or reflection. This is, of course, fertile territory for discussion and writing that promotes critical thinking, reflection, and reframing. Students begin by discussing and writing about their own educational experiences; within the first three weeks of class—drawing on students' stories alone—they raise most of the key dilemmas and issues in American education: adequate vs. inadequate funding; schools as safe or unsafe places; the importance of excellent teachers and the critical shortage of such teachers; and the pressure for parental involvement and the barriers that make it so hard for immigrant parents to comply. That early work with the students' core educational experiences builds the context that informs their later projects: analyzing the educational experiences described in an autobiography and critiquing reform proposals that might apply to their own schools. Students learn from each other as well as from experts and gradually build the shared knowledge that enables them to tackle increasingly difficult reading and increasingly complex writing tasks.

Writing Studio pedagogy also couples practice with feedback, the second key element of UID. Like most freshman composition courses today, Writing Studio employs a process approach, asking students to write multiple drafts and coaching students to use the feedback they receive from classmates and the instructor as they revise their essays. This element of course design is the norm for college freshman writing classes, so in that sense Writing Studio is a very natural choice, for EPP—colleges universally require freshman composition and nearly every program encourages a process approach.

Critical thinking and reflection on learning is the third key element of UID incorporated into Writing Studio pedagogy. If students enter CIS Writing Studio thinking, as most students do, of school readings as "manufactured" rather than as "rhetorical entities, written in response to real human exigence" (Jolliffe and Phelan 2006, 101), they have the opportunity to reframe that thinking. They enter professional conversations with their teachers, who are themselves leaders in professional organizations and authors of academic articles. The simple realization that writing matters and that student writing can matter is a developmental milestone in college composition courses. The conversations and writing in this course—about curricular innovations, antitracking pedagogy, and efforts to confront violence and harassment—engage students in reading and writing for the purpose of critical thinking, creativity, discussion and debate. Like Dorothy pulling back the curtain to see "the great and powerful Oz," students look behind the curtain separating students from teachers and school writing from real writing.

PSTL 1163: Physics by Inquiry

Leon Hsu, associate professor in the Department of Postsecondary Teaching and Learning and faculty coordinator for Physics by Inquiry, published an extensive description of the pedagogy for this course (Hsu 2005), and we have relied extensively on that description for this section. Hsu describes Physics by Inquiry as a physics course designed for non-science majors and future elementary teachers. It focuses on having students learn about and participate in the process of scientific discovery; rather than emphasizing the application of fundamental physics principles to solve complex problems, the course emphasizes knowing the evidence that supports a theory. The best candidates for this course are students who want to learn more about physics but who are unsure of their mathematics preparation, are interested in more hands-on learning, or are considering elementary teaching as a career.

The goal of this course is to help students create their own understanding of selected fundamental concepts in physics by working in a way similar to the way real scientists work. Students work in groups to perform short experiments and to analyze what is going on; they make observations, develop models about how things work, discuss the results with peers, and test and refine the models through further experimentation. Emphasis is placed on the ability to make scientific arguments based on experiments performed in class. The aim is not just to know the concepts, but also to know *how* you know them (what the evidence is) and to be able to apply them in new situations. The course uses the text *Physics by Inquiry* (McDermott 2005).

Physics by Inquiry meets the university's liberal education requirement for a four-credit, lab-based physical science. Students enrolling in Physics by Inquiry must be juniors or seniors in the academic middle, between the 50th and 80th percentile of their class. They must also have earned a B or better in a rigorous high school algebra I class or have the recommendation of a teacher, or both.

Physics by Inquiry pedagogy incorporates the key elements of Universal Instructional Design. First, it is interactive. As the course description shows, Physics by Inquiry relies heavily on students learning from and with each other. Working in groups of three to four, students learn about the scientific method by *doing* it: they observe physical phenomena and develop one or more hypothesis about what is happening—how things are working. Together they then create experiments to test their hypotheses; they likely will need to conduct further observations, develop further hypotheses, and conduct more experiments before arriving at a final theory. No instructor is explaining to them the workings of the phenomena they are observing. Working in these long-term groups, students get to know each other well; thereby creating their own support group that fosters academic achievement as well as promoting retention and consistent class attendance.

The pedagogy employed in Physics by Inquiry also incorporates practice coupled with feedback. The course includes few if any lectures; instead students work in a laboratory setting almost all the time, interacting with their peers and receiving nondirective coaching from the instructor. This pedagogy furthers the course goals, namely helping students refine their thinking and reasoning skills by developing theories based on experimental evidence. A typical class session begins with a fifteen-minute introduction to the question of the day which includes students taking a pre-test; then students work with their lab partners to complete the lab activities in a section of the text. At regular intervals, the group is instructed to call over the instructor, who asks the students questions to make sure they understand the material they have worked on. Finally, students gather for a whole-class discussion of the day's question and take a post-test.

Critical thinking and reflection on learning, the third element of UID, permeates Physics by Inquiry. Students must not only observe physical phenomena closely, they must also exercise rigorous thinking skills to identify whether the outcomes of the experiments they have created support the hypothesis or theory they have articulated. And, if they do not, they must review their thinking to identify the components of their hypothesis that need changing and then devise a new theory and a new experiment that will effectively test their new hypothesis. In other words, they must learn to think critically.

An additional key goal of this class is for students to develop meta-cognitive skills. Physics by Inquiry requires two activities that help students first become aware of the study strategies they use and, then evaluate how well those strategies work. The first required activity is completing weekly journal assignments, which necessitate students' explicitly identifying how they are studying and reflecting on their own study strategies. The second required activity is an evaluation of their group's work and of individual students' roles in the group's learning process. While students do learn basic physics concepts, they also learn how to think and reason. They come to understand themselves better *and* they learn what science is, how scientists work, and how the universe and everyday technologies work.

PSTL 1006: Mathematical Modeling and Prediction

Susan Staats, associate professor in the Department of Postsecondary Teaching and Learning and faculty coordinator for the Mathematical Modeling and Prediction course, has also published descriptions of the course design and pedagogy (Staats 2005; Staats and Batteen 2009); we have relied extensively on those publications for the description here. Mathematical Modeling and Prediction introduces students to the art of mathematical prediction through algebraic modeling and elementary probability theory. Students learn to develop equations that accurately represent the behavior of real-world data. Problems are drawn from various disciplines of interest to College of Education and Human Development majors. While students practice traditional algebraic methods, they also use Excel spreadsheet software extensively to investigate the behavior of data sets. The class also strengthens students' ability to communicate and evaluate mathematical reasoning.

This course does not contain trigonometry and is often used, in the high schools, as an algebra III course. The course satisfies the University of Minnesota's liberal education requirement for mathematical thinking coursework. Students enrolling in Mathematical Modeling and Prediction must be juniors or seniors in high school and in the academic middle, between the top 50th and 80th percentile of their class, or must have instructor approval to participate. They must also have completed high school algebra I and II courses with grades of at least a C−.

Mathematical Modeling and Prediction uses Harshbarger and Yocco's *College Algebra in Context with Applications for the Managerial, Life, and Social Sciences* (2009). Alternative textbooks can be used with approval from the faculty coordinator.

Pedagogy in this math class is highly interactive. Staats describes the pedagogy specifically as a constructivist pedagogy, noting that it uses small-group discussions and full-class guided Socratic discussions of homework problems or new material being introduced by the teacher. Some class time is devoted to the context of mathematics, material that lies just outside of algebraic procedures—geographical and demographic information, policy debates, and perspectives on social issues—all topics that are associated with, but not fully defined by, math applications. In one project, public health and economic issues associated with worldwide infectious diseases serve as the enriched context for studying algebra topics like the slope formula or exponential growth. Class discussions focus on the difference between infectious and noninfectious diseases, the geographic distribution of the three major infectious diseases, the association between disease and poverty, and the debate over treatment or prevention for HIV in Africa. After researching an epidemiological issue of their choice and collecting relevant data, students write an analysis of their data using class methods. Emphasizing the social relevance of mathematics applications counters the perception that students must leave behind their personalities and subjective perspectives when they enter a math class. Instead, the discussions that inform these projects enhance student understanding and engagement by explicitly asking students to link mathematics to real-world problem solving on social issues they already care about.

Mathematical Modeling and Prediction emphasizes practice that is coupled with timely feedback. Like most mathematics courses, this one asks students to attempt problems outside of class as homework that is turned in for teacher review. As noted above, students debrief their work during class discussion and in small-group work. Critical thinking and reflection on learning occurs on a daily basis. Students improve their ability to communicate mathematical reasoning and they compare and evaluate mathematical arguments. The modeling assignments in which students develop mathematical strategies for solving realistic problems encourage students to both sharpen their quantitative skills and to express the relevance of mathematics in the world.

Evaluation

In the project's pilot year, EPP courses enrolled 262 students, taught by 13 teachers at 13 schools (49 students in Physics by Inquiry, 189 students in Writing Studio and 24 students in Mathematical Modeling and Prediction). CIS staff implemented a formative evaluation process that included surveying students, interviewing a small number of teachers, reviewing grade reports, and comparing the grades of EPP students with those of students taking the same courses on the University of Minnesota campus. (See the student survey in Appendix 9.2.) To determine whether EPP had met its goals and to identify ways in which we might modify the project to better serve students in the future, we asked these questions:

1. Did EPP enroll a student body more academically diverse than the historic CIS?

2. Did EPP serve more students of color, students from low socioeconomic families, first-generation college-bound students, and English language learners?

3. Did EPP students improve their college readiness?

4. Did students increase their sense that when they get to college, they will belong there?

5. How could we improve EPP for future students?

The pilot-year data presented in the sections that follow—based on grade reports and responses to the student survey—indicated a successful start in serving the target audience, facilitating students' academic development, promoting engagement with course content and class activities, and increasing students' sense that when they get to college they will belong there.

Question 1: Did EPP Enroll a Student Body More Academically Diverse than Historically Represented in CIS?

We lack GPA or test data about students whom the "historic" CIS courses served, so to answer this question we compared CIS course eligibility requirements and used student self-reporting on high school GPAs. We do know that the student eligibility requirements for EPP courses differ significantly from those of most of the other courses in the CIS portfolio. For example, the only other math course available through CIS is a calculus course, which requires students to have earned an A or A– in a rigorous high school pre-calculus class. The EPP math course requires students to have earned C or better in high school algebra I and II classes. CIS also has two physics courses in its portfolio: Introductory College Physics from the College of Science and Engineering, and Physics by Inquiry from PSTL. The first course requires students to be in the 80th percentile or higher of their high school class and to have earned a B or better in a rigorous high school algebra II or trigonometry course; the second has no student eligibility requirement other than being at least in the 50th percentile of the high school class. Writing Studio requires students to have a GPA of 3.0 or better; score 3 or better on a PSTL Commanding English qualifying essay; have passed the state exams in writing and reading; and have teacher or counselor recommendation. The University Writing course, also in the CIS portfolio, requires students to be in the 80th percentile or higher of their high school class.

We did ask EPP students to tell us what their cumulative high school GPA was and we found that 64% of Writing Studio students, 78% of Physics by Inquiry students, and 47% of Math Modeling students had GPAs between 3.01 and 4.0. The value of this data is highly limited, given that it is self-reported and because we believe it reflects as much about the variety of schools, school curricula, and school populations as it does about EPP students.

Question 2: Did EPP Serve Students of Color, Students from Low Socioeconomic Families, First-Generation College-Bound Students, and English Language Learners?

Using data from the university's Office of Institutional Research, we determined that the proportion of students of color was significantly higher in the Entry Point Project courses than in other CIS courses at the 105 partner schools in 2009–10, and also higher than those of students in other CIS courses at the thirteen high schools that offered an EPP course. Sixty percent of EPP students were students of color; students of color are 16% of the students in other CIS courses, and 25% of the students in other CIS courses at the thirteen schools offering EPP courses.

Data from the Office of Institutional Research are not available regarding socioeconomic status or whether students are the first in their family to attend college. However, there are indicators from surveys of CIS student alumni indicating that the Entry Point Project enrolled higher proportions of these students as well when compared to CIS as a whole. Sixty-two percent of EPP students qualified or had qualified at some time for free or reduced-price lunches. Consistently, fewer than 21% of the respondents to surveys of students who participated in CIS from 2003 to 2008 were eligible for free or reduced-price lunch and/or self-identified as coming from a low-income background.

Forty-eight percent of EPP students came from homes where neither parent attended college. Surveys of students who participated in CIS from 2003 to 2008 consistently show that 18% to 21% of the respondents were from similar homes.

For 56% of EPP students, English was not the primary language spoken at home; unfortunately, data are not available to make a comparison with the CIS student population as a whole.

Question 3: Did EPP students improve their college readiness?

We approached this question in three ways: examining students' performance in courses subsequent to the one they took through EPP, comparing grades of EPP and on-campus students in the same course, and analyzing the student survey results.

Performance in Subsequent College Courses. Clearly, the most reliable indication of college readiness is a student's performance in college, and for the 2009–10 cohort, we have only limited data on students' performance in college. But because WRIT 1201: Writing Studio has been offered through CIS since 2002, we were able to track the grades for seventy-nine University of Minnesota students who had taken Writing Studio at their high schools through CIS. Looking at their grades in the next writing course in the sequence (WRIT 1301: University Writing), which they took on the UMTC campus, we found that EPP students did as well as students who took both courses on campus and, in fact, did quite well:

• There was no statistical difference in the performance of students who took WRIT 1201 in high school compared to students who took both courses on campus.

• Ninety percent of students who took WRIT 1201 in high school earned grades of C or better in WRIT 1301, taken on campus.

Grade Comparisons between EPP and On-Campus Students. Grade reports comparing grades of concurrent enrollment students with those of students in on-campus sections of the same courses are an excellent measure of the development of content knowledge. Of course, the only way this comparison makes sense is if grades in both settings are consistently assigned on the basis of the same standards. CIS has several policies and practices in place to ensure that this happens.[5] (See Ensuring University Quality in Appendix 9.3.) A grade of A in an EPP course is comparable to an A in the same course taught on the university campus and reflects the same level of understanding of the content. The 232 students in the 2009–10 EPP cohort performed at levels comparable to students on the UMTC campus: 91% of students in EPP courses earned grades of C or better, which is nearly identical to the performance of university-admitted

5. Note also that National Alliance of Concurrent Enrollment Partnerships standards require that concurrent enrollment students be held to the same standards as students taking courses on the postsecondary institution campus.

students enrolled in the on-campus sections of the same courses (where 92% of students earned grades of C or better).

Analysis of Student Surveys. Grade reports are important indicators of success, but we were also concerned about whether students perceived themselves as developing critical thinking skills, content knowledge, and sense of belonging in college. For that information, we relied on our student surveys. Conley's "Big 4" indicators of college readiness, which we had found important for our own understanding of college readiness, also helped us analyze student responses to both the quantitative questions and the open-ended narrative questions on the student surveys. We asked, "What aspect of your experience as a CIS student had the most impact on you? Why?" and "Has this class influenced your thinking about going to college? If so, how? If not, why not?" We saw student responses as directly related to three of Conley's college-readiness indicators: key cognitive strategies; content knowledge and skills; and academic behaviors or self-monitoring skills.

In quantitative responses, the vast majority of students rated themselves as developing "some" or "a lot" on core goals of the courses. Eighty-nine percent of Writing Studio students responded that they had developed as writers "some" or "a lot"; 90% of Mathematical Modeling and Prediction students reported developing "some" or "a lot" as math students; and 91% of Physics by Inquiry students reported developing "some" or "a lot" in their ability to figure things out for themselves.

In the open-ended survey questions, 38% of the comments mentioned disciplinary skills gained through taking the CIS course. Writing Studio students mentioned the revision process, writing in new genres (e.g., a research project), or improving their editing skills. Physics by Inquiry students mentioned being able to apply what they had learned in other contexts, and Mathematical Modeling and Prediction students mentioned learning how to do models.

Here are some representative examples of responses we received from students in each course:

Writing my narrative paper was the start of me finding my voice as a writer. (Writing Studio)

As a CIS student, what impacted me the most was the writing process and being able to analyze and use different types of writing genres. (Writing Studio)

I am able to apply what I have learned to other experiences and figure out problems. (Physics by Inquiry)

Learning tough equations had the most impact . . . being more focused and attentive. (Mathematical Modeling and Prediction)

College Readiness: Key Cognitive Strategies. Being expected to "think more deeply" in every class and for every assignment is often the biggest shock of the first semester in college. In quantitative measures, students reported that they felt challenged by their EPP courses and that their instructors had high expectations for their learning; in their narrative responses, students explained what that meant.

As a CIS student I am more confident in going with my own ideas and what I know to support and answer questions/problems and not need such explicit instructions. I am able to apply what I have learned to other experiences and figure out problems. (Physics by Inquiry)

Having all of the discussions that we had really opened my eyes to how other students think. (Writing Studio)

Yes, this class has influenced my thinking by challenging what I do. I have to be more detailed and specific. (Writing Studio)

All the work we did with rethinking education [had the most impact] because it just really got me to get my thoughts out on controversial issues. (Writing Studio)

The modeling process developed my thinking patterns more because it made me think rationally like a problem solver. (Mathematical Modeling and Prediction)

College Readiness: Academic Behaviors. Conley emphasizes students' ability to assume responsibility for their own learning, engage with course content and activities, collaborate with classmates, join class discussions, and respect diverse perspectives. In their responses to the open-ended survey questions, students indicated that they perceived themselves as performing well in these areas. Thirty percent of survey respondents said they now knew more about what college teachers expect, what college students need to be able to do, and what challenges college students face. Many comments were nonspecific (e.g., "I was looking forward to experiencing college and I got a little of it in the class"). Others, however, specifically mentioned feeling more prepared or more confident about their potential as college students. These adjustments to the faster pace and greater personal responsibility that characterize postsecondary study made them feel like "serious students," as reflected in the following sample comments.

> . . . doing labs makes me feel as though I can solve things on my own. They make me feel much more independent and I have much more responsibility. (Physics by Inquiry)

> It's made me realize college is more on your own and how much you put in determines how much you will get out of it. (Physics by Inquiry)

> As a CIS student I am more confident in going with my own ideas and what I know to support and answer questions/problems and do not need such explicit instructions. I am able to apply what I have learned to other experiences and figure out problems. (Physics by Inquiry)

> CIS has taught me to become a better writer. It also taught me that in order to get help from teachers in college, you have to approach them and ask for help and not just rely on teachers to come ask you if you needed help. (Writing Studio)

> I got a good look into how it feels like to be a college student as a CIS student. It was more work, more deadlines, and more independence. (Writing Studio)

> I believe the aspects of having to really commit and become serious in the studies had the most impact. I say so because since this is a college course; first it's more challenging, second we are treated more like college students than high schoolers, thus giving us more responsibilities. (Writing Studio)

> Tests counting for most of our grade [had the most impact] because it helped me be more organized with my homework and note taking. (Mathematical Modeling and Prediction)

I finally stopped asking for help from others and started to help myself. (Mathematical Modeling and Prediction)

Question 4: Did Students Increase Their Sense That When They Get to College They Will Belong There?

We have argued that if concurrent enrollment programs hope to serve a broader range of students, then concurrent enrollment classes must become spaces where students feel comfortable showing their capabilities and sharing their ideas, places where they know that their contributions are valued. We were pleased to see the percentages of students who responded favorably to survey questions related to sense of belonging: 93% agreed or strongly agreed that they felt comfortable discussing ideas (even controversial ideas) in class; 89% agreed or strongly agreed that they had contributed to class discussions; 90% agreed or strongly agreed that they were satisfied with the attention they received from their instructors; 94% agreed or strongly agreed that their instructors cared about their learning; 88% reported that they sometimes or often contributed to their classmates' learning. These are all strong indicators that when they get to college, these students will know what it feels like to belong in a college class.

Responding to the open-ended survey questions, 40% of the students' narrative comments related to learning the norms of college classrooms, and in 27% of the comments students mentioned feeling more confident or more excited about going to college. Ten percent of the comments related to interactions and collaborations that helped them learn.

> *The aspect of group effort had the most impact. It allowed for discussion and shared ideas. It also taught how to input your own ideas and have members comment on your thoughts/give feedback.* (Physics by Inquiry)

> *As a CIS student, working in lab groups had the most impact on me. I am not used to working with other people, especially people I don't know too well. It has helped me open up more and share my ideas on a subject.* (Physics by Inquiry)

> *The aspect that had the most impact on me was that our teacher really took time to discuss our papers with us individually. She really took an interest in giving us criticism about what to improve on and what not to do.* (Writing Studio)

Learning to open up and share ideas with other people [had the most impact] because I always thought that my ideas were not intelligent. The teacher helped me realize that sharing ideas is what could help me become a better writer. (Writing Studio)

This class has influenced me to go to college because this class proves that I am capable of doing college writing. (Writing Studio)

It taught me how to become a more advanced thinker, which made me feel more confident about going to college. Yet, I am still nervous about going to college. (Writing Studio)

Sharing ideas and actually understanding the material [had the most impact]. (Mathematical Modeling and Prediction)

By showing me guidelines about what instructors expect of you. I can actually pass my classes if I stay focused in college. (Mathematical Modeling and Prediction)

Reflections

After gathering and sorting through data, we now ask ourselves: What stood out in our analysis? What are the take-away lessons from the pilot year of EPP?

The Challenge of Doing a Thorough Evaluation with No Budget

As an accredited member of the National Alliance of Concurrent Enrollment Partnerships, CIS regularly collects data about student outcomes and monitors administrative practices and procedures. However, NACEP does not require the more in-depth analysis that we have undertaken of EPP. And, given our initial guiding principles, which included seeking no grant funds, we have had to wedge our efforts to evaluate EPP's pilot year in between our already packed schedules and workloads. None of us holds a position at the university that carries the expectation of doing research.

So, one approach to analyzing EPP's first year that promised to be extremely rich—conducting teacher interviews—was rather quickly abandoned because it was simply too time-consuming. Even in the few interviews we conducted, we encountered tantalizing comments about how teachers experienced the EPP. For example, one EPP physics teacher told us that he has taught many general chemistry and physics classes, but Physics by Inquiry is different from anything he has ever taught. In other classes, he explained, students in the academic middle "are not so interested in learning for learning's sake. They just want to finish up an assignment and move on. But in this class, they know they really have to understand Chapter 9, for example, because I'm not going to stand up and make a list of what they need to know—material that they can kick back out on the test. The ownership is very much different. The students will say the same thing—it's not like any other course!"

As the practice of employing concurrent enrollment as a means of strengthening underserved students' college readiness and sense of mattering becomes more common and intentional in Minnesota, we hope to secure grant dollars to do a more thorough evaluation, including following up with students to learn what happened to them after high school graduation.

Marketing

At our initial public information meeting to introduce the Entry Point Project and the three courses to be offered, we heard concerns that CIS was "watering down" its courses with this initiative; at this meeting and in other venues, high school teachers and administrators and college faculty questioned whether the quality in CIS classes would be compromised by expanding access. So one challenge inherent in the expansion of the CIS audience is addressing external fears about quality. We believe that such fears will be allayed only after the EPP courses have run for several years, and only if CIS continues to clearly, succinctly explain the difference between courses in its portfolio and their intended audiences.

CIS had grown accustomed to doing virtually no marketing because the University of Minnesota CIS brand was so well known and so well respected. We now realize that we need to resume marketing efforts in order to clarify our variety of "products." An effective marketing effort is doubly important, given that by encouraging schools to offer these new EPP courses CIS is essentially asking schools to pay for more courses in very difficult economic times. (In Minnesota, high schools pay for concurrent enrollment; the very small state subsidy does not significantly cut the cost for schools.)

We have found it critically important to be straightforward and honest about what taking university courses through EPP will and will *not* do for students. We specify that both Physics by Inquiry and Mathematical Modeling and Prediction satisfy University of Minnesota liberal education requirements and thus are appropriate for many students who know they are not headed for science- or math-based majors or careers and who wish to fulfill college liberal education requirements before graduating from high school. And we also state that these courses are *not* appropriate for most students who know they wish to pursue science- and math-based college majors or careers such as architecture, veterinary medicine, health sciences, or kinesiology. However, for students who want to pursue science- and math-based majors and careers but are not confident in their mathematical or science skills and seek to strengthen them before moving on to pre-calculus or algebra-based physics, these two courses are appropriate. EPP courses can help these students strengthen the skills and knowledge that prepare them for subsequent study.

Even though it is the course most often chosen by schools launching an EPP course, we found a particular challenge in explaining the value for students taking WRIT 1201: Writing Studio. This course carries regular university credit that may be used as an elective in a student's college graduation plan, but it does not satisfy the university's freshman writing requirement. Many high school administrators, counselors, and teachers ask why students should take Writing Studio given that it does not fulfill any liberal education requirement or the freshman writing requirement. Our response is this: students who truly are underprepared for college should know that succeeding in ramp-up classes is excellent preparation for the courses they will encounter on campus, and that having these courses on their preadmission transcripts looks very good to college admissions staff. We have also emphasized that WRIT 1201, like all the courses in the CIS portfolio, provides students with significant opportunities to develop the academic behavior and skills that Conley rightly deems critical to success in postsecondary study.

Helping students decide which course is best for them requires that schools and teachers accurately assess students' abilities and engage in honest, diplomatic conversations that avoid stigmatizing students or creating resentment among parents.

Matching Courses to Schools and Students

In much the same way that placement decisions require teachers and students to honestly evaluate the students' readiness for college work, deciding whether to offer an EPP course requires schools to honestly assess the level of college preparation their curriculum provides for all their students. In schools that track most or all students into a college-prep curriculum, students in the 50th to 80th percentile of their classes may have considerable experience with writing, science, and mathematics. On the other hand, in schools where large numbers of students struggle to pass minimum-standards tests, students may receive much less preparation for college-level study. High schools in the latter category may need to develop a new bridge course that builds students' skills and knowledge so they are prepared to succeed at the postsecondary level. When Sharon Ornelas, a Milken Award winner who teaches in the Minneapolis Public Schools, discovered that her students (most of whom were second-language students) were underprepared for WRIT 1201, she also realized that her school's curriculum failed to adequately prepare students for college writing courses. She developed a "pre-course" called Transitional Writing (for high school credit only) that focuses on developing academic vocabulary, expanding sentence variety, and strengthening critical reading and writing abilities. Teachers at six other schools adapted her curriculum and now offer pre-courses that ease the steep learning curve that their mostly ELL students experienced in Writing Studio. At about the same time, another school decided not to offer Writing Studio, because it was no more rigorous than the college-prep writing course they already offered for high school credit only.

Supports Outside of Class

On campus, sections of the Writing Studio course set aside for TRIO/ELL students and taught by PSTL faculty have a Writing Center consultant assigned to each section. This peer tutor attends class and establishes relationships with students, invites them to the center for further conversations and conferences about their writing, and thus builds a bridge to the Writing Center. In this model, teachers and tutors are partners, and visits to the Writing Center are not stigmatized. Similarly, Physics by Inquiry classes on campus employ several teaching assistants to circulate among the students, checking comprehension and probing for deeper thinking.

Knowing the difficulties that Writing Studio teachers had faced in pre-EPP years when they tried to approximate these supports—calling in parent volunteers or trying to access online Writing Center services—we required that schools provide EPP students with academic support outside the classroom. Each teacher applicant had to tell CIS whether their high school had an AVID program or some other similar support infrastructure.

In discussions with teachers after the first EPP year was completed, we heard that because the physics and math courses—both single semester courses on the university campus—are taught over the course of two semesters in the high schools, teachers had time to build in extra practice and support during the regular class period. They did not believe additional support outside the classroom was necessary. We have decided to not require the presence of AVID or a similar support program to be present in all schools offering an EPP course.

How Applicable Is Our Experience to Other Institutions?

We acknowledge that PSTL is an unusual university department in that its faculty represent various disciplines and willingly specialize in teaching first-year courses, using Universal Instructional Design. So where might other four-year institutions hoping to launch an effort similar to EPP find their college partners? Our strongest advice for recruiting postsecondary faculty is to look for ready-made cohorts with a shared mission, philosophical orientation, and pedagogical approach compatible with programs such as the EPP. Look for people already serving the underserved; doing so may avoid the need to wrangle over who, why, and how questions. Many universities have created First Year Experience programs, learning communities, or linked courses for their freshmen—all structures designed to ease the transition to college. Those are good places to start. Community colleges have already broadened their reach, but we believe four-year institutions need to be—and can be—equally committed to serving a diverse student body.

Making an Effective Concurrent Enrollment Model Stronger

The EPP data we have analyzed indicate that taking even a single postsecondary course during high school can contribute to students' college readiness and foster a sense of belonging in the college-going world. We are keenly aware, however, that the cafeteria-style model of concurrent enrollment that CIS has always employed has some inherent limitations. It allows high schools to select which UMTC courses in the CIS portfolio they would like to offer and allows students to choose which of the UMTC courses offered in their high school they would like to take. Students can opt to take only one EPP course, or other concurrent enrollment courses, in an academic year, even in their entire high school career. Because we do not assume that a single concurrent enrollment course will transform a student's academic trajectory, CIS will consider creating some mechanism or incentive that would result in high schools offering more than one EPP course and students taking more than one EPP course (or taking another CIS course).

Conclusion

CIS has greatly appreciated the fact that former University of Minnesota president Robert Bruininks has been a strong supporter of not only the traditional CIS but also of EPP. Though administratively far removed from CIS, Bruininks's practical and moral support helped calm our early worries that serving a broader academic and demographic range of students would be criticized by university faculty and staff. Bruininks has now retired and it is still unclear how much support the current president will provide. We believe that preparing underserved students will never be at the center of what the university does, but we do know that there is a community within the university that supports the work of EPP. We also remain keenly aware that the demographic projections for Minnesota's future demand that we continue this very important work.

Serving at-risk students is difficult; ramping up to college is hard work for students, and coaching students along this path requires energetic interventions from their teachers. The students EPP has served have been excluded by class rank requirements, discouraged from participating, and/or have self-selected out of concurrent enrollment courses. Better prepared for the transition to postsecondary study, the students themselves will benefit, but so too will the workforce and all citizens of Minnesota and the United States. Now, more than ever, we must acknowledge the importance of doing all we can to ensure greater diversity among student bodies and more diverse perspectives on campus; this diversity is critical to the vitality and relevance of higher education. There are various ways to do that; EPP is one promising approach.

Appendix 9.1. Demographics of 2009–10 EPP Schools

Schools	# of Students	Race/ Ethnicity	Free and Reduced Lunch	Limited English Proficiency
St. Paul Central	2,134	Am Indian 1.0% Asian 27.1% Hispanic 5.0% Black 32.7% White 34.3%	55%	21%
Shakopee	1,220	Am Indian 1.9% Asian 8.3% Hispanic 7.7% Black 5.0% White 77.1%	20%	5%
Irondale	1,548	Am Indian 1.6% Asian 6.9% Hispanic 3.2% Black 6.1% White 82.4%	24%	3%
Richfield	1,420	Am Indian 1.1% Asian 7.7% Hispanic 16.0% Black 28.9% White 46.2%	46%	15%

Schools	# of Students	Race/ Ethnicity	Free and Reduced Lunch	Limited English Proficiency
Edison	1,020	Am Indian 2.3% Asian 9.0% Hispanic 21.3% Black 55.6% White 11.9%	84%	39%
Chaska	1,935	Am Indian 0.3% Asian 3.6% Hispanic 5.6% Black 2.5% White 88.0%	12%	4%
El Colegio	100	Am Indian 6.0% Asian 0.0% Hispanic 57.0% Black 28.0% White 9.0%	86%	28%
Community of Peace Academy	179	Am Indian 1.1% Asian 70.9% Hispanic 4.5% Black 16.2% White 7.3%	80%	24%
Hmong Academy	330	Am Indian 0.0% Asian 98.2% Hispanic 0.9% Black 0.9% White 0.0%	93%	77%
Patrick Henry	1,202	Am Indian 1.3% Asian 36.4% Hispanic 3.8% Black 44.5% White 14.0%	74%	16%
Roosevelt	1,126	Am Indian 3.4% Asian 9.1% Hispanic 27.3% Black 45.3% White 15.0%	80%	41%

Schools	# of Students	Race/ Ethnicity	Free and Reduced Lunch	Limited English Proficiency
St. Anthony Village	638	Am Indian 0.8% Asian 6.7% Hispanic 4.5% Black 6.6% White 81.4%	16%	3%
White Bear Lake	1,360	Am Indian 0.5% Asian 7.6% Hispanic 2.5% Black 2.9% White 86.5%	16%	1%

Appendix 9.2. CIS Entry Point Student Survey

When answering questions, think about your experience as a student in WRIT 1201: Writing Studio.

1. To what extent do you agree or disagree with the following statements regarding your CIS class? *Please check one response for each item.*

Item:	Strongly Disagree	Disagree	Agree	Strongly Agree
I formed friendships with students I met in my CIS class.	○	○	○	○
I felt comfortable discussing ideas (even controversial ideas) in class.	○	○	○	○
My instructor cared about my learning.	○	○	○	○
My instructor had high expectations for my learning.	○	○	○	○
I am satisfied with the attention I received from my instructor.	○	○	○	○
Overall, the course work was challenging.	○	○	○	○

2. How often have you had the following experiences in your CIS class? *Please check one response for each item.*

Item:	Never	Rarely	Sometimes	Often
I contributed to class discussions.	O	O	O	O
I learned from my classmates or received helpful feedback from them.	O	O	O	O
I contributed to my classmates' learning or taught them something.	O	O	O	O
I challenged others' ideas in class.	O	O	O	O
I felt interested in class.	O	O	O	O
I came prepared and ready to participate in class.	O	O	O	O
I did not complete homework on time.	O	O	O	O
I missed class.	O	O	O	O

3. Outside of class, how often have you done these activities? *Please check one response for each item.*

Item:	Never	Rarely	Sometimes	Often
Talked with classmates outside of class about course related content	O	O	O	O
Talked with my instructor about non-course related topics (college, life, etc.)	O	O	O	O
Asked for help on work for this class	O	O	O	O

4. To what extent are you satisfied or dissatisfied with the following supports? If you have not used the service, please select "N/A." If the support was not offered, please select "N/O." *Please check one response for each item.*

Item:	Very Dissatisfied	Dissatisfied	Satisfied	Very Satisfied	N/A	N/O
Resource people at high school (AVID, Upward Bound, etc.)	O	O	O	O	O	O
U of M Writing Center Tutors	O	O	O	O	O	O
U of M online writing advice	O	O	O	O	O	O
U of M online library research	O	O	O	O	O	O
Media center at high school	O	O	O	O	O	O
Individual conference with CIS instructor	O	O	O	O	O	O

5. To what extent has your CIS course contributed to your growth in these areas? *Check one for each item.*

Item:	Not at all	A little	Some	A lot
Developing as a writer	O	O	O	O
Becoming more proficient and comfortable with the steps in writing (gathering ideas, planning, drafting and revising)	O	O	O	O
Understanding what is expected in college writing	O	O	O	O
Becoming more skilled at using outside information and ideas from others to support your own ideas	O	O	O	O

Item:	Not at all	A little	Some	A lot
Becoming more skilled at citing sources and using correct documentation when using information and ideas from others	O	O	O	O
Using computers for word processing, editing, revising and research	O	O	O	O
Becoming more skilled at editing for grammar, punctuation and style	O	O	O	O

Please write out a brief answer for each question below.

6. What aspect of your experience as a CIS student had the most impact on you? Why?

7. Would you have been more successful in this class if you had outside support? If so, what type of support would have helped you succeed?

8. Has this class influenced your thinking about going to college? If so, how? If not, why not?

9. What factors will most affect your decisions about college (finances, friends, getting accepted, etc.)?

10. What are your academic plans for Fall 2010? Please describe briefly in the space below.

Demographic information. Please answer the items below to the best of your ability.

11. What is your year in school? (*check one*)
_____ Junior   _____ Senior

12. What semester did you take this CIS course? (check one)
_____ Fall   _____ Spring

13. What is your high school GPA? *Check one response.*
_____ 3.51–4.0   _____ 3.01–3.5   _____ 2.51–3.0   _____ 2.01–2.5
_____ 1.01–2.0   _____ 0.00–1.0

14. Did one or both of your parents attend college (whether they graduated or not)?
   Father: _____ Attended college   _____ Did not attend college
   Mother: _____ Attended college   _____ Did not attend college

15. Have you ever qualified for free or reduced-price lunch?
_____ Yes   _____ No

16. What language (or languages) does your family speak at home? (*Please list all languages*)

   Primary language:

   _____

   All other languages:

   _____
   _____
   _____

Appendix 9.3. Ensuring University Quality:
Policies and Practices

College in the Schools, University of Minnesota–Twin Cities

1. All UMTC courses taught through College in the Schools (CIS) are courses that carry university degree credit and have been approved through normal university processes. They are catalogued UMTC courses, available to all students on the university campus as well as to qualified students in high schools participating in the CIS program.

2. A UMTC faculty or academic staff person is appointed by the relevant academic department to oversee the course(s) available through CIS and the instructors teaching CIS sections. The faculty coordinator or liaison:

    a. Accepts or denies teacher applications;

    b. Defines student qualification requirements;

    c. Plans and delivers a minimum of three course-specific workshops each year that address the content, pedagogy, and assessment of the course(s) taught by CIS instructors;

    d. Reviews each CIS instructor's syllabus annually to ensure it meets campus standards;

    e. Reviews sample student work graded by CIS teachers to ensure that University grading standards are followed;

    f. Observes CIS instructors teach, to ensure that the pedagogy and content match that in college-campus sections;

    g. Reviews official University reports of grade distribution in CIS sections; and

    h. Reviews Student Rating of Teaching surveys completed by CIS students.

3. CIS instructors must meet minimum academic and experience requirements. The minimum requirements are developed by the University faculty liaison/coordinator in consultation with and on behalf of the sponsoring academic department. CIS teachers are appointed as teaching specialists in the College of Continuing Education.

4. University courses taught through CIS use the same or comparable texts as are used in the course on the college campus.

5. Every year that they teach through CIS, instructors are *required* to participate in discipline-specific workshops led by the UMTC-CIS faculty liaison/coordinator. These workshops address the content, pedagogy, and assessment of the University course(s).

6. The UMTC-CIS program is accredited by the National Alliance of Concurrent Enrollment Partnerships (NACEP). To become accredited, UMTC-CIS demonstrated that it met or exceeded standards of excellence applying to curriculum, students, instructors, assessment, and program evaluation. See NACEP standards at www.nacep.org.

References

ACT. 2010a. *The Condition of College and Career Readiness, Minnesota, Class of 2010.* http://www.act.org/newsroom/data/2010/pdf/readiness/CCCR_Minnesota .pdf.

———. 2010b. *ACT Profile Report–Minnesota, Graduating Class 2010.* http://www.act .org/newsroom/data/2010/pdf/profile/Minnesota.pdf?utm_campaign=ccc r10&utm_source=profilereports&utm_medium=web.

Bailey, Thomas R., and Melinda M. Karp. 2003. *Promoting College Access and Success: A Review of Credit-Based Transition Programs.* Washington, DC: Office of Adult and Vocational Education, U.S. Department of Education.

Barnett, Elisabeth, and Katherine L. Hughes. 2010 (Oct.). "Supporting Middle-Achieving High School Students in College Courses." Paper presented at the 2010 conference of the National Alliance of Concurrent Enrollment Partnerships, Minneapolis, MN. Archived at http://www.nacep.org/docs/news /conference-archives/conference-archives-2010/NACEP_Conference2010 _BarnettHughes.pdf.

Complete College America. 2011. "Minnesota 2011" web page. Accessed June 21. http://www.completecollege.org/docs/Minnesota.pdf.

Conley, David T. 2007. "The Challenge of College Readiness." *Educational Leadership* 64(7): 23–29.

———. 2009. *Creating College Readiness: Profiles of 38 Schools that Know How.* Eugene, OR: Educational Policy Improvement Center.

Espinosa, Jessica, and Amanda L. Ziebell-Finley. 2010 (Oct. 20). "Changing Demographics–Concurrent Enrollment's Role in Educational Equity." Presentation at the 2010 conference of the National Alliance of Concurrent Enrollment Programs, Minneapolis, MN.

Golann, Joanne Wang, and Katherine L. Hughes. 2008. *Dual Enrollment Policies and Practices: Earning College Credit in California High Schools.* New York: Community College Research Center, Teachers College, Columbia Univ. Funded by and published with James Irvine Foundation, San Francisco, CA.

Guinier, Lani. 2002. "Race, Testing, and the Miner's Canary." *Rethinking Schools* 16(4): 13–23.

Harshbarger, Ronald, and Lisa Yocco. 2009. *College Algebra in Context with Applications for the Managerial, Life, and Social Sciences.* New York: Pearson.

Hsu, Leon. 2005. "Teaching Thinking and Reasoning Skills in a Science Course." In *The General College Vision: Integrating Intellectual Growth, Multicultural*

Perspectives, and Student Development, edited by J. L. Higbee, D. B. Lundell, and D. R. Arendale, 333–53. Minneapolis, MN: Center for Research on Developmental Education and Urban Literacy, Univ. of Minnesota.

Johnson, Dawn Rene, Matthew Soldner, Jeannie Brown Leonard, Patty Alvarez, Karen Kurotsuchi Inkelas, Heather Rowan-Kenyon, and Susan Longerbeam. 2007. "Examining Sense of Belonging Among First-Year Undergraduates from Different Racial/Ethnic Groups." *Journal of College Student Development* 48(5): 525–42.

Jolliffe, David A., and Bernie Phelan. 2006. "Advanced Placement, Not Advanced Exemption: Challenges for High Schools, Colleges, and Universities." In *Delivering College Composition: The Fifth Canon*, edited by K. B. Yancey, 89–103. Portsmouth, NH: Heinemann-Boynton/Cook.

Karp, Melinda M. 2007. *Learning about the Role of College Student through Dual Enrollment Participation*. New York: Community College Research Center, Teachers College, Columbia Univ.

Karp, Melinda M., Juan Carlos Calcagno, Katherine L. Hughes, Dong Wook Jeong, and Thomas R. Bailey. 2007. *The Postsecondary Achievement of Participants in Dual Enrollment: An Analysis of Student Outcomes in Two States*. St. Paul, MN: National Research Center for Career and Technical Education, Univ. of Minnesota.

Karp, Melinda M., and Katherine L. Hughes. 2008. "Study: Dual Enrollment Can Benefit A Broad Range Of Students." *Techniques: Connecting Education and Careers* 83(7): 14–17.

Karp, Melinda M. and Katherine L. Hughes and L. O'Gara. 2010. "An Exploration of Tinto's Integration Framework for Community College Students." *Journal of College Student Retention* 12(1): 69–86.

McDermott, Lillian C. 2005. *Physics by Inquiry*, custom edition for the Univ. of Minnesota (ISBN 9780471788119). New York: Wiley.

Minnesota Department of Education. 2011. "Data Reports and Analytics" web page (Student Data). Accessed June 23. http://w20.education.state.mn.us /MDEAnalytics/Data.jsp.

Minnesota Office of Higher Education. 2011. "Race/Ethnicity: Enrollment Statistics at a Glance" web page. Accessed June 14. http://www.ohe.state.mn.us /mPg.cfm?pageID=755.

College Readiness Consortium. 2011. *Ramp-Up to Readiness*. University of Minnesota. Accessed June 28. http://www.collegeready.umn.edu/programs/ramp _up.html.

Staats, Susan K. 2005. "Multicultural Mathematics: A Social Issues Perspective in Lesson Planning." In *The General College Vision: Integrating Intellectual Growth, Multicultural Perspectives, and Student Development*, edited by J. L Higbee, D. B. Lundell, and D. R. Arendale, 185–99. Minneapolis, MN: General College and the Center for Research on Developmental Education and Urban Literacy.

Staats, Susan K., and Chris Batteen. 2009. "Context in an Interdisciplinary Algebra Writing Assignment." *Journal of College Reading and Learning* 40(1): 35–50.

Stebleton, Michael J., Ronald L. Huesman, and Aliya Kuzhabekova. 2010. *Do I Belong Here? Exploring Immigrant College Student Responses On The SERU Survey Sense Of Belonging/Satisfaction Factor.* Research and Occasional Paper Series, UC Berkeley (CSHE.13.10).

University of Minnesota. 2011. "Campus and Unit Enrollment by Race/Ethnicity for Spring 2011." Office of Institutional Research website. Accessed June 16, http://www.oir.umn.edu/student/enrollment/term/1113/current/12189.

Weber, Tom, and Madeleine Baran. 2011 (Jan. 21). "Duncan: Minn. Must Address Achievement Gap." *MPR News.* http://www.mprnews.org/story/2011/01/21/education-secretary.

PART THREE | **State Focus**

10

Promoting Quality

State Strategies for Overseeing Dual Enrollment Programs

ADAM I. LOWE

This chapter documents the strategies that six states employ to ensure that college courses offered to high school students are of the same high quality and rigor as courses offered to matriculated college students. It highlights the main approaches used by these states to encourage colleges and universities to align their dual enrollment programs with state and national quality standards. The states use seven main strategies to oversee dual enrollment programs: program approval, periodic program reviews, student outcome analysis, regular collegial meetings, course approvals, review of district/college agreements, and annual reporting.

Introduction

Context

In many states across the country, legislative and policy changes have led to rapid expansion of dual enrollment programs in recent years—especially concurrent enrollment programs—defined as the opportunity for

An earlier version of this paper was originally published by the National Alliance of Concurrent Enrollment Partnerships (NACEP) in October 2010. This revised version is printed with permission of NACEP. Research was conducted in 2010 with financial support from the Indiana Commission for Higher Education (ICHE) and the Oregon Department of Community Colleges and Workforce Development (ODCCWD).

high school students to take college-credit-bearing courses taught by college-approved high school teachers.[1]

Concerns about dual enrollment course quality often follow periods of growth and expansion, particularly as many states embark on initiatives to raise the rigor of the high school experience through accelerated coursework and to increase access to dual enrollment for students who are underrepresented in higher education. Observers and advocates of this expansion have cautioned that merely enrolling greater numbers of students is unlikely to achieve these policy goals with adequate quality assurance mechanisms in place (Brown-Lerner and Brand 2006; Hoffman, Vargas, and Santos 2008).

Forty-two states have adopted policy provisions related to the quality of courses offered by postsecondary providers of dual and concurrent enrollment (Borden, Taylor, Park, and Seiler 2013). The most common relate to instructor eligibility and selection, course content and rigor, and transcript requirements (Borden et al. 2013; Dounay Zinth 2014). Quality standards vary widely across the states, but a common intent lies behind these standards—that college courses offered to high school students are of the same high quality and rigor as the courses offered to matriculated college students, regardless of their location, delivery method, or instructor.

Typical faculty standards adopted by states require institutions to apply the same academic credential requirements to concurrent enrollment as other faculty teaching on the college campus, conduct classroom observations, and/or provide professional development specific to the course being taught. Course quality standards variously include requirements for academic department oversight over course syllabi, assessments, textbooks, grading policies, and/or course evaluations (Dounay Zinth 2013).

---

1. There is considerable variation across the country in the use of the terms *concurrent enrollment, dual enrollment,* and *dual credit.* NACEP considers *concurrent enrollment* to be a subset of dual enrollment opportunities for high school students to take college credit-bearing courses, typically for both high school and transcripted college credit. *Dual enrollment* courses can be taught by high school and/or college/university instructors and can occur on the high school campus, the college/university campus, or via distance education.

As the only national set of standards of excellence for concurrent enrollment partnerships, NACEP's standards serve as a model for state-wide quality standards in seventeen states. While each of these states has adapted NACEP's standards to the local circumstances and needs, they share a common framework in addressing the areas of faculty, assessment, curriculum, students, and program evaluation.

Cases Selected for Comparison

Few states have, however, established comprehensive systems for over-seeing dual enrollment programs to encourage institutions to align their practices with quality standards.

Of the states that model their standards on NACEP's, eight have adopted policies that additionally require, provide incentives, or encourage colleges and/or universities to obtain NACEP accreditation: Arkansas, Indiana, Iowa, Kentucky, Minnesota, Missouri, Oregon, and South Dakota. These states have integrated NACEP's peer-review accreditation process as a component of their state's quality assurance mechanism.

While prior studies by the Education Commission of the States, the Community College Research Center, the Higher Learning Commission, and the Western Interstate Compact for Higher Education have examined dual enrollment policies across the fifty states, none had looked in depth at the processes by which states conduct program oversight.

This study sought to fill that void by illuminating dual enrollment oversight and review strategies among the following state-level entities at the time of the research (2010):

- Florida Department of Education
- Illinois Community College Board
- Oregon Dual Credit Oversight Committee
- South Dakota Board of Regents
- Utah System of Higher Education and Utah Office of Education
- Virginia Community College System

The chapter presents these six as in-depth case studies, and does not evaluate or judge the practices. This study was initiated at the request of NACEP's state agencies partners to help further knowledge and understanding of state-level policies and practices. NACEP believes in the value of nongovernmental peer-review accreditation as a mechanism for program improvement and quality assurance. Accreditation furthers institutional accountability while maintaining institutional autonomy. NACEP does not take a position favoring a particular form of governmental engagement in dual enrollment program oversight, and recognizes that government and accreditors have overlapping responsibilities to promote quality education.

Summary of Strategies Used by States

Among the six case studies, seven main strategies for overseeing dual enrollment programs were observed:

• *Program Approval.* Front-end reviews are conducted to evaluate whether a dual enrollment program meets the state's standards. Without this approval, dual enrollment providers will not be able to offer courses (Oregon) or have their credits accepted (South Dakota).

• *Periodic Program Reviews.* Each dual enrollment program is examined periodically to gauge compliance with standards and program quality and to provide feedback to the colleges.

• *Student Outcome Analysis.* Researchers use longitudinal data on student outcomes, such as persistence and grade point average in subsequent college courses. Research allows states to spot trends and monitor performance.

• *Regular Collegial Meetings.* Regularly occurring collegial meetings provide opportunities for dual enrollment administrators and state officials to share best practices, discuss standards, and resolve issues that arise. Open dialogue helps create an environment for program improvement through information exchange and professional development.

• *Course Approvals.* States with the resources to review individual course learning outcomes and/or syllabi can verify that they are college-level courses and also meet high school graduation requirements. States with existing college course transfer libraries or common numbering systems can match proposed dual enrollment courses to these approved course offerings.

• *Review of District/College MOUs.* In most states, postsecondary institutions and local school districts sign partnership agreements or

Memoranda of Understanding (MOU) describing the terms and arrangements for dual enrollment courses. MOUs submitted to state officials provide them with an opportunity to review the contents and raise concerns with postsecondary institutions. These agencies provide postsecondary institutions with templates that include provisions required by legislation and policy.

• *Annual Reporting.* States can use information from annual reports to monitor trends, learn of new developments, and aggregate data for greater understanding of how programs are operating statewide. Data from institutions can be aggregated for state-level reports on dual enrollment practices and prevalence. Without consistent data on a variety of data elements, policy makers often make decisions without knowing the extent or success of a particular program or practice. While some states' annual

TABLE 10.1

State Strategies for Overseeing Dual Enrollment Programs

	Florida	Illinois	Oregon	South Dakota	Utah	Virginia
Program Approval	[1]		✓	✓		
Periodic Program Reviews		✓	✓			[2]
Student Outcome Analysis	✓		✓	✓		
Regular Collegial Meetings			✓		✓	✓
Course Approvals	✓				✓	
Review of District/ College MOUs	✓				✓	✓
Annual Reporting	✓	✓	✓		✓	✓

1. The Florida Department of Education approves programs that offer specific dual enrollment courses to students from school districts statewide. It does not affirmatively approve the majority of dual enrollment programs, which are subject to local agreements between school districts and community colleges and public universities in nearby locations.

2. The Virginia Community College System does not have regularly scheduled program reviews, but the system's internal auditor performs program audits upon the chancellor's request.

reporting systems are limited to student enrollment, similar information is sometimes included in the MOUs submitted by colleges in those states. The large number and variance in format of MOUs, however, would make aggregation and analysis a challenge for state officials.

Each state agency implements a different combination of the seven strategies, emphasizing those aspects of oversight most relevant to their particular institutional and policy environment (see Table 10.1). Designing the right set of accountability measures can lead to program improvement, without burdensome regulatory measures. However, none of the strategies identified come without costs: all require human and financial resources at both the institution and state level.

State Overviews

Florida Department of Education

Florida has a long-standing dual enrollment program, with 85% of student enrollment concentrated in twenty-eight community colleges that are required to establish dual enrollment partnerships with school districts in their respective service areas. Some public universities voluntarily offer dual enrollment, along with a few private colleges and universities. Within the Florida Department of Education, there are two divisions that collaborate to oversee dual enrollment: the Florida Division of Colleges and the Office of Articulation.

Two Florida statutes govern dual enrollment courses: the Dual Enrollment Program statute (Fla. Stat. §1007.271) and the District Interinstitutional Articulation Agreements (IAA) statute (Fla. Stat. §1007.235). The dual enrollment statute establishes student eligibility, career pathways, alignment with the statewide course numbering system, transferability, free textbooks, and course weightings. The IAA statute requires school districts and community colleges to partner to offer dual enrollment courses and other articulated programs.

In 2007 the Council of Community College Presidents adopted a Statement of Standards Dual Enrollment/Early College Programs in the Florida Community College System, adapted from the NACEP national standards. These standards were incorporated into a State Board of Education rule on College Credit Dual Enrollment (Rule 6A-14.064, Fla. Admin. Code), which became effective in June 2010. The board's rule includes standards on placement testing, faculty qualifications, faculty liaisons, classroom observations, common course syllabi, textbooks, exams and grades, and instructional time.

The state has experienced a surge in dual enrollment participation in recent years, particularly occurring on high school campuses. This is largely due to a legislative change to the state's system of evaluating the performance of high schools. Beginning in the 2009–10 school year, the state-assigned school performance grades for high schools included calculations for student participation and student performance in accelerated coursework, including dual enrollment. Dual enrollment grew by 60% in the four-year period after this accountability system went into effect. Legislative changes to the state's dual enrollment funding model in 2013 were also predicted to cause programs to shift more toward the lower-cost concurrent enrollment model at high school locations.

The state utilizes four strategies for overseeing dual enrollment programs: (1) reviewing draft Interinstitutional Articulation Agreements; (2) ensuring that all dual enrollment courses offered are listed on a Statewide Course Numbering System for college courses; (3) approving any programs that offer dual enrollment classes statewide; and (4) tracking student enrollment and performance longitudinally in public K–12 schools into Florida public postsecondary institutions through the state's comprehensive information system.

Every college is required to annually sign an IAA with each school district in its service area, covering course offerings, student eligibility, instructional quality, and cost sharing. The department developed a template to ensure that the IAAs include the required information. Reviewing draft IAAs each year gives the Florida Department of Education staff an opportunity to provide feedback if they have concerns or when issues arise about a particular program's quality.

The department also is responsible for certifying that courses offered via dual enrollment appear in the Statewide Course Numbering System for postsecondary courses. It has developed a crosswalk for the most commonly taken academic credit courses that shows how they meet state high school graduation requirements, reducing the ambiguity of the type of high school credits students can earn through dual enrollment.

Lastly, the department also approves programs that offer specific dual enrollment courses to students statewide. The three programs that have received approval are able to operate without needing to negotiate IAAs with all school districts across the state.

Illinois Community College Board

Concurrent enrollment is the predominant form of dual enrollment[2] in Illinois, with nearly 80% of student enrollment in dual enrollment courses located on high school or career center campuses. Dual enrollment first became common in Illinois in the late 1990s, with enrollment growing an average of 13% per year in the decade that followed. A P-16 Initiative grant supported data collection and student tuition for a few years, though the grant has since ended.

The Illinois Community College Board's (ICCB) Administrative Rules set standards for community college dual enrollment programs covering faculty qualifications and selection; student academic qualifications; and placement testing and prerequisites, course offerings, and course requirements. The ICCB's standards have been in place since 2006 and were adapted from NACEP's national standards.

The 2008 Illinois Dual Credit Quality Act legislatively established similar standards, and applies them additionally to universities as well as independent and private colleges offering dual enrollment. Oversight and review of community college programs remains with ICCB. The act also directs the Illinois Board of Higher Education to oversee the implementation of the quality standards for dual enrollment programs offered by public universities and private postsecondary institutions. The 2008 act also mandates annual reporting by each program on the courses offered,

---

2. *Dual enrollment* as defined in the chapter introduction is known as *dual credit* in Illinois; *dual enrollment* is defined as a high school student taking a college course solely for college credit. The use of the term *dual enrollment* in the Illinois section of this chapter, and throughout the chapter, follows the definition in the chapter introduction.

faculty and their credentials, student enrollments, and sites where dual enrollment is offered.

ICCB's primary strategy for dual enrollment program oversight is its recognition process. In order to remain eligible for state funding, the ICCB conducts a site visit to each of the thirty-nine colleges every five years to ensure that the colleges comply with state standards and demonstrate quality programming. Highly visible reports are provided to the college's president and board of trustees, and include both quality and compliance recommendations. The college is given an opportunity to respond. The final report and the college's response are presented to the ICCB's trustees in a public meeting. The trustees can establish conditional recognition or withdraw recognition of a college if there are significant compliance concerns.

In 2006, the dual enrollment standards were incorporated into the ICCB's Recognition Manual for the Illinois Public Community College Districts, and the ICCB's director of career and technical education began making site visits to review dual enrollment programs. The two-day site visit includes a review of the college's self-study and includes an audit of student placement testing and faculty qualification files. Conversations also include discussion of program standards, agreements with school districts, and engaging high school instructors as adjunct faculty.

To help educate college administrators about its standards, the ICCB organized two statewide dual enrollment summits and regularly facilitates regional workshops and presents at other college forums and conferences.

Oregon Dual Credit Oversight Committee

All seventeen community colleges in Oregon are statutorily required to offer dual enrollment[3] opportunities to school districts within their college district boundaries. The most prevalent form of dual enrollment in Oregon is concurrent enrollment courses offered in the high school taught

---

3. The state uses the term *dual credit* to refer to a course offered in a high school where a student can earn both secondary and postsecondary credit, and the *concurrent enrollment* model as described in the introduction to this chapter is the predominant one in Oregon.

by high school teachers. Concurrent enrollment is also offered by four of the seven public universities in the state. The state first adopted an administrative rule on "Two Plus Two and Dual Credit Programs" in 1981, and the early programs were focused primarily on career and technical education. Over time, the colleges began offering more academic courses that transfer to university degrees. The 1981 administrative rule requires programs to submit their policies to the Oregon Department of Community Colleges and Workforce Development and to prepare an annual report, while a second administrative rule specifies the qualifications of community college faculty teaching under contract in high schools.

For many years, the community college dual enrollment coordinators have been meeting three or four times per year, providing a collegial environment to share program updates and best practices. Conversations began in these meetings about adopting common state program standards. A 2007–8 Dual Credit Task Force recommended that the state adopt common standards. In 2009 the task force was reconstituted as the Dual Credit Oversight Committee.

The oversight committee is comprised of three representatives from community colleges, two from public universities, and one high school representative. It is staffed by the Department of Community Colleges and Workforce Development, in collaboration with the Oregon Department of Education and the Oregon University System.

The oversight committee adopted NACEP's standards as the state's standards, and established a program approval process. From 2010 to 2013, the Committee reviewed and approved applications for every dual enrollment program in the state, any that failed to gain approval would no longer be able to offer dual enrollment in the state. Programs that hold NACEP's national accreditation are considered state-approved and do not need to be reviewed by the committee. Renewal is to be based primarily on demonstrated professional development and student outcome data, and is tentatively scheduled for 2016.

Colleges prepare annual reports tuition and fee structures and instructor qualifications. Researchers with the Oregon University System conducted two longitudinal evaluation studies, published in 2008 and 2010, utilizing data from a student information system containing data from all public higher education institutions in the state. These reports track students who took a dual enrollment course in high school and look at their subsequent performance in higher-level courses after enrolling at an Oregon community college or public university

South Dakota Board of Regents

The South Dakota Board of Regents oversees and sets policy for the state's six public universities. Historically only one public university, one community college, and one private college in South Dakota offered concurrent enrollment, though board discussions noted increasing enrollments in the model starting in 2010.[4] On-campus dual enrollment programs exist on most of the university and college campuses, but these are small and not the focus of the board's policy.

Due to the large distances between universities, numerous postsecondary institutions in neighboring states offer concurrent enrollment courses in South Dakota high schools, and many out-of-state students attend university in South Dakota. Thus the board has used its credit acceptance policy to influence the quality of concurrent enrollment programming in the region, not just among South Dakota institutions.

The South Dakota Board of Regents' interest in the quality of concurrent enrollment coursework stems from a situation in the 1990s when an institution in a neighboring state began marketing a concurrent enrollment program to South Dakota high schools. When these students matriculated to one of the South Dakota universities, the universities noticed that they were poorly prepared for higher-level college courses. Further investigation revealed that the content of these courses was not equivalent to the college's course content and that the high school instructors and the sponsoring college's faculty had little interaction.

In 2001, the Regents established a transfer policy that only accepted concurrent enrollment credit from an out-of-state institution if the institution has signed a high school–based dual enrollment agreement with

---

4. *Concurrent enrollment*, as defined in the introduction to this chapter, is referred to as *high school-based dual enrollment* in South Dakota.

the board. These agreements establish standards for student eligibility, faculty credentials, faculty mentoring, and syllabi development. Prior to signing an agreement, staff from the board conduct interviews with program coordinators and college academic officers to gauge whether the program is following the state's standards. When possible, staff visit the institutions throughout the region that send students to South Dakota universities to discuss dual enrollment. The board approved thirteen institutions between 2001 and 2010.

In addition to the program agreements, South Dakota analyzes how well students perform in advanced college classes in the same discipline after taking concurrent enrollment courses.

In a state with low population, informal networks work well to keep the Board staff informed about new developments in the schools and for resolving concerns. When a serious concern arises, staff members discuss the matter with the Regents' Academic Affairs Council, comprised of university chief academic officers whose recommendations go to the South Dakota Board of Regents and who ultimately are responsible for implementing board policy. Changes to the board's credit transfer policy in 2010 provide for credit acceptance from NACEP-accredited programs, regardless of whether those programs have signed agreements with the board.

Utah System of Higher Education and Utah Office of Education

Oversight of dual enrollment[5] in Utah is collaboratively conducted by the Utah System of Higher Education (USHE) and the Utah State Office of Education. The USHE's standards for postsecondary institutions operating dual enrollment programs are an adaptation of NACEP's program standards to the Utah context. The Utah State Board of Education's rule governs high school participation, including student eligibility standards, funding, and program delivery methods. The primary oversight strategies used in Utah include (1) regular collaborative meetings and other efforts to ensure college and school administrators and faculty are aware

---

5. Utah uses the term *concurrent enrollment* as we define *dual enrollment* in the introduction to this chapter, to cover a wide range of delivery locations and instructors.

of the state's standards; (2) course curriculum alignment and approval; and (3) close monitoring of enrollment data.

State agency staff members meet quarterly with the Utah Alliance of Concurrent Enrollment Partnerships (UACEP), comprised of postsecondary dual enrollment directors and high school administrators implementing dual enrollment. The UACEP postsecondary and school district chairs set the meeting agendas but regularly include the state representatives to explain new developments and resolve outstanding issues. The meetings also emphasize professional development, with staff and faculty from both secondary and postsecondary institutions sharing best practices.

The state also requires each high school and institution of higher education to annually sign an agreement that contains assurance statements regarding state standards compliance. These are submitted to the USHE and help ensure that administrators are aware of state policy expectations.

Utah's dual enrollment course curriculum review is designed to ensure that course content aligns 100% with college curriculum, and at least 80% with high school curriculum necessary for graduation. This review process resulted in a master list of dual enrollment courses—adopted initially for the 2006–7 school year and updated annually—for which the state provides funding to school districts and colleges. Colleges and high schools together propose new courses for the list, or adjustments to existing courses. This process has created a unique approach to curriculum alignment that must be done the year prior to a course being offered. It forces dialogue between school district curriculum specialists and college faculty, whose work is then filtered through subject area specialists at both state agencies. The process has resulted in greater focus for students taking dual enrollment courses, as the courses are better aligned with first year college requirements and career pathways.

Virginia Community College System

The Virginia Plan for Dual Enrollment, originally signed in 1988, establishes the principal framework and standards for dual enrollment in the state. Revised most recently in 2008, it encourages collaboration between Virginia's twenty-three public community colleges and local school districts. It sets standards for admissions requirements, course eligibility, credit awarded, selection of faculty, tuition and fees, and assessment and evaluation.

The plan directs the colleges to apply broadly applicable institutional policies, Virginia Community College System (VCCS) guidelines, and the accreditation standards of the Southern Association of Colleges and Schools (SACS) to dual enrollment course curricula, assessment, students, and faculty; just as the colleges would for on-campus coursework for matriculated college students.

The plan allows for local agreements between the community colleges and school districts to establish the location of the courses, whether courses are taught by high school teachers or college campus faculty, whether to mix high school and college students, and financial arrangements. VCCS provides a template to ensure the contracts contain the minimum provisions required under statute and policy. A central legal office reviews individual contracts as needed.

In 2005, multiple pressures led to an intervention by the system office to improve colleges' dual enrollment programs. These pressures included a large increase in the number of students taking dual enrollment courses, questions raised about the rigor of dual enrollment courses, ongoing negotiations with public universities regarding transfer agreements, and system office concerns about inconsistent evaluation of faculty qualifications, student placement testing, and other practices. In response, the chancellor directed the system office's auditor to conduct a policy and practice audit of nine colleges' dual enrollment programs. The primary findings related to inadequate documentation, excessive use of waivers for faculty credentialing, limited use of required student evaluations of faculty, and some high school textbooks being used instead of college textbooks. System office staff prepared a summary report with no attributions that was distributed to all twenty-three colleges' presidents and vice presidents for academic affairs.

The audit became the starting point for dialogue with the dual enrollment program directors. VCCS began holding regular meetings to create an environment for open conversations, information exchange, and professional development. The meetings were initially held three times a year. Program directors suggest agenda items. The meetings have become an opportunity for dialogue, to resolve legal and enrollment questions, and to share practices and resources such as handbooks, faculty materials, contracts, and factsheets.

Building collegial relationships and establishing an environment of transparency and trust has allowed the system office staff to deal with any issues that arise on a case-by-case basis, without the need for authority or mandates. The colleges now have greater consistency in practice, without impeding institutional autonomy.

While data reporting is limited to student enrollment in dual enrollment courses, system staff are able to monitor trends closely because enrollment and course outcome information are centrally stored in an enterprise student information system.

Conclusion

States considering implementing new strategies for overseeing the quality of dual enrollment programs have a variety of tools at their disposal. Local policy environments and institutional arrangements affect the design of a state oversight system. Policy makers should identify quality assurance mechanisms that ensure minimum standards are in place and encourage colleges and universities to adopt best practices, while respecting institutional autonomy and without establishing burdensome regulatory measures. They should consider the role of third-party peer review, and whether the resources, capacity, and institutional trust exist within the state for unbiased reviews. There are many routes to the desired outcome of a high quality seamless education system for students, where high school teachers and college faculty collaborate to align curriculum across the secondary-postsecondary divide.

References

Borden, Victor M., Jason L. Taylor, Eunkyoung Park, and David J. Seiler. 2013. *Dual Credit in U.S. Higher Education: A Study of State Policy and Quality Assurance Practices.* Chicago, IL: Higher Learning Commission. https://www.ncahlc .org/Information-for-Institutions/dual-credit.html.

Brown-Lerner, Jennifer, and Betsy Brand. 2006. *The College Ladder: Linking Secondary and Postsecondary Education for Success for All Students.* Washington,

DC: American Youth Policy Forum. http://www.aypf.org/resources/the
collegeladder/.

Dounay Zinth, Jennifer. 2013. "Dual Enrollment: 50-State Reports, Instructor and
Course Quality Component." *High School Database*. Denver, CO: Education
Commission of the States. http://ecs.force.com/mbdata/MBQuestRT?Rep
=DE1313.

Dounay Zinth, Jennifer. 2014. "Increasing Student Success in Dual Enrollment
Programs: Thirteen Model State-Level Policy Components." Denver, CO:
Education Commission of the States. http://www.ecs.org/clearinghouse/01
/10/91/11091.pdf.

Hoffman, Nancy, Joel Vargas, and Janet Santos. 2008. *On Ramp to College: A State
Policymaker's Guide to Dual Enrollment*. Boston, MA: Jobs for the Future. http://
www.jff.org/publications/ramp-college-state-policymakers-guide-dual
-enrollment.

11

Developing a Statewide Concurrent Enrollment Partnership

TED R. UNGRICHT AND CYNTHIA GRUA

This chapter describes the evolution and current status of a partnership that has developed between the Utah System of Higher Education (USHE) and the Utah State Office of Education (USOE) over twenty-three years. The Utah State Legislature has been a central factor in the evolution and development of this partnership, passing legislation that requires the USHE and the USOE to collaborate to implement a system that provides students with accelerated learning opportunities (Utah Code, Title 53A, Chapter 15, Section 101). One of those accelerated learning options is the state's concurrent enrollment program.

Funding Fuels Growth

Concurrent enrollment was first mentioned in Utah House Bill 296, passed in February 1987. In this bill, USOE was directed to develop standards and guidelines for using concurrent enrollment funds; however, no funds were allocated. During the period from 1987 to 1995, institutions of higher education offering concurrent enrollment programs funded such activities by charging students a reduced tuition. In 1991, Utah Senate Bill 196—the Minimum School Program Act Amendments—included concurrent enrollment with other special purpose optional programs, allowing districts to spend funds on concurrent enrollment. The decision to make concurrent enrollment free for students was made in 1994 with the passage of Utah House Bill 190, which prohibited institutions of higher education from charging tuition for the program. Then, in 1995, the legislature funded concurrent enrollment at a target of $1,500 per public education full time equivalent, or $33 per quarter credit hour, roughly $50 per semester credit hour (Foxley 1995; Harden 1994).

The legislature continues its commitment to funding concurrent enrollment today with an appropriation of $9.97 through the Minimum School Program (Utah Senate Bill 0001). These funds are distributed to USOE and then shared with USHE. Along with the appropriations, in 2012 the legislature allow institutions of higher education to charge

TABLE 11.1

Funding, Credits Earned, and Student Participation, 1995–2009

Year	Total Funding	Credits Earned	Students Participating
1995–96	$2,444,856	78292*	11725
1996–97	$2,761,591	105285*	13691
1997–98	$4,945,041	111447*	18033
1998–99	$4,610,898	127694	19744
1999–00	$4,701,173	126986	20506
2000–01	$5,610,838	125747	19822
2001–02	$6,149,390	133747	20663
2002–03	$5,310,029	146917	21875
2003–04	$5,354,633	153728	23384
2004–05	$5,354,633	177659	26680
2005–06	$5,541,959	189838	27396
2006–07	$8,292,311	190284	27245
2007–08	$9,215,497	191564	28277
2008–09	$9,436,669	188221	27444
2009–10	$8,705,286	194614	28185
2010–11	$8,531,186	185881	26170
2011–12	$8,531,186	189387	27012
2012–13	$8,531,200	189417	27444
2013–14	$8,893,300	187680	26879
2014–15	$9,270,600	198163	28551
2015–16	$9,766,700		

Sources: Utah State Office of Education, 2016. Utah State Legislature, 2016.

* Credits earned converted to semester rate using 2/3 ratio.

students partial tuition. The amount decided on by USHE was $5 per credit hour.

With two notable exceptions, both growth and funding since 1995 have shown steady increases (see Table 11.1). From 2002 to 2005, funding dropped then leveled off; however, enrollment continued to grow. During this period, concurrent enrollment programs slowly became underfunded. Diminished funding threatened the integrity of the programs and stimulated debate about the quality of instruction and whether students were benefiting from participation. This debate culminated in Utah House Bill 151 (2006), which authorized USHE institutions to charge partial tuition for concurrent enrollment courses. Then Governor Michael O. Leavitt vetoed this bill, and funding for concurrent enrollment was increased significantly.

The other notable exception in growth is the leveling off of enrollments since 2005. Reasons for the slowing of growth are attributed to concerns about the stability of funding for the New Century scholarship (Harden 1994), and to a persistent concern over long-term benefits of participation (e.g., questions about whether students who completed concurrent enrollment courses were graduating from college earlier).

Statewide Leadership

The state legislature exerts influence over Utah's concurrent enrollment programs by requiring USOE and USHE to collaborate to set policy and procedures. Utah State Office of Education Rule R277-713 and Utah System of Higher Education Policy R165, mirror policies, define concurrent enrollment and include requirements for student eligibility and participation, course selection, faculty approval and participation, and allocation of funds.

Utah System of Higher Education Policy R165 defines concurrent enrollment as

> enrollment by public school students in one or more USHE institution course(s) under a contractual agreement between the USHE institution and a Local Education Agency (LEA). Students continue to be enrolled in public schools, to be counted in average daily membership, and to

receive credit toward graduation. They also receive college credit for courses. Concurrent enrollment is distinct from early college admission. (2009, 1)

Utah State Office of Education Rule R277-713 mirrors the Regents definition. Both rules are updated annually after the legislative session ends. In both rules, the essential core elements of the definition have not changed significantly since 1988. They include:

• enrollment in college courses for credit by high school students who continue to be enrolled in high school and counted in Average Daily Membership;

• a contractual arrangement between a school district and a public institution of higher education in Utah to offer concurrent enrollment instruction; and

• an opportunity for prepared high school students to earn credits that count for completion of high school graduation requirements as well as college credits "corresponding to the first or second year of course-work at a USHE institution leading toward completion of a certificate or a degree." (Utah System of Higher Education Policy R165-713)

Adjunct high school instructors carry out over 80% of the concurrent enrollment instruction in Utah. The remaining concurrent enrollment is offered primarily through technology delivered (live interactive, online) systems with a small number of students enrolling in campus classes (Utah State Office of Education 2016).

USHE-USOE Curriculum Alignment

One unique feature of the Utah concurrent enrollment program is that each course curriculum is vetted and aligned to both postsecondary and secondary curriculum standards before students are allowed to enroll for concurrent enrollment credit. This business practice is illustrative of the joint leadership role the two system offices play in nurturing the program. Staff members in these offices facilitate the process, communicating legislative rule changes to program administrators and gathering best practices and needed policy changes from the field to be presented to executive staff.

Curriculum alignment begins with discussion between LEA curriculum directors and campus academic departments. These parties must agree that (1) there is sufficient match to offer a course for concurrent credit, and (2) the credit earned will be meaningful both for high school graduation and as part of a postsecondary program of study. If the parties agree, then narrative on college and concurrent learning outcomes and assessments, and on course materials including textbooks are submitted through the USHE system office to USOE curriculum specialists for validation of the alignment and approval to offer the course for concurrent enrollment. The Concurrent Enrollment Curriculum Review Data Form functions as a routing device, documents the alignment, and records approvals (Grua and Kessig 2015). Approved courses are published annually in a Concurrent Enrollment Master List (Grua and Kessig 2010–16). Only courses included on this list are approved for state funding.

Data Recording

State concurrent enrollment funds are disbursed based on a data match system between USHE and USOE. Enrollment data are gathered by both USHE and USOE. Concurrent enrollment registrations are flagged with system identifiers. A State Student Identification Number (SSID), assigned to all public education students, is used as a key data point in conjunction with LEA, demographic, and course data elements. The data match allows the two system offices to verify enrollment activity where students earned both high school and college credit. The verification of the enrollment data requires significant coordination between institutions and LEAs. Once data is verified, appropriated funds are distributed and state annual reports are prepared and published.

Annual Agreements

To standardize administration of concurrent enrollment programs in the state, both USOE and USHE have worked to standardize the annual contracts (see Table 11.2) between colleges/universities and school districts.

The contract summarizes the minimum requirements stated in legislation, state board rule, and Regent policy. Subsequent pages cover best

TABLE 11.2

Standardized State Contract

Sponsoring Institution Name
2015–2016
Concurrent Enrollment Contract

This CONCURRENT ENROLLMENT CONTRACT (Contract), is entered into by and between _____ ("Institution"), a Utah System of Higher Education credit granting institution, and _____ ("LEA"), a Utah local education agency. The Contract sets forth all rights and duties of the parties with respect to the concurrent enrollment ("CE") program.

I. DEFINITION & PURPOSE

Concurrent enrollment refers to enrollment by public school students in one or more USHE institution course(s) under a contractual agreement between an Institution and a LEA. Students continue to be enrolled in public schools, to be counted in Average Daily Membership, and to receive credit toward graduation. They also receive college credit for courses.

The purpose of concurrent enrollment is to provide an option for prepared high school students to take courses necessary to graduate from high school and to become better prepared for the world of work or complete selected general education, career and technical education, and pre-major college-level courses. Courses must correspond to the first year of course work (1000 and 2000 level courses) at a USHE institution and lead toward a certificate or degree.

II. RELEVANT POLICY

Concurrent programs are governed by Utah Code 53A-15-101 and Utah Code 53A-17a-120.5, Regent Policy 165 (Concurrent Enrollment), and Utah State Board Rule 277-713 (Concurrent Enrollment of High School Students in College Courses), and related policies.

III. USHE PARTICIPATION

Utah System of Higher Education ("USHE") institutions that grant college credit may participate in the concurrent enrollment program.

A. LEAs shall contact the USHE institution in the corresponding geographic service area to provide a CE course; the USHE institution shall respond within 60 days. If that institution chooses not to offer the course(s), another state institution may choose to offer the requested course(s) following the Right of First Refusal process.

B. Courses delivered with technology are not subject to the geographic service area requirement. Institutions may offer IVC concurrent enrollment to LEAs outside their geographic service area for the following reasons:

1. The USHE institution in the geographic service area cannot provide CE services.
2. The LEA is located a significant distance from all other USHE institutions.
3. The LEA's student population is too small to schedule a CE class; and/or
4. The LEA does not have educators qualified for adjunct faculty status at a USHE institution.

C. The Utah College of Applied Technology (UCAT) may provide concurrent instruction for high school students when a concurrent enrollment contract exists between the LEA and Institution which

1. includes the instruction being given on a UCAT campus;
2. allows for instruction provided by a third party (UCAT); and
3. outlines the responsibilities of the credit- granting institution, the UCAT ATC, and the LEA.

IV. STUDENT ELIGIBILITY

Eligibility criteria listed below assure student success in a CE course. CE eligibility is restricted to students meeting the following criteria:

A. Junior and Senior class standing; sophomores by exception with LEA and Institution department approval;

B. A grade point average, ACT score, or a placement score (generally considered to be a B average or 3.0 GPA or ACT score of 22 or higher or a C or 2.0 GPA for non-General Education CTE courses) which predicts the students' likelihood of achieving a B or better in the concurrent course;

C. For courses such as math and English, earn an appropriate placement test score or pass prerequisite course(s);

D. Parent / Guardian approval to register for CE course(s);

E. Counselor/principal and college approval to register for college credit for CE courses. College approval is not required if students do not pay for college enrollment or college credit; and

F. Current SEOP/Plan for College and Career Readiness on file.

G. Home schooled students are eligible for CE courses with principal permission from the high school they would attend. They are subject to all rules and requirements that apply to student participation in the CE program. They must have a parent affidavit (Utah Code 53A-11.102(2)) on file to participate in concurrent enrollment.

V. STUDENT PARTICIPATION

The following conditions apply to student participation in the CE program:

A. Students shall complete the application process for each USHE institution from which they intend to take concurrent courses.

B. Students are assessed a one-time admissions application fee per credit-granting institution. Payment of the admissions fee to enroll in concurrent enrollment satisfies the general admissions application fee requirement for a full-time or part-time student at an institution so that no additional admissions application fee may be charged by the credit-granting institution for continuous enrollment at that institution during or following high school graduation.

C. Students must abide by the Student Code of Conduct for each institution from which they take CE courses.

D. Students will be assigned a permanent Student ID by each USHE institution from which they take CE courses.

E. Student enrollment in CE courses will create a permanent college transcript.

F. Students are responsible for miscellaneous fees and textbooks subject to fee waiver under R277-407.

G. Students must complete all CE courses before they receive a diploma, or before their class graduates.

I. Students may attempt up to 30 concurrent semester credit hours in one academic year.

VI. COURSE DELIVERY & ELIGIBILITY

The delivery system and curriculum program shall be designed and implemented to take full advantage of the most current available educational technology. CE course offerings must meet the following criteria:

A. Course is typically taught in 11th or 12th grade.

B. Curriculum matches or exceeds the curriculum taught in the introductory level college course.

C. Curriculum taught in a core credit course must align to the public education standards and objectives at 90%.

D. Institution, the academic department, and LEA agree to offer the course.

E. The CE course utilizes the same expected student outcomes as the college course.

F. Appropriate textbooks and instructional materials are used.

G. Students have appropriate access to faculty and to equipment needed to complete the course.

H. The course is listed on the CE Master List for this academic year. Proposed new CE courses, existing course realignments, hiatus and retired status changes must be submitted to the system offices annually on or before November 30.

VII. FACULTY ELIGIBILITY & PROFESSIONAL DEVELOPMENT

Identification of qualified adjunct faculty is the joint responsibility of the LEA and the Institution. Final approval of the adjunct faculty will be determined by the appropriate department at the Institution. Public school educators who instruct CE courses as adjunct faculty must possess a current Utah teaching license and appropriate endorsements.

A. Selection criteria for CE adjunct faculty should be the same as those criteria applied to other adjunct faculty appointments in specific departments.

B. Institutions must supervise CE adjunct faculty and provide for professional development, including review of FERPA and human sexuality guidelines for secondary students.

C. Educators approved for TICE courses must participate in TICE professional development workshops, use TICE curriculum materials, and administer the TICE common assessment to all enrolled students.

D. Institution faculty shall meet the following criteria prior to teaching CE courses:

  1. Complete CE faculty training, including FERPA and human sexuality guidelines for secondary students, either by reviewing the USHE Concurrent Training document or receiving live instruction; and

  2. Pass a BCI criminal background check.

VIII. FUNDING

This Contract is for concurrent enrollment activities supported by the State of Utah Concurrent Appropriation. Appropriation funds will be disbursed to LEAs and USHE institutions by the Utah State Office of Education and the Utah System of Higher Education.

IX. PARTIES OBLIGATIONS

A. Institution and LEA agree jointly to:

  1. Coordinate college admissions and concurrent registration. LEA and Institution registrars work together to ensure CE students are:

    a. officially registered or admitted as degree seeking, non-degree-seeking, or non-matriculated students of institution;

    b. registered within Institution deadlines;

    c. enrolled both in the college course and the high school course; and

      d. awarded the same final course grade and credit hour value on both high school and college transcripts.

2. Coordinate academic advising with high school counselors and/or concurrent administrators to ensure students register for appropriate CE courses.

      a. Provide information on general education requirements at higher education institutions. Advise students how to efficiently choose concurrent enrollment courses to avoid duplication or excess credit hours, on how course credit transfers among USHE institutions and to institutions outside the USHE.

      b. Provide math and English placement testing to CE students.

      c. Monitor student academic achievement for consideration when advising on future CE course taking.

3. Collaborate to ensure a 90% systems data match of student and course data.

4. Communicate, in a timely fashion, any staffing or administrative changes that could impact CE course offerings. When possible, note impending cancellations one year in advance on the CE Master List (November 30).

5. Publish a schedule of USHE faculty-led CE courses by March 30 for the following academic year.

6. Submit annual contracts to the USHE system offices no later than 5 p.m. May 30. USHE system office will retain copies for seven years and will update the State Office of Education on completed contracts by June 30.

B. LEA agrees to:

1. Screen students for success in a CE program:

      a. Verify students have met all course prerequisites before enrolling them in a CE course; arrange placement testing if needed;

      b. Gather and maintain parent/guardian consent forms and include language that states participation in the CE program generates a permanent college transcript; and

      c. Advise students who receive poor or failing grades to reconsider other course options for subsequent enrollment.

2. Manage CE adjunct faculty and facilitator issues:

      a. Present adjunct faculty credentials to the Institution in a reasonable timeframe. Notify all students and parents the first day of class, if the educator has not received adjunct faculty approval, and that there is a possibility the course will not carry CE course credit.

      b. For technology delivered CE courses, ensure facilitators are familiar with and adhere to facilitation standards of best practice.

      c. Provide information to district personnel, students, and parents about privacy protections in the Family Educational Rights and Privacy Act ("FERPA").

    3. Monitor class enrollments to:

      a. Ensure at least 50% of the students in academic courses are earning CE course credit. Career and Technical Education ("CTE") courses are exempt from this rule.

      b. Monitor CE course taking to ensure students do not exceed the 30 credit per year limit.

C. INSTITUTION agrees to:

    1. Collect all CE course fees and partial tuition.

    2. Provide LEA with all deadlines that pertain to admission and registration into CE courses and with program enrollment data two weeks prior to the drop date. Provide LEAs with the last day students may add and/or drop a course.

    3. Monitor Institution semester credit limits.

    4. Provide guidelines for the transfer of credit among USHE institutions.

    5. Conduct student end-of-course evaluations.

X. TERM

This contract shall be effective starting May 29, 2015 and shall remain in effect for the 2015–2016 academic year.

The parties hereby execute this Contract on the dates indicated below.

for Institution   *for LEA*

_____ _____   _____ _____

by _____ date   by _____ date
Title: _____   Title: _____
Institution: _____   LEA: _____

_____ _____   _____ _____

by _____ date   by _____ date
Title: _____   Title: _____
Institution: _____   LEA: _____

Source: Utah State Office of Education, Utah System of Higher Education 2015.

practices and joint and individual responsibilities of the USHE institutions and LEAs.

Both systems have collaborated in establishing the principles and quality guidelines for concurrent enrollment programs. Utah System of Higher Education Policy R165 and Utah State Office of Education R277-713 establish requirements and monitoring authority for programs.

Program Leadership: UACEP

State-level coordination is possible because of the high level of collaboration and communication that takes place among LEA and college program administrators. The Utah Alliance of Concurrent Enrollment Partnerships (UACEP) meets three times each year. In addition, focus groups are convened as needed to address more timely or persistent issues. UACEP members include the directors of concurrent enrollment programs at each USHE institution, state public school districts, and public charter schools, and representatives from both system offices.

Because UACEP members are "in the trenches" daily, running concurrent enrollment programs, this group is often the first contact to which system offices turn to identify issues of concern as well as concurrent enrollment trends. Common UACEP coordinating functions include curriculum needs assessment, data sharing and verification, and sharing of best practices.

UACEP provides a forum to evaluate course offerings, address advising needs, and provide tools for advising. One critical issue addressed by this group is identifying course needs to meet General Education and Career and Technical Education (CTE) pathway requirements. The Concurrent Enrollment General Education pathways document, found in the *Concurrent Enrollment Handbook* provided by the Utah State Office of Education (2015, 65), shows the general education courses available through concurrent enrollment from each postsecondary institution. A CTE pathways document was also developed along with the General Education Document to show how CTE pathways are linked to concurrent enrollment courses, career information, and which USHE institutions offer concurrent enrollment courses in each CTE area of study. This document however, did not prove useful and is no longer used.

UACEP meetings also provide a forum to discuss differences of culture in the two systems. For example, an instructor at a high school may be highly qualified under the secondary education system but may not have the academic credentials required by a higher education academic department to meet adjunct status. Another example is the difference in the amount of time available in a high school schedule, as there is normally more time available to cover objectives in depth at the secondary level.

UACEP meetings are also used to share best practices on procedures, policies, and other program information such as marketing pieces. A solid body of best practices has been developed out of the information shared.

Finally, UACEP members are responsible for verifying enrollment data in advance of the system office data match. Once the data has been gathered, the informal contacts made within UACEP help to facilitate the cleaning up of errors, clarifications, and finalization of the year-end data reports. The efforts of UACEP members resulted in a 99.9% data match for the 2014–15 year. A detailed discussion of this process can be found in the Utah State Office of Education *Concurrent Enrollment Handbook* (2015, 26).

Academic Year 2015–16 Concurrent Enrollment General Education Pathway: Recommended First-Year College Experience

Concurrent enrollment provides an opportunity for prepared high school students to take selected college courses while still in high school. Students earn both high school credit for graduation and college credit corresponding to the first year at a USHE institution.

General education courses are highly advisable for concurrent enrollment because they are required for college graduation and are transferable from one USHE institution to another. Table 11.3 shows the general education requirements for each institution and how and where a student can fulfill those requirements through concurrent enrollment. Individual institutions may have additional unique requirements.

Students are instructed to select one class from each general education category. Classes listed in Table 11.3 are offered by the institution indicated in partnership with LEAs and/or by distance delivery. Institutions include: Utah State University (USU), Weber State University (WSU), Southern Utah University (SUU), Snow College (Snow), Dixie State University (DSU),

TABLE 11.3

Academic Year 2015–16 Concurrent Enrollment General Education Pathway

General Education Core (12 credits)

Credits Required for USHE Graduation	*Recommended General Education Courses*				*Institution*			
		USU	WSU	SUU	Snow	DSC	UVU	SLCC
Composition (6 credits*)	ENGL 1010 (3 credits) Intro to Writing	USU	WSU	SUU	Snow	DSC	UVU	SLCC
Quantitative Literacy (3 credits)	MATH 1030 (3 credits) Quantitative Reasoning (non-science majors)	USU		SUU	Snow			SLCC
Select ONE of these courses	MATH 1040 (3 credits) Statistics			[1]	Snow	DSU		SLCC
	MATH 1050 (3–4 credits) College Algebra	USU		SUU	Snow	DSU	UVU	SLCC
American Institutions (3 credits)	HIST 1700 (3 credits) American Civilization	USU	WSU	SUU	Snow	DSU	UVU	SLCC
	ECON 1740 (3 credits) Economic History of the U.S.							SLCC
Select ONE of these courses	POLS 1100 (3 credits) American Government	USU	WSU	SUU	Snow	DSC	UVU	

General Education Breadth (18 – 27 credits)

		USU	WSU	SUU	Snow	DSC	UVU	SLCC
Fine Arts — Select ONE of these courses	ART 1010 (3 credits) Intro to Visual Arts	USU		SUU	Snow	DSC	UVU	SLCC
	MUSC 1010 (3 credits) Intro to Music	USU	WSU	SUU	Snow	DSC	UVU	SLCC
	THEA 1013 (3 credits) Intro to Theater/Exploring Theater	USU	WSU	SUU	Snow	DSC	UVU	
Humanities — Select ONE of these courses	HU/HUM 1010/1100 (3 credits) Intro to the Humanities	2		SUU		DSC	UVU	SLCC
	ENGL 2200 (3 credits) Intro to Literature	USU		SUU	3	DSC	UVU	
	COMM/CMST 2110 Interpersonal Communication	USU	WSU			4	UVU	
Social and Behavioral Science — Select ONE of these courses	PSY 1010 (3 credits) Intro to Psychology	USU	WSU	SUU	Snow	DSU	UVU	SLCC
	CHF/FAML/FCHD/FCS/FHS(T) 1500 or PSY 1100 (3 credits) Human Development	USU	WSU		Snow	DSU	UVU	5
Life Science — Select ONE of these courses	BIOL 1010 (3 credits) General Biology	USU		SUU	Snow	DSU	UVU	SLCC
	NUTR/NFS 1020 (3 credits) Intro to Nutrition		WSU	SUU		DSU	5	5

TABLE 11.3

Academic Year 2015–16 Concurrent Enrollment General Education Pathway (*Continued*)

Credits Required for USHE Graduation	*Recommended General Education Courses*	Institution						
		USU	WSU	SUU	Snow	DSU	UVU	SLCC
Physical Science Select ONE of these courses	CHEM 1010 (3 credits) (1015 Lab 1 credit) Intro to Chemistry	USU		SUU	Snow	DSU	UVU	SLCC
	PHYS 1010 (3 credits) (1015 Lab 1 credit) Elementary Physics	USU	WSU	SUU	Snow	DSU	UVU	SLCC
	Chem 1110 (3–5 credits) Elementary Chemistry		WSU	SUU	Snow	DSU	UVU	[5]

Source: Adapted from Utah State Office of Education 2015, 65.

1. Available upon request; student registration requests will be reviewed on an individual basis.

2. Students planning to attend USU may complete USU 1320 (Civilization: Humanities). This class transfers to other USHE institutions as Humanities general education.

3. Snow offers ENGL 2230, which transfers to most USHE institutions as ENGL 2200.

4. This class is a Social Science at DSU, a Humanities at other USHE institutions.

5. This class is not a general education course at this institution. Students planning to attend UVU or SLCC should take the other class in the category.

Utah Valley University (UVU), and Salt Lake Community College (SLCC). Core courses make up the general education foundation. Breadth courses give an opportunity to explore various subjects. Note that there are many classes in each breadth category that may be substituted for those listed in Table 11-3. Students are instructed to ask a campus advisor if the class will "transfer as equivalent" credit to the institution they wish to attend before registering. Each student is provided with a list of advisors, including their respective institutions and contact information. Students are also advised to speak with an expert about classes. Before registering, they are strongly encouraged to meet with an academic adviser, preferably from the campus at which they intend to enroll after high school. An advisor can help students select classes that fit their educational goals and ensure the classes they take are part of a pre-major pathway.

In addition to information mentioned above, the following checklist is also provided to students.

Checklist: Additional Questions to Ask an Advisor

When meeting with a campus academic advisor, remember to ask:

1. What are the residency requirements for earning a degree from this institution? (Residency is about credits, not the state you live in.)

2. How many credits may I transfer from other institutions?

3. What is the maximum number of credits I can complete in a semester? A year?

4. Will the credits earned at other USHE institutions transfer as equivalent credit?

5. Can current enrollment, AP, IB, and early college classes help me work toward a scholarship?

History of UACEP

UACEP never had an official beginning; it grew from a grassroots need to seek understanding out of uncertainty. What prompted the initial contact by three concurrent enrollment directors was an issue over the Right of First Refusal, a situation where a local USHE institution is given first opportunity to provide a concurrent enrollment course in a high school in their region. If the local USHE institution chooses not to offer the course, another USHE institution may be invited to do so. In this particular situation, the rules were not clear about instructor qualifications so the local USHE institution chose not to offer the course. Another institution stepped in, felt the instructor was qualified, and offered the course.

In 1996 the director from Salt Lake Community College contacted the directors from Weber State University and Utah Valley State College to talk about the issue. The initial meeting was tense; the directors were suspicious of each other's intent. However, they agreed to meet again later in the year. The second meeting was more productive, and the directors began to open up and share their frustrations, program characteristics, and desire to continue the dialogue. These irregular meetings continued throughout the next twelve months. One goal the group set was to invite directors from other USHE institutions to meet.

Early in 1998, all USHE institutions were invited to participate. Directors from two more institutions started attending regularly. Meetings became more focused and goal-directed. One important goal of the group was to gain a voice in state-level decision-making. A USHE representative was invited to participate.

A second goal was to begin gathering data about individual programs for comparison purposes. Information on registration, assessment, course requirements, practices, and enrollment data allowed the group to begin standardizing programs and move toward consistency throughout the state.

In 1999, the directors from the five regularly attending postsecondary institutions invited the concurrent enrollment representatives from other institutions around the United States, who had been meeting informally, to Utah for their semiannual meeting. It was during this meeting of the national group that NACEP decided to become an official national organization representing institutions with concurrent enrollment programs across the nation. The five Utah institutions also adopted the name Utah Alliance of Concurrent Enrollment Partnerships to reflect a close alliance with the national organization.

Further efforts were put into recruiting higher education practitioners. In 2000, regular quarterly meetings became standard and two more postsecondary institutions became regular attendees. Representatives from both system offices also started attending. The focus continued to be on best practices and how to exert more influence at the state level.

Early in 2001, UACEP began recruiting secondary school participation: select secondary representatives were asked to attend, and the results were exhilarating. The sharing of new perspectives, ideas, and approaches began a new phase of collaboration between concurrent enrollment partners. Discussions shifted to topics such as relationships between secondary and postsecondary partners, improving program management, setting future goals, and exploring ways to include more low-income and under-represented students. As UACEP expanded, a more formal organization developed. Two members—one secondary, one postsecondary—are selected to lead the organization every two years. The combined group meets in the morning, and the public and higher education members split off in the afternoon to discuss issues specific to their systems. This quasiformal organization is the force behind the effectiveness of UACEP: partners feel free to discuss issues, dispense information, and conduct routine business either with the combined group or their particular subgroup.

UACEP has survived difficult times, including tough fiscal climates, because of the commitment of its members to the state concurrent program. Implementation of course review for the master list, stricter rules for funding distribution, funding shortfalls, and data collection protocols each put a strain on the relationships between secondary and postsecondary institutions. UACEP provides a venue for partners to vent and to work toward implementation of large, significant, system-wide changes.

UACEP Annual Conference

UACEP's efforts to gain state-level influence for concurrent enrollment programs came to the forefront in 2002, when it decided to sponsor an annual statewide conference, a seminal event in pulling members from both systems together as a cohesive and proactive group. The conference has been held each year since 2003.

Two statewide conferences were held in 2003. The first event focused on best practices in instruction and classroom management, administrative and partnership practice, and counseling and advisement. Other elements of the conference included a past, present, and future overview of concurrent enrollment in the state. An out-of-state keynote speaker presented a national perspective of concurrent enrollment. A panel of current and graduated concurrent enrollment students shared the benefits and challenges they experienced. The theme of best practices established in 2003 continues to be the theme of UACEP events. Another successful feature of the state conferences is discussion about current issues facing the state's concurrent enrollment program.

One of the original goals of having a statewide conference was to show state legislators the benefits of concurrent enrollment. Legislators were invited to speak, participate in panel discussions, and make presentations. This goal has had limited success.

One of the early realities learned from the UACEP conference was that few educators in the state had resources to attend longer than one day. Another lesson learned was that classroom concurrent enrollment instructors were not likely to attend because districts frequently will not approve time off and pay for a substitute to allow teachers to attend. Thus UACEP conference material has become focused on administrators and counselors.

Current Issues

Utah continues to deal with perennial critical issues such as funding, state data reporting, and service area commitments. A myriad of other issues—from providing proper advising to high school students to addressing the needs of lower income students and under-represented populations—ensure a future of lively meetings for the state.

Advising of high school concurrent enrollment students is essential to providing a successful transition from high school to college. From the day a high school student shows interest in participating in concurrent enrollment, proper advising should be in place to aid the student in his or her decision. The initial choice to participate should be based on whether the student is intellectually, academically, and emotionally ready to undertake postsecondary work. In Utah, the high school counselor is in the best position to determine the readiness of a student for postsecondary work. A high school counselor also helps each student develop an education and occupational plan. High schools generally have staff assigned to work as a liaison between the high school and the college. They usually update and distribute information to students concerning college admissions, registration, and prerequisites. Students are informed by the liaison about the importance of their performance in concurrent enrollment courses, including grades earned, impact their permanent college transcript. Liaisons also give out information about courses, such as mathematics and English, that have prerequisite scores on a national test such as the ACT, SAT, or Accuplacer.

Once the student decides to take a concurrent enrollment course, then the college/university and LEA work together to

• advise students on all concurrent enrollment classes and how they fulfill college credit,

• track students' progress in specific graduation requirements,

• aid in scholarship and graduation application,

• explain Advanced Placement and College Level Examination Program, challenge credit, as well as transfer credit to or from other colleges and universities, and

• assist with transitioning to college upon high school graduation.

Working with the system offices, UACEP has developed a number of resources to assist in advising students. UACEP discussions led to the widely accepted best practice for the colleges and universities to include advising as part of the services provided to high school concurrent enrollment students.

Participation rate for low-income students is another issue that has been brought forward by members of UACEP. This led to the Utah System of Higher Education publishing an annual report that found the following regarding low-income student participation:

> Concurrent enrollment (CE) provides students in 145 Utah public high school access to rigorous higher education course opportunities. Generally, students self-select to take a CE course. However, there is compelling evidence to suggest low-income students, students participating in the free or reduced lunch program, would benefit more greatly by participation:

Students taking a CE class are more likely to go to college than similar students who do not participate. Even when taking into consideration ACT score, gender, and income status, students participating in concurrent enrollment are nearly three times more likely to attend college within four years than students who don't participate.

Low-income students participating in concurrent enrollment increase their likelihood of college attendance by an additional 30% when compared to non-low-income students.

Low-income students may need to be recruited to participate in concurrent enrollment. While over half of non-low income students participate in concurrent enrollment, only 36% of low-income students participate. (Utah System of Higher Education 2015, 1)

These findings have led to some institutions initiating new initiatives and marketing strategies to increase low-income student participation.

The partnership that has developed between the Utah System of Higher Education and the Utah State Office of Education over twenty-three years provides a unique opportunity to the high school students of Utah to transition from secondary to postsecondary education. The Utah Alliance of Concurrent Enrollment Partnerships plays a critical role in fostering cooperation between two very different statewide systems. UACEP is looking to the future by developing by-laws in order to become a state chapter of the National Alliance of Concurrent Enrollment Partnerships.

References

Foxley, C. H. 1995 (Apr. 11). Memorandum: Recording of Concurrent Enrollment Courses.

Grua, Cynthia and Moya Kessig, M. 2010–16. Utah State Office of Education Concurrent Enrollment—Master Lists. http://www.schools.utah.gov/CURR/early college/Concurrent-Enrollment/Master-Lists.aspx.

———. 2014 (Oct.). FY-15–16 Concurrent Enrollment General Educ. E-mail communication.

———. 2015. 2015–16 Concurrent Enrollment Course Submission Proposal. E-mail communication.

Harden, E. R. 1994 (Aug. 23). Memorandum: Centennial Scholarships and Funding Concurrent Enrollment in Light of H.B. 190, Expanded Centennial Scholarships.

Utah Code, Title 53A, Chapter 15, Section 101. 2016 (Feb). Higher Education Courses in the Public Schools—Cooperation between Public and Higher Education—Partial Tuition—Reporting. http://le.utah.gov/xcode/Title53A /Chapter15/53A-15-S101.html?v=C53A-15-S101_1800010118000101.

Utah House Bill 151. 2006. Adjustments in Funding for Concurrent Enrollment. 2006 General Session of the Sixty-Sixth Legislature. http://www.le.utah.gov /session/2006/pdfdoc/digest2006.pdf.

Utah House Bill 190. 1994. Expanded Centennial Scholarships, 1994 General Session of the Fifty-Fourth Legislature. http://www.image.le.state.ut.us/imag ing/Viewer.asp?Image=1.

Utah House Bill 296. 1987 (Feb.). School Finance Modifications. Laws of the State of Utah Passed at the 1987 General Session of the Forty-Seventh Legislature.

Utah Senate Bill 0001. 2015. Public Education Base Budget Amendments. Laws of the State of Utah Passed at the 2015 General Session of the Seventy-Fifth Legislature.

Utah Senate Bill 196. 1991. Minimum School Program Act Amendments. Laws of the State of Utah passed at the 1991 General Session and 1991 First Special Session.

Utah State Legislature. 2016. Search Option for Bills. http://le.utah.gov/Docu ments/bills.htm.

Utah State Office of Education Rule R277-713. 2009 (June 1). Concurrent Enrollment of High School Students in College Courses. Accessed Oct. 15. http:// www.rules.utah.gov/publicat/code/r277/r277-713.htm.

Utah State Office of Education. 2015. *Concurrent Enrollment Handbook.* http://www .schools.utah.gov/CURR/earlycollege/Concurrent-Enrollment/CEHand book.aspx.

———. 2016. Annual Reports. http://www.schools.utah.gov/CURR/earlycollege /Concurrent-Enrollment.aspx.

Utah System of Higher Education Policy R165. 2009 (June 1). Concurrent Enrollment. Accessed Oct. 15. http://www.utahsbr.edu/policy/R165.pdf.

Utah System of Higher Education. 2015 (Jan.). *Concurrent Enrollment Annual Report/ Academic Year 2013–14.*

12

Dual Enrollment a Viable Credit-Based Transition Program

Partnerships in Central Ohio

GEORGE TOMBAUGH AND RICHARD SEILS

Background

This chapter presents the findings of a three-year pilot project to establish dual enrollment partnerships in Central Ohio, funded through a state grant and administered by the Educational Service Center of Central Ohio. Sixteen awards, one award to each of Ohio's regions, were made for $225,000 per region. The grant was issued for one year in fall 2006 and extended for two additional years in 2007. The total grant for each region was $225,000 per year.

Definition of Dual Enrollment

The term *dual enrollment* has a number of different definitions. As the Educational Service Center of Central Ohio implemented dual enrollment partnerships in Central Ohio, *dual enrollment* was defined as follows:
   • High schools partner with a college/university.
   • High school teachers apply for appointment as adjunct faculty on the staff of the partner college/university.
   • High school students apply for admission to the college/university.
   • Curriculum, syllabus, and assessment of the high school course reflect those of the collegiate course.

• The high school teacher receives in-service assistance from the partner college/university faculty to align course syllabi, assessments, and activities with those of the collegiate-level course.

• The course is taught by the high school teacher during the school day in the high school.

• Upon successful completion of the course, students receive transcripted college and high school graduation credit.

The History of Dual Enrollment Partnerships in Central Ohio

Dual enrollment was first introduced into Ohio in 1979 by Kenyon College. Initial partnerships were created in Northern Ohio with subsequent expansion to Central Ohio. The Kenyon program has become known as the Kenyon Academic Partnership (KAP) and has grown significantly over its first three decades. Initially in Central Ohio, Kenyon College had partnerships with several high schools in the Columbus Public School District, a large urban district; with Granville High School, a smaller school district located in Licking County; and with Mt. Vernon High School, a moderately sized district in Knox County.

More recently, Kenyon College created partnerships with two suburban Columbus districts, New Albany and Hilliard. Ohio Dominican University created a dual enrollment partnership with the schools of the Columbus Diocese in 1992. These high schools were located in the City of Columbus, as well as several smaller cities and towns in Central and Southeastern Ohio.

Implementation of the Grant by the
Educational Service Center of Central Ohio

In fall 2006, the Educational Service Center of Central Ohio (ESCCO) was awarded one of the sixteen regional grants to support the expansion of the dual enrollment model in Ohio. These grants were applicable to high schools in Region 11, which includes Franklin County and the six contiguous counties (Delaware, Licking, Fairfield, Pickaway, Madison, and Union) in Central Ohio.

The ESCCO approached the administration of the grant with the goal of utilizing the funding to promote the dual enrollment model in institutions of higher education (IHEs) and high schools in Central Ohio as a viable credit-based transition program that would:

- promote the transition from high school to college;
- help eliminate the need for remediation once a student enrolls in college;
- provide marginal students the opportunity to attempt college-level work to see if college is for them;
- reduce the student's college tuition costs;
- provide transferability and portability of college level credit;
- limit course duplication between upper-level high school courses and entry-level college courses;
- afford high schools the opportunity to provide additional high school course offerings not available in all high schools;
- increase the academic challenge of the high school experience;
- lend additional academic significance to the student's senior year;
- increase the rigor across the curriculum;
- provide professional growth opportunities for teachers.

With these goals in mind, the initial focus was to secure IHE partners. Initially, discussions were held with almost every college and university in the higher education-rich Central Ohio area. Kenyon College, Ohio Dominican University, and Hocking College, having had programs already established, became willing partners. These three institutions were followed by commitments from Ohio University–Lancaster Campus, Clark State Community College, Shawnee State University, Columbus State Community College, Central Ohio Technical College, and the Ohio State University Main Campus. During the second year of the grant, nine IHE partners had committed to be involved in partnerships.

Participation among the IHEs initially ranged from several that eagerly engaged in multiple partnerships to the Ohio State Main Campus, which engaged in one very exploratory partnership. Of the nine willing college and university partners, eight participated in grant-funded partnerships; the ninth institution participated in several partnerships that were funded outside of the grant.

The second, concurrent focus was to build an understanding of the dual enrollment model among the school districts in Region 16, and to build the awareness of the opportunity to fund dual enrollment through the Core Grant. The ESCCO conducted several meetings involving superintendents, curriculum administrators, and principals. Initially, there were a few early adopters. Many school districts approached the notion of dual enrollment with a great deal of caution. However, as school administrators began to understand the opportunities provided for students through dual enrollment partnerships, interest grew rapidly.

Participation data from the ESCCO's grant-funded dual enrollment program from 2006 to 2008 are presented in Table 12.1. Between 2006 and 2008, a total of fourteen school districts and twenty high schools participated in dual enrollment funded by the Ohio Core Support Grant.

The early adopters initially looked at the dual enrollment model as an alternative to credit-based transition programs geared to the very top tier of high school students. Partnerships were created involving a number of very high-level science, mathematics, and foreign language courses. At first, the students who enrolled in dual enrollment courses were the top scholars within the high school (i.e., the student population that had already made the decision that higher education at a four-year college or university was in their plans upon graduation).

However, during the second year of the grant, many school districts began to look at dual enrollment not just as a strategy to give the best and the brightest students a "jump start" on higher education, but also as a strategy to assist several other segments of the student population in attaining additional education beyond the high school experience. Accordingly, high school administrators started to look at dual enrollment as a strategy to:

TABLE 12.1

Growth in Dual Enrollment Classes in Ohio's Region 11

Year	Districts	High Schools	IHEs	Classes	Students	Hours Awarded
2006	8	13	4	28	418	3277
2008	13	17	8	44	924	6018

• assist those students who were bound for college but would probably need remediation once enrolled (the segment of the student population just behind the top tier of scholars);

• interest those students (first generation of their family to consider college) who had the intellectual ability to do college-level work but had neither the social support nor the parental support to continue their education beyond high school; and

• provide students a link to higher education in order to move them toward an associate's degree or a certificate in a career or technical field.

School districts began to target the "middle third" of the student body; that is, the "theoretical" middle 33% of high school students who will graduate from high school but not continue with any type of postsecondary education. Many of these students are first-generation college attendees with little or no support to enter postsecondary education. Accordingly, high schools in Central Ohio have employed a variety of strategies:

• Offer college courses that provide dual credit for required entry level general education courses.

• Offer college courses that provide dual credit leading to an associate's degree, a certificate, or an apprenticeship in a specific discipline at a two-year college (i.e., pathways).

• Convene high school and college faculties to collaborate on the alignment of high school courses to entry level college courses.

• Create counseling and advising protocols for students and parents relating to dual enrollment and college admissions and financial aid procedures.

• Inform parents and students of the cost and time saving advantages of successfully completing dual enrollment courses.

• Inform parents of Ohio's Transfer Assurance Guide that assures approved college and university level courses will be recognized at any University System of Ohio institution.

Evaluation of Dual Enrollment, 2009

In 2009, at the conclusion of the third year of the grant, the ESCCO contracted with the School Study Council of Ohio to do an independent evaluation of the dual enrollment model in Central Ohio. The remainder of this chapter will discuss the unpublished findings of the evaluation of dual enrollment in Central Ohio between 2006 and 2009.

Representatives of the School Study Council of Central Ohio (SSCO) and the ESCCO compiled a list of items to explore in surveys to be administered to the four significant populations that participated in dual enrollment classes:

- High school students
- High school dual enrollment instructors
- High school administrators
- College and university mentoring faculty

Instruments were created for each group. The target populations were those groups who participated in the forty-four grant-sponsored classes plus a small number other dual enrollment courses funded by school districts, parents, or a combination of the two. The instruments were administered via the Internet. Students were asked to complete the online questionnaires as a group in a computer lab during a regularly scheduled meeting of the class within the high school. High school teachers, high school administrators, and college/university mentors were asked to complete the surveys online at their convenience. The findings of the survey are reflective of the following respondents:

- Students: 519
- High school teachers: 28
- High school administrators: 6
- College/university teacher mentors: 13

Student Responses (n = 519)

Significant demographic data of the student respondents was as follows:

Sex
- Female: 57%
- Male: 43%

Grade in school
- Seniors: 69%
- Juniors: 22%
- Sophomores and Freshmen: 9%

Grade point average (GPA)

- >3.5: 72%
- 3.0-3.49: 21%
- 3.0: 7%

Highest level of education attained by parents

- One parent with a bachelor's degree: 36%
- One parent with a master's degree: 21%
- One parent with a doctorate degree: 8%
- One parent with some college experience: 17%
- High school degree by either of the parents: 15%
- Some high school experience by either of the parents: 5%

Final grade that students anticipated receiving in the dual enrollment course, based on their opinion of their own performance

- A: 55%
- B: 35%
- C or less: 10%

As reflected by these demographic data, the student respondents were generally high performing students in high school and tended to come from homes with highly educated parents.

Students' plans after graduation

- Attend a four-year college or university: >90%
- Attend a two-year college/technical school: 4%
- Indicated their post-high school plans had not changed: 90%

Follow-up comments from students affirmed that students' dual enrollment experiences reinforced their future plans to enroll in a four-year college/university after graduation. Students also indicated:

- They were prepared to meet the requirements of the course: 96%
- The teacher was well-prepared to teach the course: 93%
- They were satisfied with their dual enrollment class experience and would pursue additional dual enrollment courses: 90%
- The course experience was moderately more rigorous than the coursework for regular high school classes: 64%
- They would enroll in additional dual enrollment courses: 90%
- They would recommend dual enrollment courses to future students: 94%

High School Teacher Responses (n = 28)

Significant demographic data of the dual enrollment high school teacher respondents was as follows:
- Level of education, master's degree: 82%
- Teaching experience, >10 years: 82%
- Prior experience teaching dual enrollment classes: 32%

Other findings from dual enrollment high school teachers indicated:
- They felt their students were prepared to meet the college-level requirements for the class: 97%
- The structure/format was appropriate for the enrolled students: 100%
- The content was appropriate for the enrolled students: 96%
- They were satisfied with the experience of teaching a dual enrollment course: 96%
- Their abilities as a teacher improved as a result of the mentoring/professional development provided by the college/university: 67%
- Dual enrollment classes were more rigorous than other high school classes: 89%
- They would be willing to teach another dual enrollment class: 86%
- They would recommend the dual enrollment teaching experience to their colleagues: 86%

High School Administrators (n = 6)

High school administrators indicated:
- Students were well prepared to meet the college-level requirements of dual enrollment classes: 100%
- The structure/format was appropriate and the content was appropriate: 100%
- The teaching ability of the high school teacher improved from the dual enrollment experience: 86%
- The communication with the college/university was good to excellent: 100%
- The mentoring/professional development was good to excellent: 67%

• The assistance with the alignment of the college/university syllabus and methods of assessment was good to excellent: 83%

• Dual enrollment courses were more rigorous than other high school courses: 100%

College/University Mentoring Faculty (n = 13)

College/university mentoring faculty indicated:

• Satisfaction that the structure/format of the dual enrollment classes was appropriate for the enrolled high school students: 85%

• Satisfaction with the experience in the dual enrollment program: 86%

• Satisfaction with the communication with the dual enrollment teacher: 54%

• Satisfaction with the quality of mentoring/professional development provided to the dual enrollment teacher: 54%

• Satisfaction with the alignment of the syllabus and assessments of the course: 46%

• Satisfaction with the high school teacher's implementation of the college-level coursework at the high school level: 54%

• Dual enrollment courses were more rigorous than other high school courses: 77%

• Their college/university should continue to participate in dual enrollment courses: 100%

School Study Council of Ohio's Evaluation:
Conclusions and Recommendations

SSCO Conclusion: Students were very satisfied with their dual enrollment experience.

SSCO Recommendation: Consider expanding options to students who might not be aware of the Dual Enrollment Program and to students who might have GPAs in the 2.5-3.0 range.

SSCO Conclusion: There was a belief among students that dual enrollment courses were only slightly more rigorous than other high school courses.

SSCO Recommendation: Initiate dialogue between high school and college/university faculty as to whether these courses need to be more challenging to students.

SSCO Conclusion: Responses from students indicated a strong satisfaction with their dual credit experience.
SSCO Recommendation: Consider using these students to promote the dual enrollment program.

SSCO Conclusion: High school administrators were very supportive of dual enrollment and the outcomes for both students and teachers.
SSCO Recommendation: None.

SSCO Conclusion: Although high school administrators were very positive regarding the quality of professional development and the process of aligning the course syllabus and assessment, they were not as supportive of the overall communication with the college/university mentor.
SSCO Recommendation: Provide vehicles for administrators to dialogue with college/university mentors.

SSCO Conclusion: Although the college/university mentors were very satisfied with the preparedness of the students and the appropriateness of the structure and content of the courses, they were significantly less positive in regard to the communication with the dual enrollment teacher, the quality of the mentoring/professional development, and the process of aligning the syllabus and assessments.
SSCO Recommendation: Provide a forum whereby the high school faculty, administration, and the college/university faculty could discuss changes/revisions for the future of the dual enrollment program.

SSCO Conclusion: The dual enrollment program has encountered significant success in providing students with enriched academic experiences.
SSCO Recommendation: Dual enrollment opportunities should be expanded to more students in more schools throughout Ohio. Additionally, closer monitoring of the instruction and expanded dialogue

should occur among all of the stakeholders of the dual enrollment program.

Conclusion

Educational Service Center of Central Ohio: The Future of Dual Enrollment in Ohio as a Viable Credit-Based Transition Program

The findings of the SSCO's study of dual enrollment in Ohio Region 11 suggest there is a high level of satisfaction with the dual enrollment experience among students, teachers, high school administrators, and college/university mentors. The findings also suggest there is a concern for the quality of the course delivery on the part of high school teachers and administrators as well as college/university faculty. In order for the dual enrollment model to be successful, it is imperative that all stakeholders are satisfied the level of instruction reflects that of the course as it is delivered in the college/university setting.

The vast majority of the student population participating in dual enrollment courses in 2008–9 came from highly educated households, were predominantly the top students from their respective high schools, and were bound for four-year colleges and universities. The dual enrollment model can certainly have a benefit for this segment of the student population; however, the data do not reflect that the dual enrollment experience had a significant impact on the future plans of the population studied. In order to determine whether the dual enrollment experience has a positive effect on increasing the number of students pursuing higher education beyond high school, dual enrollment experiences should be made available to those populations of students other than those who are at the very top of their class and who are definitely college-bound.

Although students who are undecided about entering higher education can come from school districts with diverse demographics, many more students who are unsure about their postsecondary educational plans may come from areas that are economically disadvantaged. Additional evaluation of the impact of dual enrollment on this segment of the student population should be conducted. Unfortunately, these are students whose families cannot afford dual enrollment tuition and fees; and, in many cases their school districts cannot afford to take the additional costs from their operating budget. Accordingly, if the dual enrollment model in Ohio is to be evaluated as a method to promote the transition from high school to college among underserved students, a funding plan must be created to help this segment of the student population with tuition, fees, and other costs associated with dual enrollment.

PART FOUR | **Research and Evaluation Studies**

13

Retaining Students through Concurrent Enrollment

A Study Using Standardized Survey Instruments

DANIEL R. JUDD

Introduction and Purpose

States that have early college programs are seeing annual increases in the number of students from those programs entering institutions of higher education (Karp, Calcagno, Hughes, Jeong, and Bailey 2007; Leonard 2008; O'Hara 2008). Early college programs offer college credit to participating students to encourage them to advance to a postsecondary education. Concurrent enrollment, also called dual enrollment, is a credit-based transition program growing in popularity (Karp et al. 2007). The words *concurrent* and *dual* refer to the practice of awarding credit to fulfill both high school degree requirements and postsecondary degree requirements. Concurrent enrollment as a program most often operates within a formalized partnership between a school district and a sponsoring postsecondary institution.

Concurrent enrollment programs benefit both the students and the institutions involved (Hoffman, Vargas, and Santos 2008). Students are provided with a low-cost opportunity to "jump start" their college education while still in high school, and the sponsoring institution is given an opportunity to retain quality students.

Background

Student access to and enrollment in postsecondary education are widely accepted primary objectives for secondary education (Bailey and Karp

2003). In most states, concurrent enrollment partnerships advance these goals with contractual agreements between sponsoring institutions and school districts. In these contracts, the sponsoring institution usually agrees to support the college-level courses offered in high schools with curriculum, assessments, and supervision. Teachers of concurrent enrollment classes are high school teachers who have been approved by the sponsoring institution's academic departments to teach these courses to high school students under departmental supervision. Modality may be face-to-face, via the Internet, or as televised broadcasts (Woolstenhulme 2008). Concurrent enrollment classes may be held either at a university facility or at a high school; however, approximately 90% of the college credits earned through transition programs in the United States during the 2003–4 school year were earned on high school campuses (Waits, Setzer, and Lewis 2005).

Nationally, about 57% of postsecondary institutions in thirty-eight states have concurrent enrollment programs (Hoffman 2005; Kleiner and Lewis 2005). The number of partnerships between institutions of higher education and high schools is growing. As of August 2006, forty-seven states had approved polices related to concurrent enrollment programs (Blanco, Prescott, and Taylor 2007; Walthers and Robinson 2006). Funding mechanisms vary greatly by state. In Utah, students were initially required to pay partial tuition; however, in 1991, the Utah legislature instituted state funding for concurrent enrollment programs (Utah State Legislature 1991). Current legislation asks concurrent enrollment programs to set eligibility requirements, but most stipulate that a high school student must have a cumulative grade point average (GPA) of 3.0 or higher to register for concurrent enrollment courses (Utah State University 2008a).

Retention of undergraduate students entering college after having participated in concurrent enrollment programs is beneficial to the sponsoring institution for several reasons: (a) these students are usually qualified academically by maintaining a 3.0 GPA, (b) these are students in whom the university and its departments have invested credits, and (c) in some cases, these are students from low-income, minority, or disadvantaged communities who may otherwise not be able to afford a postsecondary education. Attracting greater diversity for the college or university adds to the institution's credibility for providing a broad, inclusive learning experience (Gurin 1999). Quantifying the contribution that concurrent enrollment programs make to the sponsoring institution's ability to attract and keep these students is, then, of utmost importance.

Tinto's Model of Integration (1993, 2002) asserts that greater student satisfaction leads to a greater likelihood of student retention (Pascarella and Terenzini 1991). The study discussed within this chapter tested the applicability of Tinto's model on a concurrent enrollment program in a third tier university as a means for quantifying programs' contributions.

Literature Review

State Concurrent Enrollment Program Policy

Jobs for the Future (Hoffman 2003, 2005; Hoffman, Vargas and Santos 2008) prepared a policy primer for those states "wishing to implement dual enrollment as a strategy for increasing college credentialing of underrepresented students" (Hoffman 2005, 5). Case studies compared concurrent enrollment programs in three states: Florida, Utah, and New York. Hoffman, Vargas, and Santos (2008) pointed out that Utah was ranked fourth in the nation in high school graduation, however Utah was ranked thirty-first in college completion rates; while this rate is affected by the fact that about 15% of the students enter two years of voluntary religious service immediately after high school, it also points to a need for policies that encourage undergraduate retention.

Karp, Calcagno, Hughes, Jeong, and Bailey (2007) researched the outcomes of concurrent enrollment in two states with long-standing programs. In Florida, they found that participation in concurrent enrollment programs increased the likelihood of initially enrolling in a four-year institution by 8%. For those students who enrolled in postsecondary education, participation in concurrent enrollment was positively related to their likelihood of enrolling in college full-time. In New York, they found that students who took two or more concurrent enrollment courses were 4% more likely to enroll full-time. Though these increased likelihoods are small, any increase supports the states' concurrent enrollment policies and establishes benchmarks for future measurement. Establishing benchmarks is necessary for measuring improvements in retention. Adoption of the methodologies from the current study could provide additional measures, which could be compared using a national database.

Retention of College Students

Tinto (1993) observed that "generally, the more satisfying those experiences (at the college/university) are felt to be, the more likely are individuals to persist until degree completion" (50). Tinto's Model of Integration suggests that a student's satisfying encounters with the tangible and intangible systems of an institution will lead to greater integration into those systems; then, as a student becomes increasingly integrated into the institutional systems, their likelihood of continuing to completion increases and the possibility of attrition decreases (Pascarella and Terenzini 1991).

Tinto (2002) observed five conditions supportive of retention: expectation, advice, support, involvement, and learning. He explained each one of these conditions: High expectations are necessary for students' success, and students, "especially those who have been historically excluded from higher education, are affected by the campus expectational climate." Students, most of whom are undecided at entry, need advising to know how to use college to achieve personal goals. The third condition is support; students "are more likely to persist and graduate in settings that provide academic, social, and personal support." Involvement, as seen by Tinto, is defined by the "frequency and quality of contact with faculty, staff, and other students" and is an important predictor of student persistence. "Fifth, and most importantly, students are more likely to persist and graduate in settings that foster learning. Learning has always been the key to student retention" (2–3).

Student Satisfaction

Informed by Tinto's Model of Integration, the literature review includes current and established research on student satisfaction. A broadly accepted definition of satisfaction is given as the difference between what a customer expected and what s/he experienced (Vavra 1997; Zeithaml, Parasuraman, and Berry 1990). This aligns with student satisfaction as conceived by Tinto (1993), which implies that satisfaction is a student's perception of the degree of goal achievement realized in the process of obtaining an education.

Astin (1993) made the following observation about student satisfaction: "Of all the types of student outcomes (e.g., G.P.A. and test scores) that have been studied so far in college impact studies, student satisfaction shows the weakest relation to student input characteristics (those that students bring with them) . . . Virtually every other type of outcome measure is more strongly correlated with student input characteristics than with environmental characteristics" (116–17). From Astin's statement, we understand that student satisfaction is an important measure of the relationship between the environment of a particular university and a student's experience of that environment. This can be interpreted to mean that the programmatic decisions that institutions make affect students' satisfaction and hence their retention.

Mavando, Tsarenko, and Gabbot (2004) developed a conceptual model for relating student satisfaction to the likelihood of students recommending an institution to prospective students. Their model included as independent variables tangible resources, such as library facilities, and intangible resources, such as student orientation and quality of teaching. The dependent variable was student satisfaction operationalized as recommendation of the institution to prospective students. Findings demonstrated that not all resources (tangible and intangible) are important in influencing student satisfaction that leads to recommendation.

Yatrakis and Simon (2002) observed, however, that the more time students spend interacting with classmates, the higher the satisfaction level as well as the retention level of information (Carmel and Gold 2007). Further supporting this, Peterson (2006) performed structural equation modeling (SEM) and found that, "in terms of student satisfaction, the factor 'Social' was the strongest (SEM score of .46) . . . to be satisfied with their educational experience students need and want a balance between social and academic opportunities" (86).

Methodology

The purpose of this study is to examine the contribution that concurrent enrollment makes to the sponsoring institution's ability to retain quality students. Based on Tinto's (1993, 2002) observations, it was hypothesized that high school students who are satisfied with their participation in a concurrent enrollment program will become integrated in the systems of the sponsoring postsecondary institution, and a large percentage will eventually enroll in that institution. Systems as understood herein include teaching systems, but extend beyond to include learning systems (e.g., libraries) and support systems (e.g., advisors). Most importantly, inclusion in the financial system of the sponsoring institution—that is, the process of exchanging a fee for services—is predicted as leading to integration.

The question of institutional satisfaction is also addressed. This variable is easily quantified because institutional satisfaction, to a large extent, can be measured in dollar amounts. Therefore, this research will seek to answer whether the investment made in providing reduced tuition to students, registered for concurrent enrollment courses, pays off in the long run for the sponsoring institution. Results are reported in terms of student satisfaction, total credits earned, and projected tuition dollars.

Study Background

This research is based on a series of studies examining the contributions that the concurrent enrollment program makes to the sponsoring university (Judd and Lafferty 2006a, 2006b, 2007a, 2007b, 2008). Drawing from this research, the current study focused on measuring the retention of students graduating from high schools within the sponsoring university's concurrent enrollment program. The opportunity to test Tinto's model for promoting retention came with the decision to seek accreditation through the National Alliance of Concurrent Enrollment Partnerships (NACEP). Organized in 1999, NACEP supports its member partnerships, in part, by providing accreditation standards and reviews.

Accreditation is necessary because concurrent enrollment programs fall outside the usual standards of accrediting bodies for colleges and universities, as they rely on qualified high school teachers rather than college faculty (personal communication, Diane Siegfried, Nov. 3, 2008). Furthermore, concurrent enrollment programs may be obligated to seek NACEP accreditation as a legislated requirement for public accountability or to ensure that students are able to transfer credit to institutions of higher education unfamiliar with the concurrent enrollment program.

Standards of the NACEP accreditation require a one-year follow-up survey of students who participated in a concurrent enrollment program and a four/five-year follow-up survey. Completion of these surveys is often the major hurdle in a postsecondary institution's preparation of an application packet for accreditation. To assist members with the challenge of developing valid measures and to meet a need to collect comparable data across partnerships, survey instruments were developed by the NACEP Research Committee. These were the survey instruments used in this study and will be referred to as the one-year (NACEP's "1 year out survey") and the five-year (NACEP's "4–5 year out survey") surveys or studies. Therefore, in addition to its stated purpose, this study also offers perspectives on the use of these two instruments as tools for determining concurrent enrollment student retention.

Research Design

As a matter of sound practice, research questions precede and direct the implementation of research (Worthen, Sanders, and Fitzpatrick 1997). Research questions used for this study were:

RQ1. What contribution has credit from the sponsoring institution's concurrent enrollment program made to students' postsecondary education?

RQ2. In retrospect, how satisfied are students with their concurrent enrollment program experience?

RQ3. Does satisfaction positively correlate to students' enrollment in the sponsoring institution?

The research design called for a random sample of 450 students and completion of approximately 200 responses for each population: one-year-out and five-year-out students. A sample of 200 has a percent margin of error of ±7%. However, to increase reliability, stratified sampling was employed to ensure that a representative sample was gathered from each of the various school districts contracted with the sponsoring institution. The research design employed an information letter approved by the Internal Review Board (IRB), a one-page questionnaire, and a business reply envelope to be mailed to the parents of students who participated in concurrent enrollment programs. An information letter, rather than a letter of consent, was approved for this survey by the IRB because no personal or identifying information was requested. Questionnaires not returned by mail were completed by scripted telephone survey.

If a student was not available, then her/his parent was asked to complete the survey. Previous research (Judd and Lafferty 2006b; Judd and Lafferty 2008) had shown that independent samples of parents and students from this population returned nearly identical results on variables related to retention and satisfaction. This research showed that concurrent enrollment students and parents surveyed separately considered as important the same five reasons for choosing an institution of higher education and both groups ranked these factors in the exact same order of priority. Therefore, for the purposes of this study, parents' perspectives were considered to be sufficiently reflective of students' perspectives to be included.

The survey instrument for the five-year study included sixteen questions on demographics, college attendance, and credit recognition for concurrent enrollment courses applicable to the undergraduate degree. Of these, thirteen questions were supplied by NACEP, and three questions were added (high school name, college attended after high school, and college attendance of second parent); these three questions were added to match data collected in the one-year study. The survey instrument for the one-year study included nineteen questions focused on demographics, educational status, transfer of credits taken through the concurrent enrollment program, and satisfaction with that program. Combined, the two instruments had thirty-nine questions, however only twelve were shared and could therefore be compared. Some key questions are reviewed below.

A question that was similar in both survey instruments, and that directly applies to RQ1, was "How did the USU [Utah State University] credits you earned apply to your undergraduate degree?" The following three responses were provided with the instruction to check all that apply:

1. I was exempted from a required course or courses. (For example, you did not need to take a required English composition course in college, because you successfully completed an equivalent college writing course through the USU Concurrent Enrollment Program.)

2. I was able to start in a more advanced course in college. (For example, you were allowed to take Organic Chemistry earlier than normal, because you had already successfully completed an introductory college Chemistry course through the USU Concurrent Enrollment Program.)

3. I am allowed to count some or all of the USU credits toward my college degree completion credits. (Counting either as electives, as meeting general education requirements, or as part of a major or minor.)

Each of the NACEP surveys also asked a question about post–high school status:

One-year survey, item 2: "I am currently enrolled in: high school, 2-yr. college, 4-yr. college, or other."

Five-year survey, item 2: "After high school graduation, did you attend a college, university, or professional school? Where?"

Names of institutions that students attended after high school were gathered in the five-year study and then, for the purpose of longitudinal analysis, were sorted into the categories that were offered to the respondents in the one-year study: (1) high school graduate working; (2) completing military or volunteer service; (3) two-year institution; (4) other four-year institution; (5) sponsoring institution.

A recognized measure of satisfaction is whether individuals will recommend a service (Berry and Parasuraman 1991; Reichheld 2006). Reichheld made the argument that no other measure of satisfaction is more important than whether individuals say that they will recommend a service. Berry and Parasuraman made a similar point, which is that when it comes to choosing a service, people rely most heavily on word-of-mouth recommendations. Therefore, a recommendation question was included in both surveys:

"Would you recommend USU Concurrent Enrollment to current high school students?"

The wording of the question item for measuring satisfaction in both the one-year and five-year survey instruments was identical:

"Looking back, rate your overall experience with the USU Concurrent Enrollment Program."

The scale—excellent, good, fair, poor—used for this question is common in satisfaction studies administered to customers (Vavra 1997). The standard interpretation of overall ratings is that combined ratings of "excellent" and "good" that exceed 90% indicate a high level of satisfaction, and "excellent" ratings that exceed 50% indicate a high level of excellence in service delivery.

Data files were analyzed using SPSS 15.0 to produce descriptive statistics such as cross tabulations, chi-square statistics, and correlations. Statistical procedures followed instructions provided by George and Mallery (2008).

Findings

Respondent Characteristics

The population for the one-year survey included concurrent enrollment program students who graduated from high school in fall 2006, spring 2007, or summer 2007. The total N was 2,766 students. As noted, if a student was not available, then her/his parent was asked to complete the survey. The random sample for the one-year study included 474 potential respondents. Of those, 74 (16%) could not be reached using the address or telephone numbers supplied or were duplicates, therefore the adjusted sample size (n) was 400. From this sample, 200 questionnaires were completed in spring of 2008 and resulted in a response rate of 50% for the one-year study. Data were collected for 117 (58%) female students and 83 (42%) males. Percentages of female students in these surveys' samples are consistent with the percentage reported for on-campus freshman students in fall 2006. Statistics showed that 56% of freshman students were female (Utah State University 2008b). For the one-year survey, respondents were predominantly students: 117 students (58%) and 83 parents (42%). Also, because the concurrent enrollment program offers courses statewide, proportionate numbers by school district were important to maintain the external validity of the study. External validity was strengthened by obtaining data from 45 (60%) of the 75 high schools served by the USU concurrent enrollment program.

The population for the five-year survey was concurrent enrollment students who graduated from high school in fall 2002, spring 2003, or summer 2003. The total N was 1,005 students. The random sample included

427 potential respondents with names, telephone numbers, and addresses. Ultimately, 80 (19%) could not be contacted using the address or telephone numbers supplied; therefore, the n was 347. From this sample, 196 questionnaires were completed in February 2008 and resulted in a response rate of 57% for the five-year study. Data were collected for 109 (56%) female students and 87 (44%) male students. Respondents were nearly equally divided: 99 parents (51%) and 97 students (49%).

For the five-year study, a comparison to 2003 county percentages of students was made. Data were collected from 17 of the 26 counties (65%) served by the concurrent enrollment program. External validity was strengthened when the percentage distribution of students by county was similar (±5%) to the percentage of the total surveys collected. It is noteworthy that, as with the population of concurrent enrollment students, the number of schools partnered with the concurrent enrollment program expanded by 80% during the time period covered by the two surveys. This is an increase of 175% in five years.

Responses to Research Questions

Findings for the study are presented by each of the three research questions below.

RQ1. What contribution has credit from the sponsoring institution's concurrent enrollment program made to students' postsecondary education?

Results of a comparison about post-high school status are shown in Table 13.1. This shows that 93% of the respondents in the five-year study and 78% of the respondents in the one-year study attended a postsecondary educational institution. These are both substantial percentages and demonstrate that the concurrent enrollment program is meeting the primary objective of transitioning students into postsecondary education. Although the one-year follow-up shows a significantly lower percentage of respondents who attended postsecondary institutions, it can be expected that in several years the population of concurrently enrolled students represented by the one-year study will show a similar percentage going on to college, because 16% of the respondents reported that they were either engaged in or preparing for voluntary religious service, which lasts two years.

TABLE 13.1

Comparison of Five-Year and One-Year Studies on Current Status of Concurrent Enrollment Students

Study	N	Working	Volunteer service	Two-year college	Other four-year institution	Sponsor institution
Five-year	196	7%	0	10%	29%	55%
One-year	200	7%	16%	13%	31%	35%
Total	396	7%	8%	11%	30%	44%

Table 13.1 shows the percentage of concurrent enrollment students who enrolled at the sponsoring institution as compared to other postsecondary options. The one-year study showed that 35% (69) of the respondents attended the sponsoring institution after high school. The five-year study showed 55% (107) enrolled in the sponsoring institution. Results from the five-year study seemed to show that students who did not immediately enroll in college (perhaps due to entering voluntary religious service) eventually enrolled at the sponsoring institution.

On the question "How did the USU credits you earned apply to your undergraduate degree," both surveys showed a positive effect on students' undergraduate program. Comparing results for this question from the one-year and five-year studies showed consistently more respondents in the five-year study marked boxes to indicate the credits, earned through the concurrent enrollment program, applied to their undergraduate program. Specifically, the five-year study showed that 82% of the students were exempted from required courses, 54% were able to start in a more advanced course, and 81% were allowed to count some or all of their credits toward a college degree.

RQ2. How satisfied are students with their concurrent enrollment program experience?

High levels of satisfaction are necessary to test the applicability of Tinto's model. In the current study, overall satisfaction ratings for the concurrent enrollment program for both the one-year and five-year surveys exceeded 90%. Combined "excellent" and "good" ratings for both was

95%. Analysis was performed to find out how many credits were earned by students who participated in concurrent enrollment programs. In the one-year study, two hundred students reported earning a total of 3,447 credits through concurrent enrollment courses. The number of credits earned was not collected in the five-year study. For the one-year study, the average number of credits was 17.24 (approximately one full-time equivalent/semester), the median was twelve credits, and the mode was six.

While students' appreciation for the opportunity to receive college credit in high school could account for the continuation of 55% of the concurrent enrollment students to the sponsoring institution's on-campus undergraduate program (see Table 13.1), the question must be asked whether similar student retention occur if the student had little or no exposure to concurrent enrollment courses. In other words, does integration through a concurrent enrollment program make any real difference in students' decision to enter into postsecondary education, and does it affect their decision to attend the undergraduate program of the sponsoring institution?

To answer these questions, the researchers performed a cross tabulation between satisfaction ratings (excellent, good, fair, poor) and groups defined by number of credits earned. Four nearly equal groups of respondents were formed when one-year student respondents were grouped by the number of credits earned (see Table 13.2).

Though not definitive, results presented in Table 13.2 begin to address the objective of this study to apply Tinto's model (1993; Pascarella and Terenzini 1991) to concurrent enrollment programs. The combined "excellent" and "good" rating for the two groups with the most credits (14–24 and 25–62 credits) was 100%. Also, students with the most USU credits (25–62 credits) gave the greatest percentage of "excellent" ratings (83%). The group that had the greatest exposure to USU courses taken through the concurrent enrollment program gave high ratings of satisfaction and perceived program excellence. However, and importantly, this group was also compensated to the greatest degree for their involvement in the USU concurrent enrollment program. The Pearson Product Moment Correlation (r) calculated between credits earned and satisfaction ratings was positive (.254) and was significant at the .01 level (2-tailed). It is important

TABLE 13.2

One-Year Study on Overall Satisfaction Ratings, Four Groups Arranged per Credits Earned

USU credits earned	n	Excellent	Good	Fair	Poor	Total
1–6 credits	60	55%	35%	8%	2%	100%
7–13 credits	52	52%	40%	2%	6%	100%
14–24 credits	41	71%	29%	0	0	100%
25–62 credits	47	83%	17%	0	0	100%

to note that the r is affected by the large percentage of students who, although they earned fewer credits, also rated their experience as either "excellent" or "good." Although credits earned were fewer, students' satisfaction remained high.

These high levels of satisfaction reflect respondents' willingness to recommend the concurrent enrollment program. If the choice "would you recommend?" is indeed "the ultimate question" (Reichheld 2006), then the concurrent enrollment program does very well with 96% of the students and parents in both the one-year and five-year studies answering that they would recommend the program to current high school students.

RQ3. Does satisfaction positively correlate to students' enrollment in the sponsoring institution?

This question was intended to discover the benefit that the concurrent enrollment program provided to the sponsoring institution. The language of the question item was: having experienced a greater level of satisfaction and earned more credits, do students who participated in concurrent enrollment programs respond by enrolling in the sponsoring institution in greater numbers? A cross tabulation was performed between the groups defined by the number of credits earned and students' current enrollment status (see Table 13.3).

As Table 13.3 shows, students in the one-year study receiving 25–63 credit hours earned through participation in a concurrent enrollment program, who thus had the greatest exposure to the USU concurrent enrollment courses, also had the greatest percentage of enrollment in the sponsoring institution, (49%). This is more than twice as many as the

TABLE 13.3

One-Year Study on Current Status of Concurrent Enrollment Students, Four Groups Arranged per Credits Earned

USU credits earned	n	Working	Volunteer service	Two-year college	Other four-year institution	Sponsoring institution
1–6 credits	60	12%	20%	13%	35%	20%
7–13 credits	52	4%	19%	14%	35%	29%
14–24 credits	41	5%	12%	10%	27%	46%
25–63 credits	47	4%	11%	13%	23%	49%

group of students that earned 1–6 credits and 20 percentage points more than those who earned 7–13 credits. Therefore, as concurrent enrollment students earned more credits from the sponsoring institution, the likelihood of them continuing with that institution increased. This supports Tinto's Model of Retention (1993; Pascarella and Terenzini 1991) as applied to concurrent enrollment programs, showing that "the more satisfying those experiences (at the university) are felt to be, the more likely are individuals to persist" (50). Significantly, this finding also demonstrates that student retention in the sponsoring institution occurs to a greater degree than if no concurrent enrollment program existed.

Discussion

Findings from these follow-up studies were very supportive of concurrent/dual enrollment as a strategy for encouraging high school students to enroll in postsecondary education and as a strategy for encouraging students to enter a sponsoring institution's undergraduate program. Additional research at a variety of sponsoring institutions, and attaining a larger n, could further substantiate these findings.

Findings show that sponsoring institutions might expect that on average, concurrent enrollment students will graduate from high school with credits equivalent to one full-time semester, and that more than half of the students served by the concurrent enrollment program will enroll in the sponsoring institution within five years of graduating from high school.

These percentages, however, depend on ratings of overall satisfaction staying at a high level (90%-plus). It also assumes that high satisfaction ratings ("excellent" and "good") will be maintained as student involvement (credits earned) increases. Most importantly, this study shows that when high satisfaction was achieved as students earned more college credit earned through participation in a concurrent enrollment program, they tended to enroll in the sponsoring institution in greater numbers. This demonstrates that concurrent enrollment is an effective tool for retaining students to continue into the sponsoring institution's on-campus undergraduate program.

This study also demonstrates how the NACEP survey instruments can be used to assist concurrent enrollment programs in quantifying their contribution to their sponsoring institution. Quantifying the contribution that a concurrent enrollment program makes is important for justifying the expense in manpower, tuition dollars, and credit that the sponsoring institution invests in its program.

Findings from this study also have implications for concurrent enrollment programs considering accreditation. First, because a majority of students participating in a concurrent enrollment program integrate into an institution's systems and enroll in the undergraduate program, the sponsoring concurrent enrollment program can be reassured that the effort and expense required to obtain accreditation is worthwhile. Second, the methodology can serve as a guide for survey administration for those institutions pursuing accreditation and relying on the instruments developed by the NACEP Research Committee. Substantiation for these findings could emerge if a nationwide database of concurrent enrollment program data is created and comparisons are made. A dialogue about use of standardized measures, such as the ones created by and available through NACEP, is critical to the realization of a national database.

The implications of the findings presented in this chapter can be seen as pertaining to two separate areas, including student retention and NACEP accreditation:

1. Retaining Students

   • Continue through concurrent enrollment courses to give each student an opportunity to experience firsthand the quality of

education offered by the institution sponsoring a concurrent enrollment program.

• Annually measure students' experience of the concurrent
enrollment program experience using satisfaction measures, with
the assumption that students who take more classes and earn more
credits have higher levels of satisfaction and enroll in the sponsoring
institution in greater numbers.

• Continue providing concurrent enrollment programs to rural
and underserved populations to encourage these students to enroll in
undergraduate programs.

2. NACEP Accreditation

• Adopt the survey instruments provided through NACEP and
continue systematic measurement as required by the accreditation
process.

• Employ the standardized NACEP measures to facilitate comparison between concurrent enrollment programs. This is critical for
benchmarking to ensure and improve program quality.

• Encourage NACEP in its efforts to create a database that will
collect and compare concurrent enrollment program data to generate
metrics for program improvement through benchmarking.

In addition to the recommendations above, the findings of this study
prompt several observations that may help to improve the NACEP surveys and questionnaires. Suggestions for such improvements include:

• Researchers should standardize the wording for the two questionnaires where such a change will reduce variation when comparing results.
Measure student satisfaction and number of credits earned.

• Wording from the five-year survey is succinct, which worked for a
telephone-administered survey, but the check box format in the one-year
survey worked better for a mailed survey and self-administration. Both
surveys should be equally adaptable to telephone (agent) administration
and self-administration.

• Combined, the two data sets had thirty-nine questions; however,
only twelve could be compared between surveys. If the two survey instruments had more variables that matched, then more comparisons could be
performed.

References

Astin, Alexander W. 1993. *What Matters in College: Four Critical Years Revisited*. San Francisco: Jossey-Bass.

Bailey, Thomas R., and Karp, Melinda M. 2003. *Promoting College Access and Success: A Review of Credit-Based Transition Programs*. Washington, DC: Office of Vocational and Adult Education, U.S. Department of Education.

Berry, Leonard L. and A. Parasuraman. 1991. *Marketing Services: Competing through Quality*. New York: Free Press.

Blanco, C., B. Prescott, and N. Taylor. 2007. *The Promise of Dual Enrollment: Assessing Ohio's Early College Access Policy*. Cincinnati, OH: KnowledgeWorks Foundation.

Carmel, Avi, and Stuart S. Gold. 2007. "The Effects of Course Delivery Modality on Student Satisfaction and Retention and GPA in On-Site Vs. Hybrid Courses." *Turkish Online Journal of Distance Education* 8(2): 127–35.

George, D., and P. Mallery. 2008. *SPSS for Windows Step by Step: A Simple Guide and Reference 15.0 Update* (8th ed.). Boston: Allyn and Bacon, Pearson Education.

Gurin, Patricia. 1999. "New Research on The Benefits of Diversity in College and Beyond: An Empirical Analysis." *Diversity Digest* (Spring). http://www.diversityweb.org/digest/Sp99/benefits.html.

Hoffman, Nancy. 2003. "College Credit in High School." *Change* 35(4): 42–49.

———. 2005. *Add and Subtract: Dual Enrollment as a State Strategy to Increase Postsecondary Success for Underrepresented Students*. Boston: Jobs for the Future.

Hoffman, Nancy, Joel Vargas, and Jose Paul Santos. 2008. *On Ramp to College: A State Policymakers Guide to Dual Enrollment*. Boston: Jobs for the Future.

Judd, Daniel R., and Vincent J. Lafferty. 2006a (June). "A Needs Assessment for Improving University Retention of Concurrent Enrollment Students." Paper presented at the National Association of Concurrent Enrollment Partnerships annual convention, Arlington, VA.

———. 2006b (Sept.). "Survey of Parents of Concurrent Enrollment Students." Unpublished manuscript, Utah State Univ., Logan.

———. 2007a. "Focus Groups of Teachers in the USU Concurrent Enrollment Program SY 2006–07." Unpublished manuscript, Utah State Univ., Logan.

———. 2007b. "Focus Groups of Counselors and Interviews with Administrators in the USU Concurrent Enrollment Program SY 2006–07." Unpublished manuscript, Utah State Univ., Logan.

———. 2008. "Five-Year Follow-Up of Concurrent Enrollment Students for NACEP Accreditation." Unpublished manuscript, Utah State Univ., Logan.

Karp, Melinda M., Juan Carlos Calcagno, Katherine L. Hughes, Dong Wook Jeong, and Thomas R. Bailey. 2007. *The Postsecondary Achievement of Participants in Dual Enrollment: An Analysis of Student Outcomes for Two States*. National Center for Career and Technical Education Grant No. V051A990006. St. Paul: Univ. of Minnesota.

Kleiner, Brian, and Laurie Lewis. 2005. *Dual Enrollment of High School Students at Postsecondary Institutions: 2002–03*. (NCES 2005-008.) Washington, DC: National Center for Education Statistics, U.S. Department of Education.

Leonard, W. 2008. "State Hoping to Boost Concurrent Enrollment." *Deseret News* (Salt Lake City), June 8.

Mavando, Felix T., Yelena Tsarenko, and Mark Gabbot. 2004. "International and Local Student Satisfaction: Resources and Capabilities Perspectives." *Journal of Marketing for Higher Education* 14(1): 41–60.

O'Hara, E. 2008. Memo to Sen. Andy Berke, Subject: (Tenn.) Dual Enrollment Demographics Follow-up. Retrieved Nov. 20. http://www.tbr.edu/uploaded Files/TBR_Offices/Office_of_Administration_and_Facilities_Development /Programs_and_Services/Legislative_Affairs/dual%20enrollment%20memo.

Pascarella, Ernest T., and Patrick T. Terenzini. 1991. *How College Affects Students: Findings and Insights from Twenty Years of Research*. San Francisco: Jossey-Bass.

Peterson, D. G. 2006. "Validation of a Procedure for Discovering a Market Position Taxonomy to Benefit Institutions of Higher Education." Doctoral diss., Utah State Univ.

Reichheld, F. 2006. *The Ultimate Question: Driving Good Profits and True Growth*. Boston, MA: Harvard Business School Press.

Tinto, Vincent. 1993. *Leaving College: Rethinking the Causes and Cures of Student Attrition* (2nd Ed.). Chicago: Univ. of Chicago Press.

———. 2002. Taking Retention Seriously: Rethinking the First Year of College. *NACADA Journal* 19(2): 5–9.

Utah State Legislature. 1991. Senate Bill 196 in Laws of Utah 1991. p. 201

Utah State University. 2008a. Concurrent Enrollment website. Retrieved July 26. http://concurrent.usu.edu/htm/policies.

———. 2008b. Office of Analysis, Assessment, and Accreditation website. Retrieved Oct. 11. http://aaa.usu.edu/FactsFigures/Admissions.asp.

Vavra, Terry G. 1997. *Improving Your Measurement of Customer Satisfaction: A Guide to Creating, Conducting, Analyzing, and Reporting Customer Satisfaction Measurement Programs*. Milwaukee, WI: Quality Press.

Waits, Tiffany, J. Carl Setzer, and Laurie Lewis. 2005. *Dual Credit and Exam-Based Courses in U.S. Public High Schools: 2002–03* (NCES 2005-009). Washington, DC: National Center for Educational Statistics, U.S. Department of Education.

Walthers, Kevin, and Jennifer Robinson. 2006 (May 24). "Concurrent Enrollment: Funding in Utah." *Policy Brief.* Center for Public Policy and Administration and Center for Public Policy and Administration, Univ. of Utah.

Woolstenhulme, David R. 2008. "Comparing Likelihood of Recruitment to University among Concurrent Enrollment Students Taking Classes Distance-Delivered and Face-to-Face." Doctoral diss., Univ. of Wyoming, Laramie.

Worthen, Blaine R., James R. Sanders, and Jodi L. Fitzpatrick. 1997. *Program Evaluation: Alternative Approaches and Practical Guidelines.* New York: Longman.

Yatrakis, Pan G., and Helen K. Simon. 2002. *The Effect of Self-Selection on Student Satisfaction and Performance in Online Classes.* Retrieved Apr. 22, 2005. http://www.huizenga.nova.edu/about/ResearchReports/HS05-22-2EffectofSelf Selectionin OnlineStud.pdf.

Zeithaml, Valerie A., A. Parasuraman, and Leonard L. Berry. 1990. *Delivering Quality Service: Balancing Customer Perceptions and Expectations.* New York: Free Press.

14

Examining the Relationship between Early College Credit and Higher Education Achievement of First-Time Undergraduate Students in South Texas

CARL A. SALTARELLI

Introduction

In his book, *Escalante: The Best Teacher in America*, Jay Mathews (1988) chronicled the exceptional teaching of Jaime Escalante at James A. Garfield High School in East Los Angeles, California. Escalante encouraged his at-risk indigent Latino students via personal concern, commitment, and an ethic of hard work and personal pride. Escalante's story was retold in the 1988 motion picture, *Stand and Deliver*, which featured Edward James Olmos as Escalante.

Many of Escalante's pupils were first-generation high school students, much like many of the South Texas students in this study. Escalante's students first gained notoriety in 1982 when the media spotlight focused on the results of their calculus Advanced Placement (AP) tests (Mathews 1988). Of eighteen students who took the calculus AP test, the scores of fourteen students were disputed. Those fourteen students were wrongly accused of copying from each other, and twelve of them agreed to retake the test.

An earlier version of this paper was originally published by the *Electronic Journal for Inclusive Education* (EJIC) in January 2010. This revised version is printed with permission of NACEP.

Mathews pointed out that the *Los Angeles Times* really missed the point in their reporting of the story. It was not significant that some of Escalante's students were accused of cheating, nor was it significant that the Garfield High School principal retaliated with charges of racial bias. The significance of the story in 1982 was how a class of eighteen inner-city high school youth from a school with 80% of the students living below the poverty level could become prepared to take and pass a calculus AP test. Early college credit via AP examination has grown since that time, becoming so universal that student scores on AP exams are now as important a measure of high school success as Scholastic Achievement Test (SAT) scores (Mathews 1988).

AP classes are more available than ever before, and they are now offered online (College Board 2005). *Newsweek* magazine now ranks colleges and universities based on percentages of students entering with AP class credits and other early college credit hours. *Newsweek*'s college ranking list orders schools based on participation in AP tests written and graded not by those teaching the AP classes, but by outside experts (Mathews 2005).

As the requirement of a college degree becomes standard in the workplace (Pennington 2004), the popularity of accelerated education by means of AP classes and other early college credit programs has increased (Ewers 2005). Interestingly, students are enrolling in early college classes not only to get a head start, but also to keep from falling behind fellow high school students (Ewers 2005). According to Pennington (2004), the goals of accelerated early college credit programs include: to increase the number of students who graduate from college, to reduce the amount of time that it takes them to do so, and to reduce disparities of educational achievement based on race and income. Accelerated education has become more and more popular, has taken many forms, and has blurred the lines of demarcation between secondary and postsecondary school (Olson 2006).

High school students can begin taking college courses as early as their freshman year (Porter 2003). Students can potentially graduate from high school with more than 60 hours of college credit, and even an associate's degree, earned at the same time (College Board 2003). Students not only become familiar with the freedoms and challenges of the college-style course schedule, but they are also allowed to adjust their personal high school schedule to take the college-level courses for which they qualify. In use in high schools across the country, early college credit programs give high school students a preview of the higher education experience and usher students through what can sometimes be a very intimidating transition from high school into college (Bailey, Hughes, and Karp 2002). Early college programs, identified by various names in different states, are made possible by state legislation and agreements among high schools, junior colleges, colleges, universities, and the College Board (College Board 2003).

Early college credit programs can accelerate degree completion, cutting as much as two years off a combined high school and college education, by minimizing course duplication between high school and college classes (Rouge Community College 2006). Early college credit programs can also represent a significant cost savings to students and parents, as students can continue to live at home (Black Hills State University 2006), and the local school district often pays for the cost of the college courses (Santa Barbara City College 2007).

In AP programs, high school students take an accelerated course taught at their own high school. Upon completion of the course, they take a College Board AP Exam, by which they can earn college credit hours and/or advanced college placement (College Board 2003). As an additional incentive, some schools will pay for the AP exam if students pass it, and other schools even reward passing students with a financial stipend for their academic success. Some high schools further encourage excellence by providing partial college scholarships to graduates who have participated in early college credit programs (Matthews 2004).

In concurrent enrollment programs in Texas, students who meet certain achievement standards take college-level courses on a college campus along with college students, while concurrently enrolled in high school (Texas Business and Education Coalition 2002). These students have the advantage of actually being on the college campus. It is thought that this arrangement best eases the transition from high school to college, which can be very difficult for some students and can contribute to their decisions to drop out (Bailey, Hughes, and Karp 2002).

In dual credit programs in Texas, students enroll in college-level courses taught either on the high school campus by college-certified faculty, or on a college campus (Texas Business and Education Coalition 2002). The college-level courses replace the high school–level courses in a given subject, so that students need not take the same courses on both high school and college levels. Generally speaking, one semester of college coursework replaces two semesters of high school coursework (Texas Business and Education Coalition 2002). It is noteworthy that over time, the distinction between concurrent enrollment and dual credit has blurred, and these descriptors are now being used interchangeably.

Porter (2003) compared the academic success of dual-enrolled high school students to their non-dual-enrolled counterparts in a study conducted in Tennessee. Porter found that dual-enrolled students had significantly higher first-semester college grade point averages (GPA) and higher overall college GPAs than non-dual-enrolled students. However, Porter also found that dual-enrolled students had higher high school GPAs and higher ACT scores than their non-dual-enrolled counterparts. The differences in college GPAs may therefore have been the result of higher individual achievement levels rather than the positive result of early college credit programs. Porter believed that students who enter college with an early college experience better understand what will be required of them, and that this experience gives them an emotional and academic advantage toward their success in higher education.

Purpose of the Study

This researcher examined the relationships between high school student participation in various early college credit programs and higher education achievement, specifically among students in South Texas, in order to determine whether being involved in an early college credit program has a positive impact on student achievement. Early college credit programs deserve investigation to determine the extent to which these programs are related to students' higher education success.

It was specifically the purpose of the current study to determine to what extent early college credit is related to higher education achievement, as measured by college GPA, while holding constant the possible effects of ACT scores and high school class ranking. Prior studies have indicated that the control variables ACT scores and high school class ranking are among the best quantitative predictors of success in higher education (Williams 2004). Although early college credit is known by several different names and is available in several different forms, the current study focused on the effect of three of the most popular early college credit programs: Advanced Placement, dual credit, and concurrent enrollment.

Research Question

The researcher utilized the following research question for the current study: While holding constant the effects of ACT scores and high school class ranking, what is the relationship between early college credit and higher education achievement, as measured by GPA, among first-time undergraduate students at Texas A&M University–Kingsville?

Procedure

The researcher sought to determine whether early college credit appears to be a reliable predictor of academic success. The study was quantitative in nature and utilized a causal-comparative research design. This type of design seeks to determine, without the use of a controlled experiment, whether there is a cause-effect relationship between a certain stimulus, known as the independent variable, and an apparent response, known as the dependent variable (Borg, Gall, and Gall 1992). The causal-comparative design is often used in educational research in situations where it is not possible to interject an experimental manipulation (Gall, Borg, and Gall 1996). The typical causal-comparative study begins by forming two groups based upon one variable and seeking out differences between the two groups on a second variable.

The population for this study consisted of 8,627 first-time undergraduate students of Texas A&M University–Kingsville who entered during class years 1997 to 2005. This window, 1997 through 2005, covered most of the years when students with early college credit could have matriculated at the university. The researcher utilized data recorded through fall 2007 for the entire population of 8,627 first-time undergraduate students and alumni. Because the study involved students from multiple class years, it included alumni, current students, and some students who had discontinued their education prior to completion of their degrees.

The study utilized data gathered by the Office of Institutional Research and the Office of the Registrar at Texas A&M University–Kingsville. Outcomes from the data analysis may be generalizable to this particular university student population. It is unknown whether the outcome can be generalized to other university student populations.

Descriptive statistics were applied to examine the obtained data. Data were analyzed using the Statistical Package for the Social Sciences (SPSS version 11.5), specifically by using a Pearson r procedure, partialing out the effects of the control variables, ACT scores, and high school class rank. The Pearson r coefficient is a "mathematical expression of the direction and magnitude" of a relationship between two sets of continuous scores (Gall, Borg, and Gall 1996, 767).

Study Participants

From fall 1997 to fall 2005, more than 10,000 undergraduate students entered Texas A&M University–Kingsville. Of these, 8,627 were first time in college students, who had never before taken college courses as part of a degree program, and who comprised the population of interest for the current study. The mean age of students in the population upon entering was M = 19.4 years, SD = 3.3.

The mean high school ranking of students was M = 58th percentile, SD = 25.6. The mean high school GPA of the population was M = 3.3, SD = 0.6, as compared to a mean university GPA of M = 2.1, SD = 1.1. The mean ACT score of the population was M = 18.7, SD = 4.0 (Table 14.1).

TABLE 14.1

Descriptive Statistics for Age, High School Rank, University Grade Point Average, and ACT Scores

Variable	N	M	SD
Age	7,474	19.38	3.345
High School Ranking	8,021	57.85	25.583
High School GPA	7,993	3.286	.5604
University GPA	8,627	2.135	1.0540
ACT Score	7,915	18.74	3.961

The variability of the population size N in Table 14.1 is due to missing values in the data provided by the Office of Institutional Research. The ethnic makeup of the population was 67.8% Hispanic, 23.8% white non-Hispanic, 6.2% African American, 2.0% others, and 0.2% unknown (Table 14.2).

Considering the entire population, the mean number of early college credit hours that students earned while in high school was relatively low: M = 1.8 hours, SD = 4.8. Within the population, 1,661 students (19.3%) earned early college credit hours via Advanced Placement, concurrent enrollment, or dual credit programs while enrolled in high school. Of those students who earned early college credit, the amount of early college credit earned per student ranged from one hour to sixty hours of credit. The mean hours of early college credit was M = 9.3 hours, SD = 7.2 (Table 14.3).

TABLE 14.2

Frequency Analysis of Ethnicity Variable

Category	N	%
White	2,049	23.8
African American	539	6.2
Hispanic	5,852	67.8
Asian	64	.7
American Indian	23	.3
Other	84	1.0
Unknown	16	.2
Total	8,627	100.0

TABLE 14.3

Descriptive Statistics for Study Variables

Variable	N	M	SD
ECC* for Total Population	8,627	1.78	4.828
ECC for ECC Earners	1,661	9.27	7.192

*Early college credit

Results

The researcher addressed the following null hypothesis: There is no statistically significant relationship between early college credit and higher education achievement, as measured by GPA, among students at a South Texas University, when controlling for the effects of ACT scores and high school class ranking. The researcher utilized a Pearson r procedure, controlling out the effects of the control variables, ACT scores and high school class ranking. The results of the partial Pearson r procedure, $r_p = .079$, p < .001, led to the rejection of the null hypothesis and indicated a small yet statistically significant relationship between early college credit and university GPA (Table 14.4).

Once the effects of the positive success indicators ACT scores and high school class ranking are controlled out, early college credit appears to be positively related to higher education achievement, as measured by GPA. That is, the more early college credit hours a student earns, the higher that student's university GPA tends to be.

To determine the relationship between early college credit and university GPA exclusively among early college credit earners, the researcher performed another Pearson r procedure with only the early college credit earners, controlling out the effects of the control variables, ACT scores and high school class ranking. The results of the partial Pearson r procedure for early college credit earners was $r_p = .096$, p < .001, which indicated a slightly stronger statistically significant relationship between early college credit and university GPA among early college credit earners (Table 14.5).

This second Pearson r procedure reinforced the evidence of positive relationship between early college credit and higher education

TABLE 14.4

Partial Correlation Coefficient of Early College Credit and University Grade Point Average, Controlling for ACT Scores and High School Class Ranking

Variable	N	r_p	p
Correlation of ECC and UGPA*	7,564	.0790	.000

*University grade point average

TABLE 14.5

Partial Correlation Coefficient of Early College Credit and University Grade Point Average for Early College Credit Earners, Controlling for ACT Scores and High School Class Ranking

Variable	N	r_p	p
Correlation of ECC and UGPA	1,584	.0956	.000

achievement, as measured by GPA, among students at Texas A&M University–Kingsville, when controlling for the effects of ACT scores and high school class ranking.

Discussion

The outcome of this study appears to indicate that South Texas high school students who prepared for higher education by participating in early college credit programs outperformed students who did not participate in such programs, in terms of their achievement in higher education. Within the population there appears to be a small to moderate, statistically significant relationship between early college credit and higher education achievement, as measured by GPA, when controlling for the effects of ACT scores and high school class ranking. It is worth restating that the current study was limited in scope to the impact of early college credit programs on the higher education success of students who have attended and graduated from a single university located in South Texas (Texas A&M University–Kingsville), and that the study investigated only the effects of early college credit programs. Other variables related to student success in higher education were not evaluated, and it may be that variables other than early college credit are even more closely related to academic success. The question lingers as to whether the academic benefit of the early college experience reflects the success of the program, or the success of the highly motivated individual students involved.

References

Bailey, Thomas R., Katherine L. Hughes, and Melinda Mechur Karp. 2002. *What Role Can Dual Enrollment Programs Play in Easing the Transition Between High*

School and Postsecondary Education? New York: Community College Research Center and Institute on Education and the Economy, Teachers College, Columbia Univ.

Black Hills State University. 2006. "Dual Credit for High School Students." Accessed Feb. 27, 2007. http://www.bhsu.edu/Admissions/Apply/DualCredit /tabid/771/Default.aspx.

Borg, Walter R., Joyce P. Gall, and M. D. Gall. 1992. *Applying Educational Research: A Practical Guide.* White Plains, NY: Longman.

College Board. 2003. "AP Program." Accessed July 31. http://apps.apcentral.col legeboard.com.

————. 2005. "AP Program." Accessed Nov. 14. http://apps.apcentral.college board.com/student/testing/ap/about.html.

Ewers, Justin. 2005. "Is AP Too Good to Be True?" *U.S. News and World Report,* Sept. 19.

Gall, M. D., Walter Borg, and Joyce P. Gall. 1996. *Educational Research: An Introduction.* White Plains, NY: Longman.

Mathews, Jay. 1988. *Escalante: The Best Teacher in America.* New York: Holt.

————. 2004. "Class Struggle: Paying Teachers and Students for Good Scores." *Washington Post,* Aug. 10.

————. 2005. "How to Build a Better High School." *Newsweek,* May 10.

Olson, Lynn. 2006. "As Accelerated Learning Booms, High School-College Divide Blurs." *Education Week,* June 20.

Pennington, Hilary C. 2004. "Fast Track to College: Increasing Postsecondary Success for All Students." Center for American Progress website. Accessed Feb. 23, 2007. http://www.americanprogress.org/kf/fasttrack-final%2012%2001.pdf.

Porter, Rubianna M. 2003. "A Study of Students Attending the Tennessee Board of Regents Universities Who Participated in High School Dual Enrollment Programs." Doctoral diss., East Tennessee State Univ.

Rouge Community College. 2006. "Early College Credit." Accessed Feb. 27, 2007, http://www.roguecc.edu/HSOutreach/2+2/.

Santa Barbara City College. 2007. "Enrollment Services." Accessed Feb. 28. http:// www.sbcc.edu/prospectivestudents/index.php?sec=44.

Texas Business and Education Coalition. 2002. Expanding Concurrent Enrollment and Dual Credit: A Policy Goal Statement of the Texas Business and Education Coalition. Adopted by the Board of Directors, Sept. 10, 2002. Accessed July 31, 2003. http://www.tbec.org/concurrentenrollment.pdf.

Williams, Magdalena H. 2004. "Achievement and Retention Patterns in a Predominantly Hispanic Serving Institution of Higher Education." Doctoral thesis, Texas A&M University–Kingsville and Texas A&M University-Corpus Christi.

15

Economic Literacy Spillovers into the High School General Economics Course from Teaching the Advanced Economics Course

An Econometric Analysis

DONALD H. DUTKOWSKY, JERRY M. EVENSKY, AND GERALD S. EDMONDS

Introduction

This chapter examines the positive effect on economic literacy when high schools allocate resources to train teachers to teach advanced economics and have those teachers teach the general economics classes as well. The argument is straightforward: High school teachers who have been carefully trained to teach an advanced economics course and then teach the advanced course generate significant spillover effects to students in the general economics courses that they also teach. The econometric evidence from our study indicates that the economic understanding of students in the advanced economics course has a significantly positive effect on economic literacy of students in the same teacher's general economics course.

Following Walstad and Buckles (2008), economics courses offered within U.S. high schools can be grouped according to two classifications, general economics courses and advanced economics courses. *General economics courses* denote non-college-level, standalone economics courses. This group is also referred to as the Basic Economics course, as in Walstad (2001) and Walstad and Rebeck (2001a, 2001b). New York State uses the term Regents Economics to designate general economics courses offered by high schools within the state.

Advanced economics courses denote college-level or college economics courses. These models include Advanced Placement (AP), International Baccalaureate (IB), and Concurrent Enrollment Programs (CEP). Walstad and Rebeck (2001a, 2001b) refer to this group as AP/Honors Economics. Dutkowsky, Evensky, and Edmonds (2006) discuss the CEP model, in which a sponsoring college or university offers its courses, taught by an appropriately trained member of the high school faculty, in participating high schools. Upon completion students receive college credit from the sponsoring institution based upon their course grade. In turn they can apply for recognition (college credit, exemption, or standing) to the college or university at which they matriculate.[1]

Positive spillover effects from the advanced economics course to the general economics course occur for at least two reasons. First, the advanced economics course typically requires additional training for teachers in economics content. The importance of formal economics training for U.S. high school social studies teachers is addressed in Walstad (2001). Second, teachers generally carry over content and materials prepared for advanced economics courses to the general economics course they teach. Walstad and Buckles (2008) find evidence that some instructional practices lead to significantly greater economic literacy for students in the general economics course. Finally, these teachers may hold higher expectations for their students on content knowledge.

The results of Walstad and Rebeck (2001a, 2001b) indicate that taking a high school economics course plays an important role in increasing economic literacy. They find that students in general economics courses score better on the Test of Economic Literacy (TEL) than higher level high school students who have not taken an economics course. Our results complement this argument. Positive spillovers imply that economic education, and thus economic literacy, is significantly strengthened by investing

---

1. See Dutkowsky, Evensky, and Edmonds (2003, 2008) for further discussion of how the CEP model offers advantages compared to AP and IB for increasing economic literacy.

resources to train a cadre of teachers to offer both advanced and general economics courses in high schools.

The next section of this chapter presents two multiple regression models to test for spillover effects. Our study focuses on the performance of students of high school teachers who teach both the Regents Economics course and the CEP Economics course offered through Syracuse University Project Advance®.[2] The chapter then reports empirical results, based on use of the TEL testing instrument. The findings indicate that a teacher from a quality advanced economics course brings a significant positive effect to the economic literacy of students who take his or her general economics course. The largest gain in economic understanding occurs in microeconomics and fundamental economic concepts. The chapter concludes by discussing the implications of these findings.

Models for Testing Spillover Effects

Walstad and Rebeck (2001b) conducted testing in one hundred high schools throughout the United States to determine economic literacy among high school students. They report student performance on the TEL based upon four different norming groups, referred to as Basic Economics, AP/Honors Economics, Basic Social Studies, and AP/Honors Social Studies. In this way, their study sets national norms for economic literacy for these populations. The main results are summarized in Walstad and Rebeck (2001a). Walstad (2001) states that the TEL is the most widely used measure for voluntarily testing economic literacy in the Basic Economics course.

Walstad and Rebeck (2001b) define these national norming groups based upon whether the students have taken a high school economics course and whether the courses are considered general or advanced. We focus on the first two norming groups. The Basic Economics group

2. Project Advance (http://supa.syr.edu) is one of the largest concurrent enrollment programs in the United States. In the 2006–7 school year, the program had 10,980 student enrollments in Syracuse University courses in 176 high schools encompassing a five state area. Syracuse University began offering principles of economics courses through Project Advance in 1988. In the 2006–7 school year, the program in economics consisted of 32 high schools throughout New York, serving nearly 1,250 students.

consists of students in a general economics course. The AP/Honors Economics group is made up of students in an advanced economics course.

Our models were tested within the following framework. Consider a representative high school in New York State. The school offers sections of two different economics courses, Regents Economics and CEP Economics. The same teacher teaches both courses. The Regents Economics course is the high school's general economics course. It fulfills state high school graduation requirements but is not college level. The CEP Economics class represents the high school's advanced economics course. It draws college-bound students with relatively higher aptitude for and interest in economics.

We offer two multiple regression models that examine the economic literacy of students taking the Regents Economics course. Each equation provides a test for spillover effects resulting from the teacher instructing the CEP course. Economic literacy is based upon the performance on the TEL, which consists of 40 multiple choice questions. Let N denote the number of high schools in the sample.

The first model, which we call the Advanced Course Spillover Model, is as follows. For the ith question on the TEL ($i = 1, 2, \ldots, 40$) and the jth high school ($j = 1, 2, \ldots, N$), the equation is given by:

$$\textbf{REGEij} = \alpha j + \beta(\textbf{TELBEi}) + \theta(\textbf{CEPij}) + \mu ij. \quad (1)$$

The variables are defined as follows. **REGEij** denotes the percentage correct on the ith question from students taking the Regents Economics course in the jth high school. **TELBEi** is the percentage correct on the same question from the Basic Economics norming group of the TEL. **CEPij** denotes the percentage correct on the same question from students taking the CEP Economics course from the teacher in this high school, and μij is the regression residual.

The β parameter measures a peer effect, based upon the percentage correct on the given TEL question from students nationally who took a general economics course. It examines the effect of question difficulty, described by the performance of the national peer group in relation to students in the Regents Economics course. The coefficient would be expected to have a positive sign and a magnitude of one.

The αj parameters measure individual school effects. Since the model controls for the peer effect, if students in the Regents Economics course are entirely representative of those in the TEL Basic Economics national norming group, then the αj parameters should equal zero. However, the student in the New York State Regents Economics course may perform less well than those in the Basic Economics group. At least two character-istics account for this distinction.

First, all high school students in New York State are required to take an economics course for graduation, while many high school students outside of New York can opt out of economics entirely.[3] Second, many high schools in the United States do not offer an advanced economics course of any type. In this case, even the best students would be found in the general economics class. These factors imply that even though the Basic and Regents Economics *courses* serve the same curricular function, the average score on the TEL of students taking the Regents Economics course may be lower than for the national Basic Economics group. Con-trolling for the peer effect, this behavior implies that the αj parameters would have negative sign.

The θ parameter represents a possible spillover effect. Spillovers imply a positive sign. In the absence of spillovers, the performance of students in the advanced economics course would have no bearing on the group tak-ing the general economics course with the same teacher. Spillover effects imply that the teacher of the CEP Economics course will carry over train-ing, materials, and content expectations into his/her Regents Economics class(es). This activity will increase the economic literacy of this teacher's Regents Economics students as a result.

The second model seeks to test for spillover effects due to the quality of the advanced economics course alone. TEL performance from students in the advanced course stems from two factors—the relatively higher aptitude of the students themselves and the quality of the advanced eco-nomics course. This equation presents a test for spillovers that looks to

---

3. As of 2007, only seventeen states carried this requirement (National Council on Eco-nomic Education 2007).

subtract out the former effect. We refer to this model as the Value Added Spillover Model. This equation is given by:

$$REGEij = \alpha j + \beta(TELBEi) + \theta(CEPij - TELAPHEi) + \mu ij, \quad (2)$$

where **TELAPHEi** refers to the percentage correct on the ith question from the AP/Honors Economics norming group of the TEL. The αj and β parameters have the same roles as in equation (1).

As in the previous equation, the θ parameter represents a possible spillover effect, with spillovers implying a positive sign. However the corresponding variable, **CEPij – TELAPHEi**, measures the increase in economic literacy acquired by the CEP Economics students from the quality of their college economics course alone. The variable measures the gain beyond the higher level students' innate ability in economics plus the training they would have received from a representative advanced economics course. Dutkowsky, Evensky, and Edmonds (2006) provide evidence of increased economic literacy of students in CEP Economics courses beyond those of the AP/Honors Economics norming group.

Empirical Findings

This study had several Syracuse University Project Advance Economics teachers administer the TEL to both their CEP Economics classes and their Regents Economics classes at the end of the fall 2003 semester. The CEP class is a one-semester course on the principles of micro- and macroeconomics, with Evensky (2005) as the primary text. We sent the TEL materials just before the exam was administered, so the teachers did not have time to "teach to the test." We gave the TEL within four participating high schools (i.e., **N** = 4), reflecting a total number of students of 118 from Regents Economics and 136 from the CEP Economics course. All students took Form A of the TEL. An observation of the dependent variable **REGE** is the percentage of students taking the Regents Economics course from a given high school who answered the given TEL question correctly. Thus the sample for the estimated models consists of 160 observations, 40 TEL questions multiplied by four high schools.

Table 15.1 reports sample means for the Regents and CEP Economics classes along with the corresponding information for the TEL norming

TABLE 15.1

Sample Means, Percentage Correct on the Test of Economic Literacy (TEL)

Sample Group	TEL National Norming Sample	CEP High Schools
General Economics		
Overall Exam	60.7	54.9
Fundamentals	64.3	55.8
Microeconomics	62.2	56.2
Macroeconomics	58.2	55.4
International	54.4	50.0
Advanced Economics		
Overall Exam	71.0	78.4
Fundamentals	74.1	80.7
Microeconomics	71.7	79.2
Macroeconomics	69.9	77.0
International	64.5	74.3

Notes: Results are based upon Test A of the TEL. Statistics for the TEL norming samples come from Walstad and Rebeck (2001b).

groups. The means in Table 15.1 present a contrast for the TEL performance of the high schools in New York State versus the national groups. Regents Economics students average nearly six percentage points less than the Basic Economics group. The largest differences occur in microeconomics and fundamentals. On the other hand, CEP Economics students score over seven percentage points higher than the AP/Honors Economics group.[4] The difference is fairly uniform throughout the field areas.

Table 15.2 reports regression findings. All estimated models include an intercept and dummy variables for three of the four schools. The first

4. The spread in the average score between the CEP students and AP/Honors Economics students here is larger than in Dutkowsky, Evensky, and Edmonds (2006). This time we had the teachers maintain tighter standards for students to take the exam seriously. In the previous study, we found that outliers in the exams skewed the means downward.

column of estimates presents results from a model with no spillover effects. The school-specific effect is negative and significantly different from zero at the 5% level. The estimated peer effect, corresponding to the variable **TELBE**, is positive, highly significant from zero, and close to one. Statistical testing cannot reject the null hypothesis of a unitary value for this parameter at any reasonable level of significance.

TABLE 15.2

Estimated Models: TEL Performance in the Regents Economics Course

Variable/ Model	*(No Spillover)*	*(1)*	*(2)*	*(3)*	*(1a)*	*(2a)*
Intercept	−12.095					
(5.857)	−15.137					
(5.961)	−11.512					
(5.756)	−4.589					
(8.116)	−16.297					
(5/041)	−5.809					
(1.956)						
TELBE	1.128					
(0.091)	0.956					
(0.120)	1.095					
(0.260)	1.383					
(0.255)	1.000	1.000				
CEP	—	0.174				
(0.081)	—	—	0.155			
(0.060)	—					
CEP-TELAPHE	—	—	0.222			
(0.085)	0.227					
(0.085)	—	0.234				
(0.084)						
TELAPHE	—	—	—	−0.571		
(0.301)	—	—				
R^2	0.51	0.52	0.53	0.53	0.07	0.08
SE	12.13	11.99	11.91	11.89	11.96	11.91

Notes: Standard Errors appear in parentheses. Regressions include dummy variables for individual schools.

The next column reports estimates from equation (1), the Advanced Course Spillover Model. The findings provide evidence of a positive spillover effect, as the estimate for **CEP** is significantly different from zero at the 5% level. The coefficient of 0.174 indicates that every 5.75 percentage points that the CEP students achieve on a given TEL question leads to a 1-percentage-point gain in the score of the Regents Economics classes taught by the same teacher.

The third column of estimates presents findings from equation (2), the Value Added Spillover Model. The results support a positive spillover effect here as well. The estimated spillover parameter is positive and significantly different from zero at the 5% level. The magnitude of the estimated spillover effect is larger, though, compared to the Advanced Course Spillover Model. The estimated coefficient of 0.222 indicates that Regents Economics classes score 1 percentage point better on a given TEL question for every 4.5-percentage-point achievement on the same question from students in the CEP Economics course beyond those of the AP/ Honors Economics norming group. For both estimated spillover models, the school-specific effects have a negative sign and are significantly different from zero.

To further investigate the robustness of the estimated spillover effect, we estimate a variant of equation (2), also presented in Table 15.2. Model (3) separates the CEP and AP/Honors Economics effects. The estimated coefficient for **CEP** is positive and significantly different from zero, while the estimate for **TELAPHE** is negative and insignificant. Statistical testing cannot reject the restriction that the effects are of equal absolute magnitude with opposite sign (the **t**-statistic for testing the null hypothesis equals 1.21). This finding provides evidence for the validity of the value added variable **CEP-TELAPHE**.

For all the estimated spillover models, the peer effect, represented by the variable **TELBE**, is significantly different from zero and close to unity. In addition, the null hypothesis that $\beta = 1$ cannot be rejected at any reasonable level of significance in all cases. Therefore, we estimate the spillover models with the restriction of a unitary peer effect. These results appear in the columns labeled (1a) and (2a). The findings again indicate a significantly positive spillover effect. The estimated spillover effects have magnitudes close to those in their corresponding estimates in equations (1) and (2). The increased estimator efficiency appears in the lower standard errors, notably the intercept.

Table 15.3 reports estimated models with the sample decomposed by fields, based upon the Value Added Spillover Model (Table 15.2, model (2a)). We use the model with the unitary peer effect restriction due to the smaller number of observations for each equation. Very similar findings come from the corresponding estimated Advanced Course Spillover Model separated by fields (see Table 15.4).

The results reveal positive estimated spillover effects in all cases. The strongest evidence comes from microeconomics. The estimated parameter has the largest magnitude across all fields and is significantly different from zero at the 5% level. The estimated coefficient of 0.306 indicates that Regents Economics classes score 1 percentage point better on the TEL question for every 3.25-percentage-point achievement on the same question from CEP Economics students beyond those of the AP/Honors Economics norming group. The spillover coefficient for fundamentals is significantly from zero at the 10% level. On the other hand, the estimated spillover effects for macroeconomics and international are not

TABLE 15.3

Estimated Spillover Model by Field: Value Added Spillover Model

Variable/ Field Area	*Fundamentals*	*Micro*	*Macro*	*International*
Intercept	−5.333	−11.961	−2.737	−2.457
	(3.535)	(3.569)	(3.855)	(4.724)
TELBE	1.000	1.000	1.000	1.000
CEP-TELAPHE	0.264	0.306	0.229	0.166
	(0.158)	(0.139)	(0.176)	(0.289)
R^2	0.17	0.24	0.08	0.13
SE	12.88	10.99	11.02	11.13

Notes: Standard Errors appear in parentheses. Regressions include dummy variables for individual schools. Estimates are based upon model (2a) (see Table 15.2).

TABLE 15.4

Estimated Spillover Model by Field: Advanced Course Spillover Model

Variable/ Field Area	Fundamentals	Micro	Macro	International
Intercept	−21.969	−29.878	−12.696	−5.661
	(9.428)	(10.564)	(8.532)	(13.211)
TELBE	1.000	1.000	1.000	1.000
CEP	0.227	0.254	0.153	0.057
	(0.111)	(0.129)	(0.098)	(0.180)
R^2	0.19	0.22	0.10	0.12
SE	12.72	11.12	10.91	11.20

Notes: Standard Errors appear in parentheses. Regressions include dummy variables for individual schools. Estimates are based upon model (1a)(see Table 15.2).

significantly different from zero at the 10% level. The estimated spillover effect is smallest for the international field.[5]

Conclusion

The evidence indicates that investing in teacher training for an advanced economics course carries positive effects beyond those received by students in the higher level class. Preparing for and instructing the advanced course brings about enhancements in expertise, materials preparation, content coverage, and increased standards that teachers can bring to the more populated general economics class, all of which contribute to increasing the economic literacy of general economics students. Estimates indicate that students taking general economics courses improve their score on the TEL by an average of 1 percentage point for every percentage point increase achieved by students in the advanced economics course

5. It should be noted that the findings may also reflect the significant role of a highly talented teacher in economics. One way to control for teacher talent might be to compare TEL results from the general economics course for the same instructor before and after undergoing programmatic training, which includes teaching the advanced economics course. We plan to pursue this experiment in future research.

taught by the same teacher. The strongest spillover effects come from microeconomics and fundamentals.

The implications of our findings for design and delivery of the high school economics curriculum are substantial. A very efficient and effective model is to establish a set of economics teaching specialists who are trained for and teach a quality advanced economics class and who deliver the general economics instruction as well. Implementation of this model would make a significant contribution toward increasing economic literacy.

References

Dutkowsky, Donald H., Jerry M. Evensky, and Gerald S. Edmonds. 2003 (Dec. 3). "Improving Economic Literacy: The Role of Concurrent Enrollment Programs." Available at Social Science Research Network (SSRN). http://ssrn.com/abstract=476146.

———. 2006. "Teaching College Economics in the High Schools: The Role of Concurrent Enrollment Programs." *Journal of Economic Education* 37 (Fall): 477–82.

———. 2008. "Economic Literacy Spillover Effects from Concurrent Enrollment Programs to the High School Basic Economics Course." Unpublished manuscript, Syracuse Univ.

Evensky, Jerry M. 2005. *Economics: The Ideas and the Issues*. Boston, MA: Pearson Custom Publishing.

National Council on Economic Education. 2007. *Survey of the States: Economic and Personal Finance Education in Our Nation's Schools in 2007, A Report Card*. Washington, DC: National Council on Economic Education, June 7, 2007.

Walstad, William B. 2001. "Economic Education in U.S. High Schools." *Journal of Economic Perspectives* 15 (Summer): 195–210.

Walstad, William B., and Stephen Buckles. 2008. "The National Assessment of Educational Progress in Economics: Findings for General Economics." *American Economic Review* 98 (May): 541–46.

Walstad, William B., and Ken Rebeck. 2001a. "Assessing the Economic Understanding of U.S. High School Students." *American Economic Review* 91 (May): 452–57.

———. 2001b. *Test of Economic Literacy: Examiner's Manual*, 3d ed. New York: National Council on Economic Education.

16

Income Effects on Concurrent Enrollment Participation

The Case Study of UConn Early College Experience

BRIAN A. BOECHERER

Introduction

The effects of household income on educational opportunities are not only a well-researched area in scholarly literature, but also a popular topic in the mass media. Scholarship indicates that high schools in less affluent areas may struggle to provide the educational opportunities that schools in more affluent areas are able to provide. Conversely, areas of higher affluence offer greater academic programming. Many scholars claim that the more affluent the area, the stronger the culture for academic competition and achievement (Blossfeld and Timm 2003; Breen and Goldthorpe 1997; Breen and Jonsson 2005; Kerckhoff 1995). Given the access, students will choose the academic opportunity that offers them the greatest reward at the smallest cost. While there have been few academic studies on concurrent enrollment programs, a normative assumption would be that, given the access to college classes at the high school, students would enroll in these classes because it provides them with more opportunities and greater benefits as they apply to and attend college. However, when one investigates the University of Connecticut's concurrent enrollment program, UConn Early College Experience (ECE), the scholarship is not supported by the data; rather it shows the opposite tendency. That is, in the upper quartile of median household income, as household income increases in a linear fashion, student participation decreases exponentially. Contradicting scholarship even further, in the middle and lower income quartiles, there appears to be no relationship between the median household income and participation. What does this mean and what would cause this to occur?

While the relationship between income and participation in the upper quartile is clear to see (although the reasons may not be clear), the absence of a correlation in the middle and lower quartiles is equally interesting. That is, if income and participation have no relationship, this indicates that economic factors do not bear relevance when students enroll in the program. More to the point, there do not seem to be economic barriers for students to participate in UConn ECE.

To better understand this relationship, a survey was administered to the UConn ECE site representatives (designated high school liaisons who administer the program, register the students for the UConn courses, and disseminate program information to faculty, administration, students, and parents at the high school; usually in the guidance department). Based on the survey data, primarily two things affect program growth (positively or negatively) across all three quartiles: (1) students' ability to earn UConn credits that are accepted not only at UConn but also transfer to other universities and colleges, and (2) instructor interest. If the instructors see value in the program, the participation at the high school grows, and likewise, if enrollment at the high school is declining, the faculty is generally not in favor of the program.

UConn Early College Experience

Concurrent enrollment is an educational opportunity that allows high school students to take university courses at their high school for college credit. High schools that participate in such programs are not only offering their students access to college credits, but also allowing them the benefit of applying to college with a university transcript, thereby making them more competitive during the admissions process. Moreover, once students matriculate to a university or college, they have an academic advantage compared to their peers because they have an established transcript. These credits offer students greater flexibility in scheduling their semesters and may allow them to take more advanced courses earlier in their academic career, thus increasing the opportunity for students to double or dual major, as well as increasing early or on-time graduation rates.

Established in 1955, UConn ECE is the oldest continually active concurrent enrollment program in the Unites States, as well as one of the largest in the nation by student enrollment and numbers of classes offered per year. While some of the community colleges offer concurrent enrollment in Connecticut, UConn ECE is by far the most expansive (in terms of programming and student enrollment) and the only accredited member of the National Alliance of Concurrent Enrollment Partnerships (NACEP). At its inception, the program had seven partner high schools and just over two-dozen students. During the 2009–10 academic year, UConn ECE had 139 active partner high schools and more than 7,500 students enrolled in one or more UConn courses. UConn ECE is a robust program that seeks to work with highly motivated high school students. In the program's recent history, there has been an effort to offer a broader array of courses so that it is not an exclusionary program that caters to the top 15% of students. Rather, as is central to the mission of the program, UConn ECE seeks to help develop students who excel in specific academic areas and/or who have diverse academic backgrounds and motivations. Students in the top rankings also enjoy this diversity, along with the traditional core courses of a rigorous academic program (e.g., calculus, chemistry, and freshman English). The broadening of course options allows students to follow their academic interests, thereby allowing students who may be hesitant about going to college to realize their potential in higher education.

Student Access to the Program

The first step in establishing a concurrent enrollment program is certifying high school instructors. Certified high school instructors are the bedrock of the program and the certification process is quite extensive. Indeed, UConn ECE instructors are certified by the university's departments as adjunct UConn faculty. This means that the standards used to hire an adjunct to teach a specific course on campus is the same standard applied to certify UConn ECE faculty. Using this as a panoramic of the program, such a system creates great specificity when one looks at how each department conducts certification, because certification is centralized at each department.

Because certification is conducted at the department level, the system as a whole offers a panoramic of approaches that can be used to carry out the certification process. It is not a traditional "access" program that works exclusively with underserved populations; rather it is an open access program for students who are academically motivated. During the first four decades of the program, UConn ECE catered to "academically superior" students. High school students who applied to the program had to have a combined SAT of 1200 or be ranked in the top 15% of the high school class by grade point average. As of fall 2000, the program disposed of such regulations and gave the course gatekeeping responsibilities to the UConn ECE faculty and site representatives, with the instructions that the UConn courses should be for students who not only have an interest in the course but also can keep pace with the rigor of a university course. In fall 2005, UConn ECE started its efforts to broaden course offerings in an effort to provide greater access to a greater number of students. While courses such as calculus and freshman English would always remain for the honors students who fit the former acceptance standards, there was a new effort to offer courses to all motivated high school students. Environmental science, political science, and human development and family studies are just some of the disciplines that appeal to the interests of students, and these courses may not require prerequisite coursework.

Financial Restrictions

Broadening the course offerings was one method of increasing student access to university coursework. The other primary means for keeping UConn ECE an access program was keeping the cost structure manageable for all students. Prior to the academic year 2000–2001, students who took UConn courses through UConn ECE did not have to pay for the opportunity. All courses were free. The following year, the university decided that in order to increase administrative oversight, a nominal cost of $5 per course would be applied to the program. Over the years, as the program's costs increased and its vision was to increase benefits and opportunities for students, the student fees were raised incrementally to $25 per credit.

Compared to taking a course at the university through Continuing Education, the student fees are still quite low. Nevertheless, the central office has been sensitive to the needs across the state, and those students who are part of the federally subsidized Free and Reduced Lunch Program are given a full fee waiver. Moreover, in high schools that have a student population where 85% or more are part of the Free and Reduced Lunch Program, the entire student body receives a fee waiver from UConn ECE. This ensures that all students who are motivated to take college courses can do so. There are no economic barriers to the students, but there are limited financial costs that are incurred by the district: high schools do not pay for participating in the program, but they do have to allow their UConn ECE faculty to come to the university for scheduled professional development once every other year. Thus, the cost to the district is a substitute teacher for a day, while the UConn ECE faculty person completes his or her professional development.

Literature Review: Educational Decision Making

The idea of educational decision making will serve as the theoretical framework for understanding student participation in concurrent enrollment programs. In the social sciences, scholars have spent years studying elite decision making, voting behavior, and civil participation. In some ways all three categories address the idea of educational decision making, and at the same time none of them truly focuses on or explains the rationale. That is, elites are making decisions for their nation usually in reaction to some event; voters are making decisions for themselves as individuals and for the country as a collective; and civil participation (political protest, volunteering, etc.) is generally cause-based. Educational decision making is individualized, the results are not delayed, and the effort invested in one's education is converted to personal gain. Thus, educational decision making is truly a separate category from the collective decision making studied by social scientists.

Currently there is a deficit of literature on educational decision making; rather, the emphasis is placed on educational access. Educational access is different from educational decision making because "access" implies restrictions from, or allowances to, education. Thus, the term is most often connected to ideas of poverty. Most scholars are concentrated on minority access to educational opportunities and/or educational access in economically challenged areas. However, very few scholars are focused on educational decision making. This is the next step in the process once opportunities are available. This is truly the focus of our study as we are trying to understand why participation in UConn ECE decreases as household income increases. While there are but a few scholars who focus on educational decision making, this study benefits greatly from their approaches.

Breen and Goldthorpe (1997) examine "educational differentials" and construct a model of decision making that mirrors political game theory. For example, making the decision to stay in high school opens up a number of other decisions, perhaps to take advanced coursework, focus on the arts, or choose from a series of other options. This model differs from traditional game theory in that, under these circumstances, microdecisions affect only one person or at most the family unit. They focus on educational opportunities, aspects of gender, and differences in resources. Before testing their proposed model, Breen and Goldthorpe establish a few important benchmarks. Their model begins with the assumption that educational differentials, the differences in educational attainment, can be divided into two categories—primary and secondary. Primary effects are those that stem from class origins and academic ability. Breen and Goldthorpe support the notion that children from more advantaged backgrounds generally have higher educational performance on tests (both standardized and other forms of examination) than children with less privileged backgrounds. Secondary effects, however, are those that come from actual choice—what the student (and perhaps the parent) chooses to do for their educational future. Breen and Goldthorpe state that children and their parents make rational decisions about their educational opportunities, a formula that considers costs, benefits, values, and norms. Breen and Goldthorpe's general approach is supported by scores of everyday examples where individuals make decisions that determine personal gain, while not adversely affecting others. Duncan and Brooks-Gunn (1997) and Breen and Jonsson (2005) approach educational inequality from the same perspective. While taking less theoretical approaches, they add to Breen and Goldthorpe by emphasizing that parent socioeconomic status, cultural assets, and other networks impact the educational deci-sions of their children. Thus, the wealthier the family, the more actively involved parents and students are in the student's own education; con-versely, the less affluent the family, the weaker the culture for academic involvement. This model reflects the understanding that income and edu-cational attainment are related.

Absent from the literature discussed above is that students may not make decisions with a clear understanding of the facts or full informa-tion. That is, when students and their parents make decisions based on cost and benefits, they may be well informed, poorly informed, or work-ing under a set of mixed assumptions. Further, it is worth noting that stu-dents may not even know the full list of options at their disposal. This is important as we try to understand why students, with or without parental guidance, make their decisions.

Taking a different perspective on the issue of affluence and educational access and decision making, Karabel and Astin (1975) determine that so-cial class and where students attend college are linked together. More-over, their research indicates that at levels of high affluence (social rank), academic ability is only a factor if the student is exceptionally talented or an exceptionally poor performer. If academic ability is held constant, the scholars found that even in terms of financial support (scholarships and endowments), funds are more often and more generously offered to stu-dents who have more affluent backgrounds, compared to students with less affluent backgrounds. Using many layers of regression analysis, they finally conclude that social rank does not necessarily determine where a student will attend college; however, high-ranked colleges will select students of higher affluence and social background. Moreover, the authors support the notion that patterns of elite access perpetuate themselves in the culture.

Methods and Data

Participation/Income Data

This study employs both quantitative and qualitative methods of inquiry. It not only establishes a relationship between household income and student participation, but also seeks to understand why this relationship could possibly exist. The investigation will examine the issue on a macro level for one key reason: UConn ECE does not collect income data on the student household. However, income is not what the study is trying to understand; rather it is student participation. Student participation has many more aspects than one may originally estimate.

A major component of student participation is student enrollment (se), which is our dependent variable. Student enrollment is defined as the nonduplicated tally of students enrolled in a UConn course at the high school. If the student registers for one course or five courses, the student is counted only once. If we were to count the number of courses per student, that would potentially show the diversity of student interests or the academic background of enrolled students. That variable, however, would be used for a different study.

While student enrollment is a crucial indicator of participation, there are two interaction variables that help explain student participation and are two of the study's three independent variables. First, in order for students to participate in a concurrent enrollment program there must be a certified instructor; that is, there must be an actual course offered. The number of courses offered per high school (cph) is defined by how many certified instructors were actually offering courses. The tally does not include duplicate sections. In other words, if there were three sections of freshman English, the course was counted once regardless of whether there were one or three UConn ECE instructors. Second, upon reviewing the data on student enrollment in the program in relation to courses offered, there were glaring disparities between the two. For example, some high schools have as many as fifteen courses offered, but no more than forty students enrolled. This is a critically important variable because it shows a tendency toward participation. The ratio in the example above would indicate low participation, whereas if the reverse occurred it would show high participation. Thus, the variable students per course (spc) is derived by taking the total nonduplicated student enrollment at the high school and dividing it by the total nonduplicated courses offered at the high school. All student and course offering data is pulled from the 2008–9 academic year.

The final independent variable used in this study is median house-hold income (mhi). Since UConn ECE does not collect data on student household income, the data on household income that will be used is town median household income. While it would also be ideal for this study to include a time series analysis tracing the changes in median household income over ten years in relationship to student participation, household income data are not collected on a regular basis. Rather, town data is col-lected depending on the size of the town. The American Community Sur-vey from the United States Census Bureau collects socioeconomic data on all towns with a population of 65,000 or greater on an annual basis. Towns with a population that ranges between 20,000 and 65,000 are surveyed every three years. Towns with a population less than 20,000 are surveyed every five years.[1] Thus, annual household income data would consider only fifty-three towns in Connecticut, which would misrepresent the study. Therefore, this study uses 2008 median household income data (the only data available) provided by the Connecticut Economic Resource Cen-ter, Inc. The 2008 median household income data corresponds with the student enrollment data for the 2008–9 academic year.

This study, however, is not looking at the town median household income; it is using town median household income as a proxy for the high school. In most cases one high school serves the community of one town. In Connecticut there are a number of very rural towns that do not have their own high school and thus send their students to a regional high school. In order to stay consistent with the proxy described above, regional high school median household income is the average of the send-ing-town's median household incomes. For example, High School X is a regional high school that receives students from seven area towns. The median household incomes of the seven towns are tallied and divided by seven. This average of medians is designated as the median house-hold income for the high school. In none of the cases does a regional high school have a town where the median household income is an outlier. In only two regional high schools are the individual towns in two different

1. Connecticut State Data Center (http://ctsdc.uconn.edu).

income quartiles. Each of these high schools has only two towns that compose the district.

As median household income is ascribed to high schools in this way, it forces the study to remove the private and parochial high schools that charge tuition. Students who attend private schools come from a variety of towns with different backgrounds; some students receive tuition waivers, while other families pay the full rates. These nuances and the selection requirements established by the high school make the issue of student participation much different in these schools, and thus these high schools are arguably outliers to this study.

Finally, the high schools are segmented into three quartiles by the median household income. The UConn ECE program median is $76,390. The upper income quartile range includes high schools with a median household income between $87,066 and $190,636; the middle quartile includes high schools between $65,056 and $87,007; the lower quartile includes high schools between $30,379 and $64,405. When all the high schools are presented on a scatter plot, there is a slight skew to the left (see

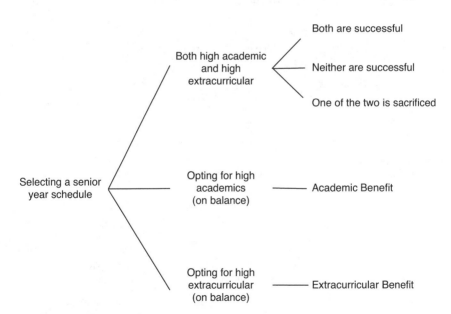

Figure 16.1. UConn Early College Experience (ECE) Income and Student Enrollment

Figure 16.1). This indicates that the distribution of schools with the highest enrollment is "middle America." Not only does the graph show the area of highest enrollment, but also it shows the density of participating schools. Additionally, the graph shows the utility in segmenting the data into quartiles in order to determine a relationship between participation and income.

Upper Quartile

Using the segmented data the study uses STATA 10 to run regressions on the data to determine the strength of the relationship between student participation and income. Upon looking at the graph of the upper quartile of median household income (see Figure 16.2) it is apparent that the relationship is not linear. As income increases in a linear fashion, participation decreases exponentially. Indeed, when a basic OLS-regression is used to test the hypothesis, there is no relationship between the variables.

A better estimate occurs when we adapt the equation to a more functional form, using a log-log model. Log-log regressions are very typical for demand models when all the values are known and no value drops

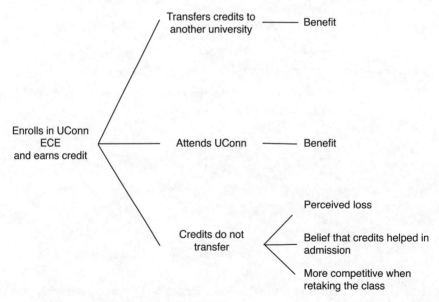

Figure 16.2. UConn ECE Upper Quartile

TABLE 16.1

Variables and Log Student Enrollment

Variables	*Log Student Enrollment (se)*
Avg. Students per Course (spc)	.0695783 *
	(.0128906)
Number of Courses per HS (cph)	.1408301 *
	(.0342958)
Log Median Household Income (mhi)	−1.238437 ***
	(.6663778)
Constant	16.38114 **
	(7.870349)

N = 23
R^2 = 0.7160
* p < .01
** p < .05
*** p < .10

below zero. When the model is run, the results show a relatively strong relationship between the variables. R^2 = 0.7160, which means that there is a relatively high accuracy to the regression (see Table 16.1). Further, all of the variables are statistically significant between .10 and .01.

$$\ln(se) = 16.38114 + -1.238437 \ln(mhi) + .0695783spc + .1408301cph$$
$$(7.870349)\quad (.6663778)\quad (.0128906)\quad (.0342958)$$

Middle and Lower Quartiles

When linear and nonlinear regressions are run for the middle and lower quartiles, a relationship cannot be established between student enrollment (se) and median household income (mhi) (Figure 16.3 and Figure 16.4). For the middle quartile, neither a log-log model regression (the expected model) nor a linear regression produces a relationship that supports a correlation between student enrollment and median household income. In both cases the regression lines fit well; R^2 = 0.8375 and R^2 = 0.9243, respectively, but the only significant variables are students per course (spc) and courses per high school (cph). Similarly, when a log-linear model (the

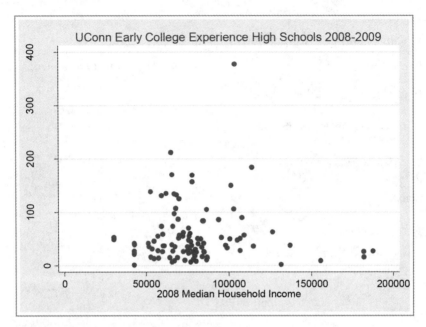

Figure 16.3. UConn ECE Middle Quartile

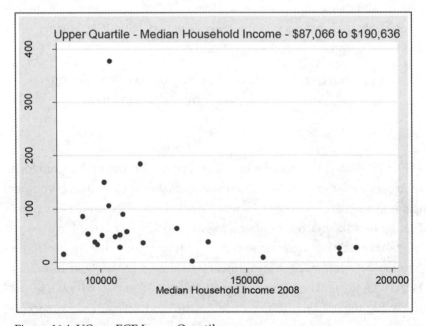

Figure 16.4. UConn ECE Lower Quartile

expected model) and a linear regression are run for the lower quartile, the regression lines are strong; $R^2 = 0.9256$ and $R^2 = 0.8259$, respectively. The only variables with statistical significance, however, were students per course (spc) and courses per high school (cph). Median household income (mhi) and student enrollment (se) were not statistically significant in either case. Therefore, this indicates that there is no relationship between median household income (mhi) and student enrollment (se) in these quartiles.

Analysis and Results

Upper Quartile

The regression for the upper quartile not only shows a relatively high correlation, but also all of the variables of the upper quartile are significant or highly significant. What this shows is that as median household income increases, student enrollment decreases. While this is the general trend, the explanation requires a bit more discussion. First, as the median household income increases by 1,000 units (i.e., $1,000 increase in household income) and all other units are held constant, student participation will decrease by 8.344, approximately 8 to 9 students. As this is a log-log model, however, this rate is not a constant rate; it is elastic. Thus, at a 10,000-unit increase, the rate of decrease is 11.20, or approximately 11 to 12 students. Clearly, due to the nature of the independent variables, student enrollment (se) will never slump below 1 student. Students per class (spc) and the average courses per high school (cph) are both highly statistically significant. This makes sense, as without a course being offered, there can be no student enrollment. Likewise, if there are no students per class, then student enrollment will be zero. This is something that does not stand out in the regression equation, but it is a matter of logic and an important distinction in this discussion.

Middle and Lower Quartiles

The middle and lower quartiles indicate that there is no relationship between household income and student participation. It is not surprising that both students per class (spc) and the average courses per high school (cph) are highly statistically significant. The reason for their significance is that, as previously explained, if there is a class being offered, then there must be a student in the class; if there are no students in the class, then the course is removed from the list of active courses offered. While the regression line is strong, our dependent variable is not significant. This is not to say that we cannot learn from the regression. Having no correlation between median household income (mhi) and student enrollment (se) indicates that economic barriers do not restrain students from enrolling in UConn ECE in the middle and lower quartiles. While it does not indicate why students enroll in UConn ECE, it contradicts many scholars who make a connection between educational access and income. This is not only true in the middle quartile, but also it is true in the lower quartile. One potential factor that impacts household income and participation is UConn ECE's fee waiver program, which exempts students on Free and Reduced Lunch from paying student fees. In the lower quartile, five of the twenty-seven high schools receive a fee waiver for all the students, due to the 85% Free and Reduced Lunch rule. Thus, the lack of relationship between income and participation is a welcome indicator for UConn ECE.

Educational Decision Making

Returning to the logic of educational decision making, after a student has access to make choices for his/her education, the student then weighs the costs and the benefits of the educational opportunity. Let us apply this logic to students in the upper quartile faced with the decision to enroll in a UConn course at high school. Students in the upper quartile are perceived to be highly competitive candidates when applying to college. The rank and reputation of their high school, the student's personal class rank, and extracurricular activities all account for college admissions decisions. On a high school transcript, generally all honors courses are ranked the same. The benefit of taking an honors course, a UConn course, or an Advanced Placement (AP) course is usually the same on a high school transcript. It is understood that college admission opportunities increase with a greater amount of student activities (sports, after school jobs, and volunteering). When making a decision about where to invest the most time, a student may consider the balance of time spent on extra coursework versus extracurricular activities. In affluent high schools with a good reputation, a student's knowledge of that reputation enters into the cost/benefit trade-off. That is, if the student thinks that his/her high school has a good reputation, s/he may opt to devote more time to extracurricular activities. Depending on a student's class rank, there may be a dramatic difference in decisions if the student is in good academic standing or if s/he is in poor academic standing. (See Figure 16.5.) Finally, if we are to follow Karabel and Astin's conclusions, social class/affluence also has a bearing on the decision, but students would not know this. What they would know is that there is a culture in their town and high school that students go to high ranked colleges.

In the upper income quartile, cost of education is less of an issue than in the middle and lower quartiles. Depending on one's perspective, a student in the upper quartile might sign up for as many UConn courses as possible because cost is no object. Conversely, one could also assume that students would not register for the UConn courses because they can afford college next year and do not need the advancement. Further, college

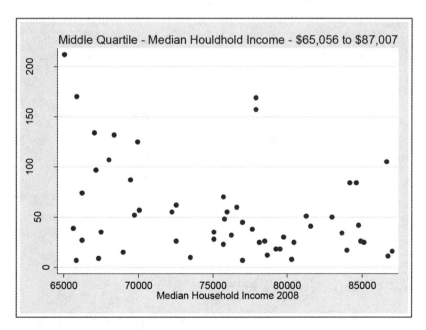

Figure 16.5. Decision Making and Outcomes Based on Student Priorities

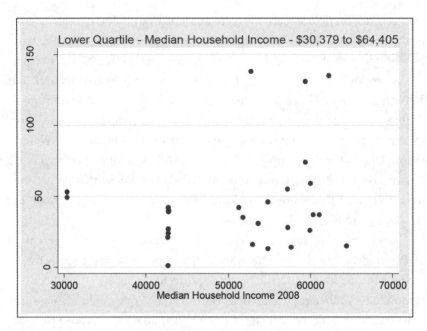

Figure 16.6. Decision Making Based on Benefits of UConn Credit

selection might be focused on the private liberal arts colleges. While many private liberal arts colleges accept UConn credit earned through UConn ECE, the student might not believe the credits transfer or might not want to sacrifice extracurricular activities to other time investments.

Students and parents in the middle and lower quartiles, however, are worried about college costs next year. If a student can graduate from college in three years versus four, then they are likely to take advantage of the opportunity to do so. Moreover, students want to maximize their opportunities when applying to college, and applying with a university transcript may prove to be an advantage. While students do not know exactly how universities and colleges admit students, they know that having a college transcript does not diminish their chance of admission. (See Figure 16.6.)

Site Representative Survey: Method and Results

The decision-making (game theory) diagramming is useful in mapping a student's choices. Given the theoretical background, in conjunction with the regression results, it is a convincing argument. In addition to this approach, a survey also was distributed to the site representatives to see if they could offer greater insights on the program. The survey asked the site representatives to identify the benefits of UConn ECE at their high schools, whether UConn ECE conflicted with other educational opportunities like Advanced Placement, as well as what motivated the high school's partnership with UConn ECE. The survey was used in an attempt to understand the culture that existed at the high schools and whether the culture supported the partnership with UConn ECE.

In addition to the survey, each high school site representative received a program growth chart that showed the UConn ECE student enrollment at his or her high school over the past eleven years in relationship to the county average and the program average. The site representative also received a growth chart illustrating the number of nonduplicated courses offered at their high school over the past five years, again in comparison to the county average and the program average. The data sheets offered the site representatives a long-range view of their participation in UConn ECE and allowed them to answer such questions as "Has your student enrollment in UConn ECE grown over the last eleven years (or since you have been a partner high school)?" Ninety-eight site representatives responded. While surveys were anonymous, one of the questions asked the respondent to identify the county where the high school is located. All eight Connecticut counties fit on a spectrum of median household income; the two polar ends have a variance of more than $30,000. Thus, knowing the county of the respondent may indicate preferences by affluence.

Of the site representatives who responded, 79% have a growing UConn ECE program, 18% have a declining UConn ECE program, and 3% of respondents are in their first year of the program. From the total pool of respondents, 65% of site representatives indicated that their program has grown because students earn a UConn transcript; 86% of all respondents reported that the credits transfer well to other universities and colleges. This seems to indicate that while having a UConn transcript is important, the convertibility of credits as college currency is very important. It is interesting to note that there are more schools that enjoy the fact that the credits transfer well than there are schools with a growing UConn

ECE program. Naturally, one of the reasons for this is that site representatives are usually guidance staff and do not teach the courses; rather, they organize the program.

After the singular importance of the earning and transferability of credit, the most important factor that determines student participation is instructor interest in UConn ECE. With regard to program growth, 50% of site representatives report instructor interest as an impacting cause, the second most important factor after transcripts and transferability. Likewise, in the 18% of schools with declining UConn ECE student enrollment, the most cited cause for the decline in the program is instructor interest (38% of respondents) and difficulty in getting instructors certified (19%). Combining the aforementioned percentages that relate to instructor interest, 64% of respondents link instructor interest, lack of interest, or certification standards preventing certification as impacting program growth. Thus, instructors have as much to do with student participation as does the value of earning a UConn transcript.

When asked whether instructors prefer UConn ECE over other advanced programs such as AP or International Baccalaureate (IB), only 26% responded positively. Furthermore, while the majority of instructors do not prefer UConn ECE over other programs, students prefer it to AP or IB by 39%, or 13 points more. Interestingly, in schools with declining UConn ECE programs, respondents say that 10% of parents prefer AP to UConn ECE, and another 24% say that the student interest is declining or the academic level of students is declining.[2] In all cases, the responses to the survey are nearly identical on the program level as they are on a county level; thus, no inferences can be made based on affluence. What can be gleaned from this survey, however, is that transcripts and instructor interest are the two most impactful reasons for program growth. Although the opinions of the site representative are not necessarily the opinions of the students and parents (who are ultimately making the decisions), it is arguable that the views of faculty and staff at the high school do affect the

---

2. In the free response section of the survey, 14% said that the academic ability of students has decreased and therefore the school cannot offer the course.

decisions of the students. As the site representatives (and presumably the UConn ECE faculty) put a high value on the transferability of the credits and are the ones advising the students, it is even more curious to see low student participation in the upper quartile of the program.

Conclusion

Taking the results of the regressions from all three income quartiles and the information gathered from the site representative survey, it is valuable to revisit the theoretical framework of this chapter as a road map for understanding the data at hand. Educational decision making is difficult to understand when there is a relationship between decision making and affluence. Scholarship often focuses on the lack of access to education among the economically disadvantaged. It is not often the case that affluence is the focus of a study. It is a positive indication that there is no relationship between affluence and participation in the middle and lower quartiles. Indeed, Figure 16.1 shows a left skew to the graph, which indicates that the bulk of the students in the program are from the middle and lower quartiles. Given a game theory approach, students in these two quartiles are participating because they want to get a head start on their college work, presumably to reduce the time and tuition costs once they are enrolled in a degree program at a college where the cost of education will be higher. In the upper quartile, given the decline in participation as income increases, it indicates that students are focused on something else. There are two issues that may explain this: (1) conflicting opportunities for these students, and/or (2) a confidence in the culture of college participation that is grounded on a casual disregard for costs. The first issue refers specifically to a conflict between UConn ECE and other advanced credit programs like AP, IB, and online programs. Given the responses of the site representatives, there is a high understanding that UConn credits earned through UConn ECE transfer to other institutions. There does not seem to be such a conflict in the middle and lower quartiles; it would seem improbable that such a conflict could not be overcome in the upper quartile. Given the survey data, high schools in all areas of Connecticut seem clear on the benefits of the program, which would seemingly reduce such conflicts between programs.

What remains to be argued is that in the upper quartile there is a culture of college participation that is not impacted by cost. This cannot be judged by the regression data, nor can the survey data offer deeper explanation. However, the theoretical framework allows for the comparison of resources to register in decision making. Karabel and Astin, Breen and Goldthorpe, and Breen and Jonsson all discuss the culture of access to education and that affluence allows access and opportunity to education. These authors were not referring to concurrent enrollment; they were referring to the culture of access and opportunity to college. Concurrent enrollment is a partnership that increases student access to higher education. But if the access is already there, why is there a need to increase it? In the middle and lower quartiles, where attending college is only now starting to institutionalize in the culture, students are encouraged to use available opportunities because the competition for college admission and scholarships is difficult. In these areas, concurrent enrollment performs much better than in the upper quartile. Indeed, the first eight high schools in the poorest areas have a larger student enrollment than the first eight high schools in the wealthiest areas.

In terms of concurrent enrollment programs throughout North America, the findings of this study are more than just interesting. In the middle and lower quartiles, access to concurrent enrollment partnerships should be opened with as few economic restrictions as the program can manage. Students who earn college credits while in high school can realize their potential for college and the experience will allow them greater opportunities once in college. In the upper quartile, the immediate need for concurrent enrollment may not yet be realized because access to higher education is more easily attainable and with fewer restrictions. However, the trends revealed in this study are not all one way. There are already a few high schools in affluent areas with robust partnerships and high student participation. As college applications increase and access starts to tighten, this trend may shift. It is the responsibility of the concurrent enrollment program and NACEP to increase awareness of these rich opportunities through research and advocacy. Concurrent enrollment is a program where all students can benefit and student success is determined by effort, not affluence.

References

Blossfeld, Hans-Peter, and A. Timm, eds. 2003. *Who Marries Whom? Educational Systems as Marriage Markets in Modern Societies*. Dordrecht, Netherlands: Kluwer.

Breen, Richard, and John H. Goldthorpe. 1997. "Explaining Educational Differentials: Towards a Formal Rational Action Theory." *Rationality and Society* 9: 275–305.

Breen, Richard, and Jan O. Jonsson. 2005. "Inequality of Opportunity in Comparative Perspectives: Recent research on Educational Attainment and Social Mobility." *Annual Review of Sociology* 31: 223–43.

Duncan, Greg J., and Jeanne Brooks-Gunn, eds. 1997. *Consequences of Growing Up Poor*. New York: Russell Sage.

Karabel, Jerome, and Alexander W. Astin. 1975. "Social Class, Academic Ability, and College 'Quality.'" *Social Forces* 53(3): 381–98.

Kerckhoff, Alan C. 1995. "Institutional Arrangements and Stratification Processes in Industrial Society." *Annual Review of Sociology* 21: 323–47.

17

The Effect of Syracuse University Project Advance on College Student Performance and Persistence

KALPANA SRINIVAS

Introduction

This study examines student performance and persistence in college in relation to participation in the Syracuse University Project Advance (SUPA) concurrent enrollment program. To explore this relationship, the researcher has focused on:

• examining two groups: (1) undergraduates at Syracuse University (a four-year, private institution) who had participated in SUPA courses while in high school; and (2) undergraduates at Syracuse University who had not taken SUPA courses in high school (non-SUPA);

• understanding and getting acquainted with the overall data set used for this study and all subsequent analyses;

• extracting and querying the data from the Syracuse University Student Records System and creating an observation matrix;

• listing and defining all of the independent and dependent variables used in the study as noted in Appendix 17.1;

• utilizing descriptive statistics to describe the basic features of the data and provide details regarding SUPA students and non-SUPA students; and

• applying statistical tests to identify the difference in means with respect to the independent variable between the group that had taken SUPA courses and the group that had not.

Background

An important indicator of the quality of college preparation at the secondary school level is reflected in how well students perform subsequently in higher education. Adelman (1999) found that the strongest predictor of degree completion in college was the intensity of the curriculum at the high school level. There is a national debate on whether our high school students are "college ready" and whether our schools are indeed preparing students adequately to fulfill their requirements to successfully graduate from college. Venezia, Kirst, and Antonio (2006) report that "eighty-eight percent of 8th graders expect to participate in some form of postsecondary education and approximately 70 percent of high school graduates actually do go to college within two years of graduating" (3). Interestingly, Bailey, Hughes, and Karp (2002) found that 37% of students entering college for the first time had left after two years without earning a degree. There seems to be a disconnect here, and hence both high schools and colleges are interested in tracking the effects of high school interventions on student performance and persistence, especially through the early semesters of college.

Decades ago, when few students aspired to attend college, it was appropriate to treat K–12 and postsecondary education as separate units. In recent years, however, with the masses of high school students desiring to attend college, Venezia, Callan, Finney, Kirst, and Usdan (2005) argue that state policies should require partnerships between the two units to improve college readiness of high school students.

About a quarter of high school students did not enroll for postsecondary education, and one approach to address this problem would be through dual enrollment (Windham and Perkins 2001). The lack of standard nomenclature is confusing, and these programs are interchangeably called dual credit, dual enrollment, and concurrent enrollment. One way that Syracuse University (SU) addresses this issue is by creating a wider range of learning experiences and opportunities for high school seniors through its Project Advance concurrent enrollment program. SUPA is designed to bridge the high school–college gap by providing introductory Syracuse University courses in high schools to qualified seniors, enabling them to earn college credits at tuition rates much lower than the main campus college tuition rates. SUPA was started in 1972 when six principals from local high schools approached Syracuse University with a request to start a program for competent high school seniors who had completed their required courses. They sought a solution to senior year boredom that would challenge students without duplicating coursework that they would then have to take again in their first year of college. Such concurrent enrollment programs are "seen as a way to encourage students who might otherwise 'slack off' to engage in demanding coursework during their final year of high school" (Bailey, Hughes, and Karp 2002, 9), which then prepares them for the rigor of subsequent college coursework.

The U.S. Department of Education reported that 71% of the nation's high schools and 51% of its postsecondary institutions allowed high school students to take college courses in 2002–3, with 813,000 high school students taking a college-credit course in that academic year (Waits, Setzer, and Lewis 2005). In that same year, the SUPA program had 6,646 student enrollments.

Dutkowsky, Evensky, and Edmonds (2006) report that in the 2006–7 school year, SUPA had approximately 10,900 student enrollments in classes taught at 180 high schools in a five-state area (New York, New Jersey, Maine, Michigan, and Massachusetts). Faculty members at SU continuously work with the high school teachers to ensure that college standards are maintained in the off-campus sections of their courses. Thirty-two SU faculty members work with high school teachers in twenty-two different disciplines to improve teaching strategies. About twenty-nine courses are taught in high schools by more than seven hundred high school teachers who have attended graduate seminars in their subject areas and have been appointed adjunct instructors at SU (Edmonds and Signorelli 2009).

The SUPA courses offered in high schools are similar in content and course rigor to the corresponding courses offered to first-year and sophomore students on the SU main campus. SUPA students are assessed for each course in the same way and are held to the same standards as students on SU's main campus; however, SUPA students earn both high school and college credits. "Recent research has shown that 93% of SUPA graduates who sent an official transcript to another university or attended

SU received recognition (credit, placement, and/or exemption) for their SU courses" (Edmonds and Signorelli 2009).

Waits, Setzer, and Lewis (2005) note that evidence suggests that student participation in concurrent enrollment programs is almost equal to that of student participation in Advanced Placement (AP) programs, signifying the need for further research on the effectiveness of these programs.

Karp, Calcagno, Hughes, Jeong and Bailey (2007) noted in their study that further research should be conducted on determining the effectiveness of concurrent enrollment programs to continue the debate on whether these programs should be offered to a larger audience of students, as typically they are only offered to select students in high school.

SUPA's guidelines state that the program's courses are typically offered to students who have completed their high school work successfully with a B average or better. But in reality, if the high school guidance counselor believes a specific student is motivated and committed to doing well in the college-level course, then the student is enrolled for the course. Of course, the guidance counselor is then expected to monitor the student's progress and advise the student to either continue, just audit the course, or drop the course.

Swanson (2008) has argued that concurrent enrollment program participation may influence a change in students' attitudes and reinforce retention and graduation rather than attrition from college. She has also noted that participation in concurrent enrollment programs may increase students' confidence as future college graduates, and this may prove to be one of the most important reasons to enroll in such programs in high school.

Conceptual Framework and Purpose of the Study

This study was designed to address two questions:

1. Are the outcomes data consistent with the assertion that concurrent enrollment participation is beneficial to student academic performance and persistence, using SUPA as the specific case?

2. Is there any relationship between SUPA and student performance and persistence outcomes in college?

This is an ex post facto research design that tests the hypothesis of association as the two student groups chosen are assumed to differ on some important variables, and are compared to see if they also differ on other variables as well. This study uses a formal hypothesis to look at the effectiveness of the SUPA program as a strategy for increasing students' postsecondary achievement/outcomes.

According to Bailey, Hughes, and Karp (2002), AP and concurrent enrollment students have an advantage over students not in these programs that should correlate to more success for AP and SUPA students. Some studies have found that concurrent enrollment students are more likely to graduate from college, while other studies have found the opposite. The following hypothesis will be analyzed in this study.

This study examines a select population of students, as SUPA requires that students be academically successful with at least a B average or above both in the particular subject and overall high school grade point average (GPA) prior to gaining admission into the SUPA program.

The question of persistence has been a subject of research since 1975, when Tinto first explored the topic in his study of student attrition. Pascarella and Terenzini (2005) have noted the importance of continuing educational and sociological research to pursue possible explanations of student departure from college.

The literature on persistence has focused on why students depart from an institution of higher education after matriculation. But not much is addressed in terms of how students navigate their way from high school to college in terms of the overall systems model. As Venezia, Callan, Finney, Kirst, and Usdan (2005) point out, "States need to make sure that what students are asked to know and do in high school is connected to postsecondary expectations—both in coursework and assessments. Currently, students in most states graduate from high school under one set of standards and face a disconnected and different set of expectations in college. Many students enter college unable to perform college-level work" (ix).

SUPA has been in existence since 1972, and claims to make the transition from high school to college easier. Not much is known about the effectiveness of SUPA on students who decide to pursue their undergraduate education at SU in terms of increasing their postsecondary achievement/outcomes. The primary purpose of this study is to examine the relationship between high school students' participation in SUPA and their subsequent commitment to early years in college (performance) and short-term retention and degree attainment (persistence).

Duffy (2008) observes that very few outcome studies have controlled for students' pre-college entry variables, and that of the few studies that have controlled for these variables, the results have been mixed. He recommends that since the interest in concurrent enrollment programs is growing tremendously, future empirical studies should focus on student outcomes as they are significant to further implementation of these programs. Swanson (2008) argues that "defining efficacy of dual enrollment, in terms of college persistence, academic achievement, and degree attainment, merits scholarly investigation" (9).

Limitations of the Study

This study is based on one single institution (SU) with its own concurrent enrollment program, Syracuse University Project Advance. Therefore, the generalizability of the results to the general population is limited. This is not a multi-institution study and does not control for any pre-entry college student characteristics, so isolating the effects as relating to participation in SUPA may be difficult. This study also does not control for possible differences in the quality of high schools and does not address the differences in populations between schools that offer SUPA courses in their curriculum. The non-SUPA group may have taken other concurrent enrollment courses from other programs, but this study does not address that issue.

Literature Overview

In 2003, Bailey and Karp's review of the literature revealed a lack of strong quantitative data supporting the proposed benefits of dual credit courses, making it difficult to assess the real effect of the dual credit programs. The Illinois Dual Credit Task Force (2008) has pointed out that without the data to explain the differences in students specific to their pre-college entry characteristics in the dual credit programs in which they participated, it is hard to validate claims of success by dual credit programs. Most research on dual credit is not published in refereed journals.

Many studies on dual enrollment programs refer to Adelman's 1999 study as "strong justification for establishing dual credit programs in high school," but with the rapid growth of these dual credit programs, concerns about these programs have also have increased as to whether the learning is truly at "college level" (Duffy 2008, 19).

Dutkowsky, Evensky, and Edmonds (2006) at Syracuse University examined the performance of high school students who took SU's one-semester micro/macroeconomics course through SUPA. They found that SUPA students "averaged nearly one percentage point higher than the AP/Honors economics group in the test for economic literacy and scored considerably better in fundamentals and international economics" (1). Their study also showed that "SUPA students scored over 4 points in the knowledge area, and exhibited better performance on application questions" (1). In addition, Dutkowsky, Evensky, and Edmonds (2009) examined both the AP and concurrent enrollment models and compared the expected benefits to AP students versus concurrent enrollment students. They concluded that evaluating the effectiveness of concurrent enrollment programs as well as a direct comparison of effects of AP versus concurrent enrollment is an important area for future research.

Kim (2008) provides a thorough literature review on terms and definitions (as these programs are referred to in many different ways; e.g., dual credit, dual enrollment, concurrent enrollment); how concurrent enrollment policies and implementation have evolved; connection between dual credit and technical preparation; types of students who enroll in concurrent enrollment programs; and the effect of dual credit participation on student outcomes in college. However, some of the studies Kim references do not control for pre-college entry characteristics, and he does not make reference to the huge body of research on persistence and performance.

Karp, Calcagno, Hughes, Jeong, and Bailey (2007) studied postsecondary achievement of dually enrolled students in the state of Florida and in New York City, and this study has been cited many times in the literature. They used nonexperimental, multiple regression statistical methods and found that Florida showed a positive relationship between concurrent enrollment programs and educational outcomes in college, whereas New York City showed negative impacts on both short-term and long-term outcomes after controlling for student demographics, prior achievement, and high school characteristics. The study did show evidence that dual enrollment programs do help a range of students in closing the gap from high school to college. These authors recommended that future research should determine program effectiveness by using control variables such as student background and motivation. Their study addressed the effectiveness of dual enrollment as a reform strategy for high schools and career and technical education. However, this study examined students in Florida who went on to community colleges and not a four-year private institution.

Similarly, Thompson and Rust (2007) followed AP students in college and compared their college GPA to that of other high-achieving students in natural science and English courses. Their sample size included forty-one students from a state-supported university based in the southern United States. They used a survey instrument with sixteen items pertaining to AP courses, English and natural science course grades, high school GPA, and ACT/SAT scores. They hypothesized that AP students would rate the benefits of their high school AP courses higher than the benefits of their general education courses, and the results supported this hypothesis. But their "findings contradicted expectations that AP students would earn significantly higher college grades when their grades were compared to those of other high-achieving students. Likewise AP students did not rate the benefit of their high school courses higher than did their high-achieving peers who did not take AP courses" (1). Their sample size was very small, so there could be issues of generalizability.

Duffy (2008) also studied whether significant differences existed in college students' performance and persistence between dual credit students, Advanced Placement students and the non-dual credit/Advanced Placement students while controlling for student pre-college entry attributes at a four-year public university in Tennessee. His results showed that when controlling for student pre-college entry attributes, no significant differences existed in student college persistence and performance outcomes among the respective student groups. Duffy found that "the only pre-college entry attribute that showed a significant relationship with college persistence and performance outcome measures in every regression model was the achievement composite variable: composite ACT/SAT, high school GPA, and high school rank" (v).

Klopfenstein and Thomas (2009) used rigorous regression analysis to investigate taking AP courses as a potential cause of early college success. The study focused on a group of Texas public school students who entered the Texas public universities directly after graduating from high school in May 1999. The data set was unique in that the authors included variables describing the students' non-AP curricular experience. This study showed that when students' non-AP curricular experiences were not controlled for, it led to positively biased AP coefficients. But when the researchers controlled for these factors they found no evidence that taking AP courses increased the likelihood of early college success beyond what was predicted by the non-AP curriculum for the average student, irrespective of race or socioeconomic status.

Even though Tinto (1987) stressed the connection between pre-college entry characteristics and persistence/performance, Duffy (2008) has noted that very few research studies pertaining to concurrent enrollment programs have controlled for pre-college entry characteristics. Duffy's results are consistent with Tinto's 1993 research in that although there is a significant relationship between pre-college entry attributes and persistence/performance in college, this relationship explains less than 5% of variation in outcomes in every regression model run in his study.

A larger, future study conducted by this researcher will determine whether significant differences exist in performance/persistence among the SUPA, AP, and non-SUPA/AP student groups when controlling for demographic and pre-college variables, as well as AP participation.

Methodology

In this study, two groups are compared:

1. Students attending SU who have taken at least one course through Project Advance

2. Students attending SU who have not taken any courses through Project Advance (non-SUPA)

Quantitative summarization of this data set is provided below in the subsection on data classification and definitions. A major emphasis is placed on the significance level for rejecting the null hypothesis that the groups being compared are equal. The comparisons between SUPA and non-SUPA are gross, but future studies will compare the SUPA only group, AP only group, both the SUPA only group and the AP only group, and the non-SUPA/AP group.

Extraction/Querying of Data

The Institutional Review Board (IRB) approval was obtained to access the data from Syracuse University's Student Records System (SRS), which are considered to be the university's "official records." All data pertaining to the samples are solely reliant on the accuracy of the university's student database and the information reported therein. The data for this study are maintained in the PeopleSoft enterprise-level records/transaction system and are made available through the university data warehouse (via querying and extraction). The SRS contains student academic performance records (transcript data), demographic information, and pre-college entry characteristics data related to high school performance and achievement, including credit received for AP and Project Advance sections of SU courses over a period of twelve years.

The question that arises here is whether has SUPA changed or remained the same over the twelve years represented by data in this study. With respect to the fundamental components such as teacher selection, site visits, research and evaluation, and seminars, not much has changed. However, many changes have occurred on the operational side during this period. For example:

• The program has streamlined its operations.

• The program's standardized financial assistance requirements have moved from paper-based applications to bubble applications to online applications.

• Initially high school teachers collected the fees, but now there is direct billing.

• In 2002, SUPA moved away from conducting sporadic workshops to offering a summer institute that brings teachers from all disciplines to campus for a two-week session.

• A student guide was created to provide information to students and parents about the program.

The researcher worked with the Office of Institutional Research and Assessment to extract student files from the SRS database. Any student identifiers (name, student ID number) were removed from the data set prior to its release for use in this study. The subjects were assigned a unique identification number for the purpose of this study, and their performance cannot be linked back to them because there are no identifying factors other than their race and gender.

Babbie (2004) noted that using existing/extant data creates problems of validity and reliability. This study handled validity challenges by ensuring that complete information for each variable is available for each student included in the study. When a frequency analysis was performed on the 30,846 students in the two groups, it was found that 4,682 students had missing data, and these students were not included in this study. It was determined that 26,164 students had valid values recorded in the SRS database for both independent and dependent variables.

The integrity of SU's enterprise-level student records/transaction system is maintained in three ways. First, the basic system infrastructure is built with technology that includes layers of redundancy to ensure that data are not lost or corrupted. Second, the system itself uses validation rules where appropriate to validate data entered into the system. Finally, business procedures in the schools and colleges within the university, the registrar's office, and in the IT support unit are designed to ensure that institutional data are entered, changed, or deleted only by authorized personnel. System security (including surrounding processes) is audited once a year.

Data Classification and Definitions

The data can be classified within these major categories:

1. Demographics (gender, race/ethnicity, financial aid need)

2. Admissions/pre-college achievement indicators (SAT Math, SAT Verbal, high school GPA, and merit rating, which is a score of 1–7 assigned by SU's Office of Admissions; since merit rating was an artifact of GPA and SAT scores it was decided to remove this variable from future regressions but to leave it in for this initial investigation)

3. College academic achievement indicators (subsequent course grades, GPAs)

4. Retention and attrition (dropout and graduation rates)

Since this chapter will primarily look at SUPA and college persistence/performance, the dataset includes only first-time higher education matriculants; it excludes transfers-in, as most of these students completed their first- and second-year coursework elsewhere and transfer course grades are generally not available; and it excludes spring matriculants, most of whom are transfers-in.

The analysis is based on individual student records (i.e., not on aggregate data). Appropriate methods are necessary so that the statistical procedures are not compromised by the largely different group sizes. SU course information for Project Advance sections is stored on system in the same way as main-campus courses and with the same level of detail including final grade (A–F); this facilitates comparisons of SUPA sections and main campus sections of courses. If a SUPA student becomes an undergraduate student at SU, information on their program of study and major is available, which in turn provides access to the courses taken and the grades achieved in the next sequence course, first semester and cumulative GPA, and short-term and long-term retention. If SUPA students do not seek admission into SU, then they are considered nonmatriculated students and are not included in this study. Certain variables in the multiple regressions (e.g., course grades, GPA) are quantitative, while others (persistence) are qualitative. Quantitative variables include SAT scores, high school GPA, college course grades and college GPA (GPA scale: $F = 0.0$; $A = 4.0$). Qualitative variables include SUPA participation, AP participation, course subject, demographics, admissions merit rating, financial aid need, and persistence category. Thus both linear and nonlinear regression modeling will be used in the larger, future studies. The qualitative variables will all be indicator (i.e., dummy) coded for regression modeling.

Descriptive Statistics

The data were analyzed using Statistical Package for the Social Sciences (SPSS) software. The sample was split into two groups:

1. Students who attended SU with SU credit earned through Project Advance only for any course, and

2. Students who attended SU with no SU credit through Project Advance.

Students who got a D or an F on the Project Advance course did not earn any credits. However, their grades are recorded on the SU transcript if they matriculate into SU.

Descriptive statistics for all key predictor (student characteristics) and outcome variables were computed to examine the differences among SU students who enrolled for SU courses through Project Advance when compared to students who did not enroll for SU courses through Project Advance in terms of both demographic variables and academic characteristics.

Measures of central tendency (mean, median, mode, standard of error mean), measures of dispersion (standard deviation, range, minimum/maximum value), measures of distribution (skew, kurtosis), and effect sizes were generated for all continuous variables. Frequency distribution and mode were generated for all categorical variables to count the number of times each score occurred on a single variable. The information from the SPSS output file was then exported into an Excel worksheet (Appendix 17.2) and both significant and practical effect sizes were calculated.

With the large sample used in this study, statistical significance can be found even when the differences or associations are weak. However, a significant result with a small effect size means that we can be confident that there is a meaningful difference or association.

One could argue that just because there is a statistical difference there need not be a practical significance. No causal claims are made. Correspondingly, effect sizes measure the strength of the relationship and/or the magnitude of the difference between levels of the independent variable with respect to the dependent variable. The attempt here is to understand whether these differences are due to reasons beyond a quirk of the sample. Effect sizes are used to alert the reader to the fact that an estimate of practical significance is being reported. Practical significance involves a judgment by the researcher and the end users. Hedrick, Bickman, and Rog (1993) define effect size "as the proportion of variance accounted for by the treatment or as the differences between a treatment and control group, measured in standard deviation units" (75). Also, Levin (1993) argued that that the p value shows the statistical significance, and effect size shows the practical significance. Levin urges readers that statistical significance (p value) and practical significance (effect size) are complimentary concepts rather than competing ones.

In order to judge the magnitude of effects, this study uses the following diagnostic method to calculate effect size (ES):

$$ES = (SUPA \ Mean - non\text{-}SUPA \ mean) \ / \ (non\text{-}SUPA \ mean)$$

TABLE 17.1

Student Characteristic Variables

Student Characteristic Variables (IV)	Dependent Variables (DV)
Race/Ethnicity (nominal variable) • Asian Pacific Hawaiian • Black/African American • Hispanic/Latino • Native American • Non-resident alien • White • Other (Multiple, Unknown)	Drop Out Rate • 1st year • 2nd year
Gender (nominal, dichotomous variables) • Female • Male	Graduate within • Four years • Five years • Six years
High School Academic Performance • SAT Math • SAT Verbal • High School GPA • Merit Rating 1–7 (1 being best. Assigned by the Office of Admissions to each student upon receipt of complete application)	College GPA (interval variable) • 1st Semester GPA • 1st Year cum GPA • 2nd Year cum GPA
Financial Need • Did not apply for aid • Applied, but no need for aid • Low need for aid • Medium need for aid • High need for aid	Course Grade** • In subsequent course (in a two-level course) This is not included in this data set yet. Is used for a future study

A positive sign means that the SUPA mean is higher and a negative sign means that the non-SUPA mean is higher. The purpose of this diagnostic method was to find out if there were any meaningful differences and if the differences were even worth noting. However, this study takes into consideration that this diagnostic method is more subjective relative to statistical significance.

Table 17.1 lists a set of variables (available on the SU database) that are compared between the two subgroups. They are classified into the two categories:

- Student Characteristic variables (predictor)
- Dependent variables (outcome)

More complete descriptions of these variables are noted in Appendix 17.1.

Analysis

The effect sizes evaluated in the context of this study are reported below. Note that the interpretation of the effect sizes does include some subjective judgment: to determine benchmarks for standardized differences between means, one must ask whether the value of the effect size estimate is trivial, small, medium, large, or gargantuan. The answer really depends on the context of the research. In some contexts a **d** of .20 would be considered small but not trivial, in others it would be considered very large. According to Cohen (1998) the significance levels are:

- Small (but not trivial) Effect Size: .2 to .49
- Medium Effect Size: .5 to .79
- Large Effect Size: .8 and higher

The findings presented in the sections below use the significance levels described by Cohen. Effect sizes that are significant are indicated in bold. Statistical significance (Z statistic) is indicated by **(S)** if significant, and by (NS) if not significant.

Race/Ethnicity

Race and ethnicity, as defined by the United States Census Bureau, "are self-identification data items in which residents pick the race or races with which they closely identify." In this study, the SUPA group has a higher representation of White students when compared to the non-SUPA group, (74% SUPA, 66% non-SUPA). Conversely, SUPA has lower proportions of African American (3% SUPA, 6% non-SUPA), Asian American (7% SUPA, 8% non-SUPA), and Hispanic/Latino (3% SUPA, 6% non-SUPA) students. Very few (<1%) SUPA participants are Native American. The effect sizes are:

- Asian/Hawaiian: −0.035 (NS −0.352)
- White: 0.117 **(S 6.067)**
- Black/African American: −0.465 **(S −5.501)**
- Hispanic/Latino: −0.435 **(S −4.621)**
- Native American: −0.088 (NS −0.210)

Gender

The SUPA group has a higher representation of female students (62% SUPA, 56% non-SUPA). The effect sizes are:

- Female effect size: 0.093 **(S 3.679)**
- Male effect size: −0.120 **(S −3.679)**

This is a meaningful difference, as this study suggests that fewer males participate in SUPA. In 2005, *USA Today* reported that nationally the male/female ratio on campus was 43/57 (a reversal in the trend from the 1960s) (Marklein 2005). These effect sizes would be of concern if one were looking for gender parity, as high schools may serve as the ideal place for addressing the issue of getting male students in the college conduit. Of course, another possibility could be that the male students are enrolling for other accelerated courses like AP instead of SU courses through Project Advance. These demographic data are comparable to other concurrent enrollment programs and AP programs.

According to Klopfenstein (2003), females in particular tend to take advantage of concurrent enrollment programs, and though this is consistent with the gender gap and college graduate rates, not much is known about the reasons behind these trends.

Financial Aid Need

Financial need is an indicator of a student's general socioeconomic status. In general, it is calculated as the cost of attending college minus the expected family financial contribution. It is an approximate expression of the amount of financial aid needed to "close the gap." There are five categories of financial need that can be rank-ordered from low to high:

1. no financial aid application
2. application, but no need
3. low financial need
4. medium financial need
5. high financial need

By comparing the proportions of SUPA and non-SUPA students who fall into each of the five categories, we can get a sense of similarity or differences between these two groups in terms of financial need. Category 1 (no application) contained 18% of the SUPA students versus 28% of non-SUPA students (effect size: 0.35). On the other hand, the top category (5, high need) contained 55% of the SUPA students versus 44% of non-SUPA students (effect size: 0.25). Based on this pattern, one can conclude that on average, SUPA students have greater financial need than non-SUPA students. Proportions of filers who had no application for need, low financial need, or medium financial need were comparable for the SUPA and non-SUPA groups. The effect sizes are:

- No financial aid application filed: −0.350 **(S −8.564)**
- Applied, but no need for aid: −0.084 (NS −1.183)
- Low need for aid: 0.043 (NS 0.395)
- Medium need for aid: −0.054 (NS −0.540)
- High need for aid: 0.252 **(S 7.547)**

There is evidence from previous studies that these concurrent enrollment programs are not being offered to students from lower socioeconomic groups; according to the National Center for Education Statistics, schools with the highest minority enrollment were the least likely to offer dual enrollment courses when compared to schools with lower minority enrollment—58% to 78% (Krueger 2006). Some policymakers believe that these programs, therefore, are not accessible to low-income students. It is also possible that minority students have lower GPAs and, because of the guidelines for admission, may be less prevalent in SUPA. But SUPA assures us that this decision is left up to the guidance counselors. Students are allowed to audit the SU course and take the class for college-level experience and just a high school grade. Because students in this case are auditing the course, the grade does not then transfer to SU.

Going into this study the assumption was that most of the SUPA students would be from the upper socioeconomic status (SES) group. However, the effect size for financial need in this study suggests otherwise; the effect size of 0.252 for high need for financial aid indicates that students who enroll in SUPA courses and then subsequently enroll at SU do come from lower-income families and have a high need for financial aid. This finding is in alignment with SU's mission to provide exceptional support for a diverse population.

Also, the effect size for students who applied for financial aid but had no need for aid was −0.350, which is also meaningful and practical, as colleges and universities do see the multiple benefits of admitting students who can pay full tuition.

Admissions/Pre-College

Nationally, the debate continues on whether our high schools are preparing students adequately to compete in higher education and fulfill their requirements successfully to graduate. Both high schools and colleges are interested in tracking the effects of high school interventions on student performance in the early semesters of college. SUPA is designed to help students who are planning to attend a college/university; the belief is that SUPA bridges the gap from high school to university by helping students successfully complete some academic requirements early, preparing them for the rigor of university study.

This study finds that SUPA and non-SUPA students had the following pre-college academic credentials:

SAT Math (comparable scores)
Mean of 597 for non-SUPA group
Mean of 599 for SUPA group

SAT Verbal (comparable scores)
Mean of 576 for non-SUPA group
Mean of 580 for SUPA group

The effect sizes are:
- SAT Math effect size: 0.004 (NS 1.173)
- SAT Verbal effect size: 0.008 **(S 2.145)**

The effect sizes are small in both SAT Math and Verbal. However, SAT Verbal is statistically significant. This suggests that the SUPA group is being compared to matched non-SUPA students. This suggests that SUPA group is representative of the population from which it was drawn, thus satisfying one of the assumptions of multiple regressions in the future studies.

Merit Rating

Merit rating is a single indicator of a student's general level of academic preparation for college. Assigned by SU's Office of Admissions and based largely on high school GPA and test scores (e.g., SAT), merit rating takes a value from 1 (top) to 7 (low). By comparing the proportions of SUPA and non-SUPA students who fall into each of the seven categories, we can get a sense of similarity or differences between these two groups in terms of academic preparation. Of the seven categories, three showed significant differences of proportions of SUPA and non-SUPA students.

A merit rating value of 2 was assigned to 20% of the SUPA students versus 15% of non-SUPA students. A merit rating value of 3 was assigned to 17% of the SUPA students versus 13% of non-SUPA students. Conversely, the bottom merit rating value of 7 was assigned to 19% of the SUPA students versus 29% of non-SUPA students. For these three merit rating categories, effect sizes ranged from 0.26 to 0.37. This suggests that on average, SUPA students have greater academic preparation than non-SUPA students (the top category, 1, contained 8% of the SUPA students versus 7% of the non-SUPA students, though this difference is not significant).

The effect sizes are:
- Merit rating 1 effect size: 0.107 (NS 0.975)
- Merit rating 2 effect size: 0.318 **(S 4.079)**
- Merit rating 3 effect size: 0.260 **(S 3.192)**
- Merit rating 4 effect size: 0.137 (NS 1.632)
- Merit rating 5 effect size: 0.081 (NS 0.899)

- Merit rating 6 effect size: −0.078 (NS −0.917)
- Merit rating 7 effect size: −0.370 **(S −9.483)**

Merit ratings 2, 3, and 7 are statistically significant and have meaningful effect sizes, too (merit rating 2 being the highest). Understandably, this suggests that SUPA is attracting high caliber students into the university but not the best. Based on their merit rating, SU also provides financial scholarships to entering first year students regardless of financial need, so many SUPA students receive merit scholarships. These scholarships are renewable each year as long as the student maintains a minimum GPA of 2.75 on a 4.0 scale. Based on the kinds of students enrolling in SU courses through Project Advance, SU can improve its retention/graduation rates as these students continue to strive for higher levels. The post-graduate student survey (2005 high school students in their senior year of college) results show evidence of this. Some quotes from students are as follows:

From what I could remember the project advance program made the transition from high school work to college level work a lot easier because my teacher made us ready for the workload. Additionally the program allowed for greater self-expression and greater freedom. Overall I know what was expected from me as I transitioned in my first year of college!

I appreciate the opportunity you give high school students to take a college level course and earn credit before attending a university. It was a unique experience and I wish I had taken advantage of the other SUPA classes offered at Guilderland.

I believe more courses should be available for High School students to take at the college level. The courses were challenging but helped to prepare me for the college classroom experience. Offering courses at a highly reduced rate for all students helps promote an equal opportunity for higher education.

I enjoyed the program very much. The most valuable aspect of the course for me was the ten page synthesis paper I was required to write. I hadn't written a paper that length in high school and didn't know how to utilize sources in writing a research paper. In college I chose to double major in music (which I had expected to do) and in history as well. My major in history has required many, many twenty (and longer) page research papers that I was already prepared to do and knew how to do as a result of doing sociological research for the Syracuse University program in high school. Now I will go on to pursue a master's degree in musicology, which will also require heavy research and writing, and feel that I am well prepared. The SUPA program is an excellent preparation tool for college level research papers.

High School Grade Point Average

High School GPA is a measure of a student's achievement in high school, which is calculated by dividing the total number of grade points received by the total number of credits attempted. In this study, SUPA students were found to have a higher GPA than non-SUPA students—on a scale of 0–4.0, the mean of SUPA students is 3.72 versus the mean of non-SUPA students, which is 3.52. The effect size is:

• High School GPA effect size: 0.057 **(S 17.773)**

Tinto's research (1987) determined that students' educational expectations correspond to their "goals and commitments" and if students successfully complete SU courses offered through Project Advance in high school and simultaneously form relationships with college faculty while in high school they may be more inclined to continue in college. High school students who take SUPA courses have access to SU faculty for consultation on projects and mentoring, if needed. University faculty review papers, review tests, and visit each class during the semester to ensure that the grading standards applied are consistent with those applied in the same courses on campus. Non-SUPA students who matriculate into SU may not have similar opportunities or exposure to SU faculty.

College Academics

Grade point averages at Syracuse University are based on a 4.0 scale. The GPAs for both groups are comparable, but SUPA students consistently show a slightly higher GPA than non-SUPA students.

	SUPA mean	*Non-SUPA mean*
First-semester GPA	3.06	3.05
First-year cum GPA	3.10	3.06
Second-year cum GPA	3.13	3.11

The effect sizes are:
- Historical Cum GPA (first-semester GPA) Fall Year 1: 0.003 (NS 0.590)
- Historical Cum GPA (first-year cum GPA) Spring Year 1: 0.015 (S 2.683)
- Historical Cum GPA (second-year cum GPA) Spring Year 2: 0.007 (NS 1.399)

Most important, if students use their transfer credits to get exemptions from entry-level college courses they could reduce the time and money necessary to finish their undergraduate degree. Added to the economic benefit, the students would get more time to take other courses thereby advancing their studies even further. They also could take some electives that they are interested in. The post-graduate student survey (2005 high school students in their senior year of college) results show evidence of this as follows:

Having course credits from Syracuse University allowed me to be able to take courses I wanted to take because I was not concerned with having to fulfill required credits. The psychology course was extremely helpful because I took three more psych courses at Hartwick which made me confident in the classes and have a better background in the field. I highly suggest that students take advantage of this program because I had such a great experience with it.

Extremely helpful course, especially to develop college level writing abilities. Also believe that it helped with the Analytical writing section on the GREs. Counted as the required freshman English course as well as another English course at Gettysburg, which allowed me to have 2 transfer credits. This ultimately led me to go abroad 2 semesters rather than 1. An excellent program I would highly recommend to other high school students.

Retention

Dropout Rates

Comparisons of dropout rates after the first and second years of college, and four-, five-, and six-year graduation rates, are suitable characterizations of the differences in academic success between SUPA and non-SUPA students. All five-year rate comparisons were statistically significant and seemed to favor the SUPA group. Rates for SUPA and non-SUPA students, respectively, were: 7% versus 9% (one-year dropout), 11% versus 14% (two-year dropout), 77% versus 71% (four-year graduation), 84% versus 81% (five-year graduation), 87% versus 82% (six-year graduation). This finding suggests SUPA students persist and graduate at a rate higher than non-SUPA students. The effect sizes are:

- Second year: −0.220 **(S −2.646)**
- Third year: −0.214 **(S −3.028)**
- Fifth year: −0.197 **(S −2.737)**
- Sixth year: −0.172 **(S −1.995)**

Even though both effect sizes and Z-values are significant here, no causal claims are being made. The effect sizes suggest that SUPA students are less likely to drop out of college when compared to the non-SUPA students. This is very important as attrition affects the individual student from a personal and social point of view and also hurts the university's reputation. Also, in times of limited financial and general resources it is a direct loss of tuition income for a university.

It is important to note here that some students may be entirely dropping out of the academic system, while others may be transferring to another institution for various reasons. This study does not take in to account why a student dropped out of SU. It is possible that these observed and predictable differences are due to other factors that resulted in some students being in SUPA and others not being in SUPA because of socioeconomic status; parents' education; and/or family income. These differences will be examined in a future study using multiple regressions.

Stillman (2009) noted that graduating from college has benefits such as "less dependence on public assistance, increased tax revenues, greater civic participation, and access to higher income jobs," and that when a student drops out of college it is looked upon as "wasted talent" not only for the student but for the society as a whole. It is also well known that the gap in the capacity for earning between those who graduate from high school and those who graduate from college is sizeable. The Bureau of Labor Statistics (2010) reported that an educated individual is more likely to receive higher earnings and lower unemployment rates. The agency reported that as of February 2010, the unemployment rate for high school students with no college was 10.5%, compared to college graduates at 5.0%. The median weekly earnings in 2008 for high school graduates was $453, while for students with a bachelor's degree it was $1,102. Also, if students drop out of the education system, society as a whole faces the burden of providing public assistance at a later date.

Graduation Rates

The SUPA group consistently shows a higher rate of graduation in all three years at which rates are assessed (Table 17.2). Once again, no causal claims are being made—just correlational. Although the effect sizes are small if one looks at the means, the SUPA students have a higher percentage of both persistence and graduation rates, suggesting that SUPA could be providing a positive environment in high schools that helps students transition into the college environment and persist until graduation.

High schools track whether their curricula are adequately preparing their students for the rigor of college courses. The gap that exists between high school teachers' expectations and the expectations of college faculty explains some of the attrition from colleges and universities (Achieve, Inc. 2008.)

Previous research studies have also found that positive experiences in concurrent enrollment programs may bring about a change in a student's attitude and reduce the chances of attrition (Swanson 2008). The U.S. Department of Education (2010) claims that earning college credits before matriculation into a college or university will reduce the time

TABLE 17.2

Effect Size SUPA

	SUPA rate	*Non-SUPA rate*	*Effect Size*
Five-year	77%	71%	0.084 **(S 3.702)**
Six-year	84%	81%	0.041 **(S 2.112)**
Seven-year	87%	82%	0.063 **(S 3.074)**

to degree attainment, noting that the average time to graduate with no credits earned in high school is 4.65 years when compared to students who have earned nine or more credits who graduate in 4.25 years. This study could identify SUPA students' likelihood of accumulating credits, entering SU, and graduating with a bachelor's degree in less than 4.65 years. As Duffy (2008) points out, most of these concurrent enrollment programs have been established for the purpose of increasing access to higher education through reducing college costs by reducing the time to graduate, and also to increase college enrollments and revenue. Using Tinto's model of student departure, we understand that academics and social integration are core constructs, and that pre-entry college characteristics do impact a student's commitment to an institution and commitment to graduate from that institution.

Relevance for Theory and Practice

Pascarella (1982) noted that often theories are viewed as abstract and difficult to understand, and not really applicable to a college's situation. Studying the relationships between SUPA and college performance and persistence outcomes using formal models, detailed rich data, and robust statistical methods will help high school administrators and faculty to put into practice more effective concurrent enrollment programs in the best interest of students, parents, institutions, and society.

The relevance of this study becomes apparent, given the tremendous increase in SUPA enrollment from the 1970s through the present and the lack of research on the effectiveness of SUPA on student performance and persistence at SU. The findings from this and future studies will help align high school outcomes to SU's expectations and help students assess their own college readiness and their subsequent success at SU.

Conclusion

This study examined student performance and persistence outcomes among SUPA and non-SUPA college students *without* controlling for pre-entry college characteristics. SUPA course enrollment draws from students who average a GPA of B, and Sadler and Tai (2007) note that if this self-selection is ignored the outcome for SUPA course taking may be overestimated.

In summary, the results in this study without controlling for any confounding variables suggest a positive relationship of SUPA to financial need, merit rating, and retention. However, this does not rule out rival explanations, as other confounding variables were not controlled. SUPA also had a higher representation of White females than other demographic groups in the program. SUPA students have greater financial need compared with non-SUPA students, contrary to the belief that only affluent students are given the opportunity to enroll for SUPA courses. With regard to test scores, SUPA students had a higher mean for both SAT Math and SAT Verbal. Merit Ratings 2, 3, and 7 are statistically significant and had meaningful effect sizes, too. GPA for both groups was comparable, however, SUPA students show a slightly higher GPA than non-SUPA students. This study again suggests that SUPA students were less likely to drop out in the first two years of college and also had a higher rate of graduation in the three years assessed.

Whatever the findings of a larger, future study, all research on concurrent enrollment programs, as Duffy (2008) suggests, should be seen as a step forward in understanding that concurrent enrollment programs have become a viable piece of higher education in terms of planning and research. Also, SUPA can utilize the findings from this study and future studies to improve/examine their policies, procedures, and operations.

The next step will be to assess the relationship of SUPA and AP participation controlling student attributes including demographic, college pre-entry academic characteristics, and financial need variables. Multiple regression analyses will be used to examine and estimate quantitative relationships between collegiate academic persistence and performance (i.e., the dependent variables) and pertinent control (i.e., independent variables).

Given that the independent variables are attributes that are not subject to manipulation, the research approach going forward will be nonexperimental. The longitudinal nature of the data set will capture, and let us control for, demographic, pre-entry, and financial student characteristics.

Appendix 17.1. List of Variables

TABLE 17.3A

List of Demographic Variables

Variable	Definition of Variable
ID	Unique identifier of student
CohortCode	Student Records System (SRS) code for fall entering cohort
Cohort	Literal fall entering cohort
CohortFall1997ind	Indicator for Fall 1997 entering cohort; 1 = Fall 1997 cohort; 0 = otherwise
CohortFall1998ind	Indicator for Fall 1998 entering cohort; 1 = Fall 1998 cohort; 0 = otherwise
CohortFall1999ind	Indicator for Fall 1999 entering cohort; 1 = Fall 1999 cohort; 0 = otherwise
CohortFall2000ind	Indicator for Fall 2000 entering cohort; 1 = Fall 2000 cohort; 0 = otherwise
CohortFall2001ind	Indicator for Fall 2001 entering cohort; 1 = Fall 2001 cohort; 0 = otherwise
CohortFall2002ind	Indicator for Fall 2002 entering cohort; 1 = Fall 2002 cohort; 0 = otherwise
CohortFall2003ind	Indicator for Fall 2003 entering cohort; 1 = Fall 2003 cohort; 0 = otherwise
CohortFall2004ind	Indicator for Fall 2004 entering cohort; 1 = Fall 2004 cohort; 0 = otherwise
CohortFall2005ind	Indicator for Fall 2005 entering cohort; 1 = Fall 2005 cohort; 0 = otherwise
CohortFall2006ind	Indicator for Fall 2006 entering cohort; 1 = Fall 2006 cohort; 0 = otherwise
CohortFall2007ind	Indicator for Fall 2007 entering cohort; 1 = Fall 2007 cohort; 0 = otherwise
Femaleind	Indicator for female 1 = female; 0 = otherwise
Maleind	Indicator for male 1 = male; 0 = otherwise
Unspecifiedind	Indicator for race/ethnicity Unknown 1 = student did not identify race/ethnicity; 0 = Otherwise

List of Demographic Variables *(Continued)*

Variable	Definition of Variable
BlackAfAmerind	Indicator for race/ethnicity Black/African American 1 = Black; 0 = otherwise
NativeAmericanAKNativeind	Indicator for race/ethnicity Native American/AK Native 1 = Native American; 0 = otherwise
AsianPIHawaiianind	Indicator for race/ethnicity Asian/Pacific Islander 1 = Asian/Pacific Islander; 0 = otherwise
HispanicLatinoind	Indicator for race/ethnicity Hispanic 1 = Hispanic; 0 = otherwise
Whiteind	Indicator for race/ethnicity White 1 = White; 0 = otherwise
NonResAlienind	Indicator for race/ethnicity non-resident alien 1 = nonresident alien; 0 = otherwise
PersistingFallYear2ind	Indicator for persisting as of fall of second year derived from SRS 1 = Yes; 0 = No
DropoutFallYear2ind	Indicator for drop out as of fall of second year derived from SRS 1 = Yes; 0 = No

TABLE 17.3B

Persistence and Graduation Rates

Variable	Definition of Variable
PersistingFallYear3ind	Indicator for persisting as of fall of third year derived from SRS 1 = Yes; 0 = No
DropoutFallYear3ind	Indicator for drop out as of fall of third year derived from SRS 1 = Yes; 0 = No
PersistenceFallYear4	Indicator for persisting as of fall of fourth year derived from SRS 1 = Yes; 0 = No
GraduatedFallYear5ind	Indicator for graduated as of fall of fifth year derived from SRS 1 = Yes; 0 = No
DropoutFallYear5ind	Indicator for drop out as of fall of fifth year derived from SRS 1 = Yes; 0 = No
GraduatedFallYear6ind	Indicator for graduated as of fall of sixth year derived from SRS 1 = Yes; 0 = No
DropoutFallYear6ind	Indicator for drop out as of fall of sixth year derived from SRS 1 = Yes; 0 = No
GraduatedFallYear7ind	Indicator for graduated as of fall of seventh year derived from SRS 1 = Yes; 0 = No
DropoutFallYear7ind	Indicator for drop out as of fall of seventh year derived from SRS 1 = Yes; 0 = No
HistoricalSemGPAFallYear1	Semester GPA fall of first year not adjusted for retaken courses; derived from SRS—on a 4 point scale 0–4
HistoricalSemGPASpringYear1	Semester GPA spring of first year not adjusted for retaken courses; derived from SRS—on a 4 point scale 0–4

TABLE 17.3B

Persistence and Graduation Rates *(Continued)*

Variable	*Definition of Variable*
HistoricalSemGPAFallYear2	Semester GPA fall of second year not adjusted for retaken courses; derived from SRS—on a 4 point scale 0–4
HistoricalSemGPASpringYear2	Semester GPA spring of second year not adjusted for retaken courses; derived from SRS—on a 4 point scale 0–4
HistoricalSemGPAFallYear3	Semester GPA fall of third year not adjusted for retaken courses; derived from SRS—on a 4 point scale 0–4
HistoricalSemGPASpringYear3	Semester GPA spring of third year not adjusted for retaken courses; derived from SRS—on a 4 point scale 0–4
HistoricalSemGPAFallYear4	Semester GPA fall of fourth year not adjusted for retaken courses; derived from SRS—on a 4 point scale 0–4
HistoricalSemGPASpringYear4	Semester GPA spring of fourth year not adjusted for retaken courses; derived from SRS—on a 4 point scale 0–4
HistoricalSemGPAFallYear5	Semester GPA fall of fifth year not adjusted for retaken courses; derived from SRS—on a 4 point scale 0–4
HistoricalSemGPASpringYear5	Semester GPA spring of fifth year not adjusted for retaken courses; derived from SRS—on a 4 point scale 0–4

TABLE 17.3C

Historical GPA

Variable	*Definition of Variable*
HistoricalSemGPAFallYear6	Semester GPA fall of sixth year not adjusted for retaken courses; derived from SRS—on a 4 point scale 0–4
HistoricalSemGPASpringYear6	Semester GPA spring of sixth year not adjusted for retaken courses; derived from SRS—on a 4 point scale 0–4
HistoricalSemGPAFallYear7	Semester GPA fall of seventh year not adjusted for retaken courses; derived from SRS—on a 4 point scale 0–4
HistoricalCumGPAFallYear1	Cumulative GPA fall of first year not adjusted for retaken courses; derived from SRS—on a 4 point scale 0–4
HistoricalCumGPASpringYear1	Cumulative GPA spring of first year not adjusted for retaken courses; derived from SRS—on a 4 point scale 0–4
HistoricalCumGPAFallYear2	Cumulative GPA fall of second year not adjusted for retaken courses; derived from SRS—on a 4 point scale 0–4
HistoricalCumGPASpringYear2	Cumulative GPA spring of second year not adjusted for retaken courses; derived from SRS—on a 4 point scale 0–4
HistoricalCumGPAFallYear3	Cumulative GPA fall of third year not adjusted for retaken courses; derived from SRS—on a 4 point scale 0–4
HistoricalCumGPASpringYear3	Cumulative GPA spring of third year not adjusted for retaken courses; derived from SRS—on a 4 point scale 0–4
HistoricalCumGPAFallYear4	Cumulative GPA fall of fourth year not adjusted for retaken courses; derived from SRS—on a 4 point scale 0–4
HistoricalCumGPASpringYear4	Cumulative GPA spring of fourth year not adjusted for retaken courses; derived from SRS—on a 4 point scale 0–4

TABLE 17.3C

Historical GPA *(Continued)*

Variable	*Definition of Variable*
HistoricalCumGPAFallYear5	Cumulative GPA fall of fifth year not adjusted for retaken courses; derived from SRS—on a 4 point scale 0–4
HistoricalCumGPASpringYear5	Cumulative GPA spring of fifth year not adjusted for retaken courses; derived from SRS—on a 4 point scale 0–4
HistoricalCumGPAFallYear6	Cumulative GPA fall of sixth year not adjusted for retaken courses; derived from SRS—on a 4 point scale 0–4
HistoricalCumGPASpringYear6	Cumulative GPA spring of sixth year not adjusted for retaken courses; derived from SRS—on a 4 point scale 0–4
HistoricalCumGPAFallYear7	Cumulative GPA fall of seventh year not adjusted for retaken courses; derived from SRS—on a 4 point scale 0–4
NoFinancialAidAppInd	Indicator for FAFSA not filed for first year 1 = FAFSA not filed; 0 = otherwise
NoFinancialNeedInd	1 = FAFSA form filed but zero dollar need; 0 = otherwise
LowFinancialNeedInd	1 = FAFSA form filed and first tercile (lowest) dollar need; 0 = otherwise
MidFinancialNeedInd	1 = FAFSA form filed and second tercile (middle) dollar need; 0 = otherwise

TABLE 17.3D

Socioeconomic Status

Variable	*Definition of Variable*
HighFinancialNeedind	1 = FAFSA form filed and third tercile (highest) dollar need; 0 = otherwise
MeritRating1ind	1 = merit rating of one (highest rating); 0 = otherwise
MeritRating2ind	1 = merit rating of two; 0 = otherwise
MeritRating3ind	1 = merit rating of three; 0 = otherwise
MeritRating4ind	1 = merit rating of four; 0 = otherwise
MeritRating5ind	1 = merit rating of five; 0 = otherwise
MeritRating6ind	1 = merit rating of six; 0 = otherwise
MeritRating7ind	1 = merit rating of seven—lowest rating outside of SSS/HEOP; 0 = otherwise
MeritRatingHEOPind	1 = merit rating of HEOP (Higher Education Opportunity Program); 0 = otherwise
MeritRatingSSSind	1 = merit rating of SSS (Student Support Services); 0 = otherwise
MeritRatingNew1to9	1xMR1ind+2xMR2ind+3xMR3ind+4xMR4ind+5xMR5ind+6xMR6ind+7xMR7ind+8xMR8ind+9xMR9ind
MeritRatingNew1to7	1xMR1ind+2xMR2ind+3xMR3ind+4xMR4ind+5xMR5ind+6xMR6ind+7xMR7ind
SATVerbal	SAT Verbal zero to 800
SATMath	SAT Math zero to 800
ACT	ACT combined
HighSchoolGPA	High School GPA off application HS transcript (on a scale of 1.16 to 4.33)
HS_ClassRank	High School Class Rank
HS_ClassSize	High School Class Size
HS_ClassPercentile	High School Class Percentile
TestCreditsIndicator	1 = AP coursework credits transferred to SU; 0 = otherwise
TotalTestCredits	Total number of AP coursework credits transferred to SU
PACreditIndicator	1 = PA coursework; 0 = otherwise
NumberOfPACredits	Total number of SUPA coursework credits

314

Appendix 17.2. Statistical Analysis of SUPA versus Non-SUPA Z Tests

TABLE 17.3E

Statistical Analysis I of SUPA versus Non-SUPA Z Tests

Non-SUPA	Non-SUPA N	Non-SUPA Mean	Non-SUPA SD	SUPA	SUPA N	SUPA Mean	SUPA SD	Z Numerator
AsianPIHawaiianind	24943	0.08	0.27	AsianPIHawaiianind	1221	0.07	0.26	−0.00270
BlackAfAmerind	24943	0.06	0.25	BlackAfAmerind	1221	0.03	0.18	−0.02995
CohortFall1997ind	24943	0.04	0.19	CohortFall1997ind	1221	0.01	0.12	−0.02376
CohortFall1998ind	24943	0.05	0.21	CohortFall1998ind	1221	0.01	0.12	−0.03202
CohortFall1999ind	24943	0.05	0.21	CohortFall1999ind	1221	0.01	0.12	−0.03182
CohortFall2000ind	24943	0.05	0.21	CohortFall2000ind	1221	0.01	0.11	−0.03502
CohortFall2001ind	24943	0.09	0.29	CohortFall2001ind	1221	0.08	0.27	−0.01179
CohortFall2002ind	24943	0.11	0.31	CohortFall2002ind	1221	0.11	0.32	0.00926
CohortFall2003ind	24943	0.10	0.29	CohortFall2003ind	1221	0.09	0.29	−0.00357
CohortFall2004ind	24943	0.10	0.29	CohortFall2004ind	1221	0.11	0.31	0.01107
CohortFall2005ind	24943	0.12	0.32	CohortFall2005ind	1221	0.14	0.34	0.02079
CohortFall2006ind	24943	0.11	0.31	CohortFall2006ind	1221	0.14	0.34	0.03025
CohortFall2007ind	24943	0.10	0.31	CohortFall2007ind	1221	0.16	0.36	0.05315
DropoutFallYear2ind	24943	0.09	0.29	DropoutFallYear2ind	1221	0.07	0.26	−0.01997
DropoutFallYear3ind	22317	0.14	0.34	DropoutFallYear3ind	1076	0.11	0.31	−0.02949
DropoutFallYear5ind	17043	0.19	0.39	DropoutFallYear5ind	716	0.15	0.36	−0.03783
DropoutFallYear6ind	14150	0.18	0.38	DropoutFallYear6ind	549	0.15	0.36	−0.03106
DropoutFallYear7ind	11750	0.17	0.38	DropoutFallYear7ind	418	0.12	0.32	−0.05750
Femaleind	24943	0.56	0.50	Femaleind	1221	0.62	0.49	0.05255

Z Denominator	Z-statistic	Conc.	O. Sort	Effect Size	Effect Size Name	Effect size	Effect Size Name
0.00766774	−0.35266593	ns	1	−0.010261057	Less than Small	−0.035388054	Less than small
0.005444181	−5.501043833	SIG	2	−0.140045757	Less than Small	−0.465426684	Less than small
0.003564746	−6.66608789	SIG	3	−0.154475696	Less than Small	−0.630551344	Less than small
0.003607055	−8.877531135	SIG	4	−0.196098073	Less than Small	−0.696961836	Less than small
0.003606043	−8.824433448	SIG	5	−0.195130573	Less than Small	−0.695633886	Less than small
0.003428259	−10.21592805	SIG	6	−0.217195429	Small	−0.740317745	Less than small
0.008064593	−1.462384899	ns	7	−0.041692979	Less than Small	−0.125873452	Less than small
0.009326732	0.992823831	ns	8	0.029592703	Less than Small	0.087853648	Less than small
0.008470351	−0.421374029	ns	9	−0.01225701	Less than Small	−0.03745318	Less than small
0.009055011	1.222497387	ns	10	0.036624102	Less than Small	0.115046751	Less than small
0.010044224	2.069716165	SIG	11	0.062620205	Less than Small	0.1792369	Less than small
0.010029531	3.016119528	SIG	12	0.092755186	Less than Small	0.283979056	Small
0.010623028	5.003087649	SIG	13	0.158317661	Less than Small	0.506560613	Large
0.007547413	−2.646211959	SIG	14	−0.073595721	Less than Small	−0.220914848	Less than small
0.009735578	−3.02886459	SIG	15	−0.090115149	Less than Small	−0.214777437	Less than small
0.013818171	−2.737382414	SIG	16	−0.100292457	Less than Small	−0.197567273	Less than small
0.015565993	−1.995475075	SIG	17	−0.083800168	Less than Small	−0.172158616	Less than small
0.016137972	−3.562933671	SIG	18	−0.16385546	Less than Small	−0.329083125	Less than small
0.014280451	3.679650262	SIG	19	0.10692645	Less than Small	0.093413257	Less than small

TABLE 17.3F

Statistical Analysis II of SUPA versus Non-SUPA Z Tests

Non-SUPA	Non-SUPA N	Non-SUPA Mean	Non-SUPA SD	SUPA	SUPA N	SUPA Mean	SUPA SD	Z Numerator
Graduated FallYear 5ind	17043	0.71	0.46	Graduated FallYear 5ind	716	0.77	0.42	0.05996
Graduated FallYear 6ind	14150	0.81	0.39	Graduated FallYear 6ind	549	0.84	0.37	0.03369
Graduated FallYear 7ind	11750	0.82	0.38	Graduated FallYear 7ind	418	0.87	0.34	0.05166
High Financial Needind	24943	0.44	0.50	High Financial Needind	1221	0.55	0.50	0.11011
High SchoolGPA	24943	3.52	0.44	High SchoolGPA	1221	3.72	0.38	0.20087
Hispanic Latinoind	24943	0.06	0.23	Hispanic Latinoind	1221	0.03	0.17	−0.02392
Historical CumGPA FallYear1	24836	3.05	0.68	Historical CumGPA FallYear1	1216	3.14	0.56	0.08664
Historical CumGPA FallYear2	20415	3.09	0.56	Historical CumGPA FallYear2	1012	3.13	0.53	0.04284
Historical CumGPA FallYear3	17057	3.12	0.51	Historical CumGPA FallYear3	795	3.17	0.49	0.04625
Historical CumGPA FallYear4	14398	3.15	0.47	Historical CumGPA FallYear4	624	3.18	0.47	0.03353
Historical CumGPA FallYear5	1454	2.77	0.55	Historical CumGPA FallYear5	45	2.79	0.60	0.02484
Historical CumGPA FallYear6	143	2.44	0.57	Historical CumGPA FallYear6	5	2.38	0.51	−0.05408
Historical CumGPA FallYear7	56	2.34	0.54	Historical CumGPA FallYear7	2	2.04	0.68	−0.29104

Z Denominator	Z-statistic	Conc.	O. Sort	Effect Size	Effect Size Name	Effect size	Effect Size Name
0.016195214	3.702287046	SIG	20	0.136514451	Less than Small	0.08483205	Less than small
0.015947533	2.112272255	SIG	21	0.088701849	Less than Small	0.041698038	Less than small
0.016804376	3.074464637	SIG	22	0.143369143	Less than Small	0.0630709	Less than small
0.014591251	7.546533965	SIG	23	0.221549628	Small	0.251516277	Small
0.011301528	17.77377022	SIG	24	0.487774055	Small	0.057131691	Less than small
0.005177007	−4.62110112	SIG	25	−0.119083786	Less than Small	−0.434612657	Less than small
0.016528732	5.241520668	SIG	26	0.140631038	Less than Small	0.0283788	Less than small
0.017030442	2.515361546	SIG	27	0.078722377	Less than Small	0.013876185	Less than small
0.017940981	2.577773822	SIG	28	0.091994173	Less than Small	0.014804412	Less than small
0.019264179	1.740423808	ns	29	0.071135188	Less than Small	0.010657401	Less than small
0.090081404	0.275804336	ns	30	0.043374284	Less than Small	0.008979776	Less than small
0.232677224	−0.232423781	ns	31	−0.100414946	Less than Small	−0.022179457	Less than small
0.484406582	−0.600808752	ns	32	−0.47809097	Small	−0.124638656	Less than small

TABLE 17.3F

Statistical Analysis II of SUPA versus Non-SUPA Z Tests *(Continued)*

Non-SUPA	Non-SUPA N	Non-SUPA Mean	Non-SUPA SD	SUPA	SUPA N	SUPA Mean	SUPA SD	Z Numerator
Historical CumGPA SpringYear1	24230	3.06	0.63	Historical CumGPA SpringYear1	1192	3.10	0.58	0.04628
Historical CumGPA SpringYear2	19813	3.11	0.53	Historical CumGPA SpringYear2	984	3.13	0.52	0.02385
Historical CumGPA SpringYear3	16348	3.14	0.49	Historical CumGPA SpringYear3	751	3.18	0.48	0.04081
Historical CumGPA SpringYear4	13783	3.13	0.46	Historical CumGPA SpringYear4	573	3.18	0.44	0.04234
Historical CumGPA SpringYear5	1031	2.78	0.56	Historical CumGPA SpringYear5	32	2.76	0.63	−0.01403
Historical CumGPA SpringYear6	115	2.44	0.58	Historical CumGPA SpringYear6	3	2.72	0.24	0.27696
Historical SemGPA FallYear1	24836	3.05	0.68	Historical SemGPA FallYear1	1216	3.06	0.66	0.01140
Historical SemGPA FallYear2	20306	3.08	0.68	Historical SemGPA FallYear2	1000	3.11	0.67	0.03046
Historical SemGPA FallYear3	17008	3.16	0.65	Historical SemGPA FallYear3	791	3.22	0.65	0.06371
Historical SemGPA FallYear4	14390	3.15	0.70	Historical SemGPA FallYear4	624	3.17	0.76	0.01653
Historical SemGPA FallYear5	1447	2.75	0.87	Historical SemGPA FallYear5	45	2.88	1.00	0.12747
Historical SemGPA FallYear6	142	2.54	1.06	Historical SemGPA FallYear6	5	2.83	1.61	0.28559

Z Denominator	Z– statistic	Conc.	O. Sort	Effect Size	Effect Size Name	Effect size	Effect Size Name
0.017244304	2.683558891	SIG	33	0.076808993	Less than Small	0.015144339	Less than small
0.017035534	1.399999801	ns	34	0.045315528	Less than Small	0.007679069	Less than small
0.018080552	2.257388925	SIG	35	0.083616955	Less than Small	0.013002111	Less than small
0.018989557	2.229664738	SIG	36	0.093473293	Less than Small	0.01351022	Less than small
0.112160565	−0.125131291	ns	37	−0.023673332	Less than Small	−0.005052287	Less than small
0.150017735	1.846158538	ns	38	0.675774916	Medium	0.113318983	Less than small
0.019304014	0.590647525	ns	39	0.017122839	Less than Small	0.003734814	Less than small
0.021825151	1.395672915	ns	40	0.045098249	Less than Small	0.009895547	Less than small
0.023806641	2.675976766	SIG	41	0.097795943	Less than Small	0.020156346	Less than small
0.031098563	0.531390168	ns	42	0.022608015	Less than Small	0.005238149	Less than small
0.150462814	0.847196881	ns	43	0.136264531	Less than Small	0.046381888	Less than small
0.724293726	0.394297663	ns	44	0.214443022	Small	0.11240884	Less than small

320

TABLE 17.3F

Statistical Analysis II of SUPA versus Non-SUPA Z Tests (*Continued*)

Non-SUPA	Non-SUPA N	Non-SUPA Mean	Non-SUPA SD	SUPA	SUPA N	SUPA Mean	SUPA SD	Z Numerator
Historical SemGPA FallYear7	55	2.52	1.14	Historical SemGPA FallYear7	2	0.50	0.71	−2.02385
Historical SemGPA SpringYear1	24229	3.05	0.71	Historical SemGPA SpringYear1	1192	3.04	0.75	−0.00725
Historical SemGPA SpringYear2	19812	3.12	0.65	Historical SemGPA SpringYear2	984	3.10	0.72	−0.01584
Historical SemGPA SpringYear3	16344	3.17	0.62	Historical SemGPA SpringYear3	751	3.21	0.65	0.03697
Historical SemGPA SpringYear4	13773	3.08	0.74	Historical SemGPA SpringYear4	573	3.12	0.79	0.03653
Historical SemGPA SpringYear5	1025	2.71	0.86	Historical SemGPA SpringYear5	32	2.60	1.13	−0.10482
Historical SemGPA SpringYear6	115	2.61	1.16	Historical SemGPA SpringYear6	3	3.10	0.67	0.49466
HS_Class Rank	13004	59.94	64.21	HS_Class Rank	734	52.35	55.56	−7.58649

Z Denominator	Z– statistic	Conc.	O. Sort	Effect Size	Effect Size Name	Effect size	Effect Size Name
0.523096689	−3.868987492	SIG	45	−2.191347773	Large	−0.801890326	Less than small
0.022267453	−0.325776761	ns	46	−0.009950658	Less than Small	−0.002382001	Less than small
0.02330189	−0.679731284	ns	47	−0.023118094	Less than Small	−0.005082571	Less than small
0.024148547	1.531010164	ns	48	0.058158471	Less than Small	0.011648845	Less than small
0.033557753	1.088490139	ns	49	0.047699026	Less than Small	0.011858554	Less than small
0.202245719	−0.518287825	ns	50	−0.105369964	Less than Small	−0.038696792	Less than small
0.401032805	1.23345289	ns	51	0.541892741	Medium	0.189691758	Less than small
2.126606697	−3.567414288	SIG	52	−0.126685499	Less than Small	−0.12656652	Less than small

TABLE 17.3G

Statistical Analysis III of SUPA versus Non-SUPA Z Tests

Non-SUPA	Non-SUPA N	Non-SUPA Mean	Non-SUPA SD	SUPA	SUPA N	SUPA Mean	SUPA SD	Z Numerator
HS_Class Size	13044	304.21	188.45	HS_Class Size	735	319.38	162.87	15.17799
HS_ Percentile	13003	79.61	15.49	HS_ Percentile	734	83.87	12.69	4.26221
Low Financial Needind	24943	0.07	0.25	Low Financial Needind	1221	0.07	0.26	0.00301
Maleind	24943	0.44	0.50	Maleind	1221	0.38	0.49	−0.05255
Merit Rating1ind	24943	0.07	0.26	Merit Rating1ind	1221	0.08	0.27	0.00772
Merit Rating2ind	24943	0.15	0.36	Merit Rating2ind	1221	0.20	0.40	0.04724
Merit Rating3ind	24943	0.13	0.34	Merit Rating3ind	1221	0.17	0.38	0.03499
Merit Rating4ind	24943	0.12	0.32	Merit Rating4ind	1221	0.14	0.34	0.01636
Merit Rating5ind	24943	0.10	0.30	Merit Rating5ind	1221	0.11	0.31	0.00823
Merit Rating6ind	24943	0.10	0.30	Merit Rating6ind	1221	0.09	0.29	−0.00778
Merit Rating7ind	24943	0.29	0.46	Merit Rating7ind	1221	0.19	0.39	−0.10894
MeritRating HEOPind	24943	0.02	0.13	MeritRating HEOPind	1221	0.02	0.14	0.00404
MeritRating New1to7	24180	4.55	2.09	MeritRating New1to7	1181	4.05	1.99	−0.50000
MeritRating New1to9	24943	4.67	2.17	MeritRating New1to9	1221	4.20	2.12	−0.47404
MeritRating SSSind	24943	0.01	0.12	MeritRating SSSind	1221	0.01	0.11	−0.00187
Mid Financial Needind	24943	0.08	0.26	Mid Financial Needind	1221	0.07	0.26	−0.00408
Native American AKNative ind	24943	0.00	0.07	Native American AKNative ind	1221	0.00	0.06	−0.00040

Z Denominator	Z-statistic	Conc.	O. Sort	Effect Size	Effect Size Name	Effect size	Effect Size Name
6.230126418	2.436224245	SIG	53	0.086404025	Less than Small	0.049893824	Less than small
0.487559908	8.741914955	SIG	54	0.302551358	Small	0.053537858	Less than small
0.00761562	0.395469841	ns	55	0.011695819	Less than Small	0.043099272	Less than small
0.014280451	−3.679650262	SIG	56	−0.10692645	Less than Small	−0.120113765	Less than small
0.007912871	0.975568788	ns	57	0.029208931	Less than Small	0.107629251	Less than small
0.011580493	4.079499904	SIG	58	0.125556204	Less than Small	0.318135163	Small
0.010957719	3.192854621	SIG	59	0.097642616	Less than Small	0.26003154	Small
0.010025407	1.632000019	ns	60	0.049032561	Less than Small	0.136809927	Less than small
0.009150972	0.899867672	ns	61	0.026791944	Less than Small	0.081120543	Less than small
0.008478369	−0.917485841	ns	62	−0.026453618	Less than Small	−0.078173331	Less than small
0.011487257	−9.483221996	SIG	63	−0.25809744	Small	−0.370493011	Less than small
0.004133687	0.97674128	ns	64	0.030037923	Less than Small	0.245630331	Small
0.059299894	−8.431718339	SIG	66	−0.245579568	Small	−0.10989011	Less than small
0.062122019	−7.630838775	SIG	65	−0.221231571	Small	−0.10140614	Less than small
0.003241196	−0.576100535	ns	67	−0.016356411	Less than Small	−0.131940336	Less than small
0.007552181	−0.540067197	ns	68	−0.015648619	Less than Small	−0.054142972	Less than small
0.001876708	−0.210599392	ns	69	−0.006045769	Less than Small	−0.088020651	Less than small

TABLE 17.3G

Statistical Analysis III of SUPA versus Non-SUPA Z Tests *(Continued)*

Non-SUPA	Non-SUPA N	Non-SUPA Mean	Non-SUPA SD	SUPA	SUPA N	SUPA Mean	SUPA SD	Z Numerator
NoFinancial AidApplind	24943	0.28	0.45	NoFinancial AidApplind	1221	0.18	0.39	−0.09748
NoFinancial Needind	24943	0.14	0.35	NoFinancial Needind	1221	0.13	0.33	−0.01157
NonRes Alienind	24943	0.03	0.17	NonRes Alienind	1221	0.00	0.00	−0.03055
NumberOf PACredits	24943	0.00	0.00	NumberOf PACredits	1221	6.05	3.36	6.04668
PACredit Indicator	24943	0.00	0.00	PACredit Indicator	1221	1.00	0.00	1.00000
Persisting FallYear2ind	24943	0.91	0.29	Persisting FallYear2ind	1221	0.93	0.26	0.01997

Z Denominator	Z-statistic	Conc.	O. Sort	Effect Size	Effect Size Name	Effect size	Effect Size Name
0.011382561	−8.563603438	SIG	70	−0.233913899	Small	−0.350034182	Less than small
0.009778987	−1.183219646	ns	71	−0.034106905	Less than Small	−0.083533343	Less than small
0.001089683	−28.03535079	SIG	72	−0.355027216	Small	−1	Less than small
0.096230491	62.83541726	SIG	73	3.596471864	Large	#DIV/0!	
0	#DIV/0!	Ns	74	#DIV/0!	Less than Small	#DIV/0!	
0.007547413	2.646211959	SIG	75	0.073595721	Less than Small	0.021957113	Less than small

TABLE 17.3H

Statistical Analysis IV of SUPA versus Non-SUPA Z Tests

Non-SUPA	Non-SUPA N	Non-SUPA Mean	Non-SUPA SD	SUPA	SUPA N	SUPA Mean	SUPA SD	Z Numerator
Persisting FallYear3ind	22317	0.86	0.34	Persisting FallYear3ind	1076	0.89	0.31	0.02865
SATMath	24943	597.02	76.53	SATMath	1221	599.53	73.02	2.51717
SATVerbal	24943	576.00	78.71	SATVerbal	1221	580.57	72.27	4.56222
TestCredits Indicator	24943	0.34	0.47	TestCredits Indicator	1221	0.36	0.48	0.01627
TotalTest Credits	24943	3.38	6.12	TotalTest Credits	1221	3.48	6.08	0.09573
Unspecified ind	24943	0.11	0.31	Unspecified ind	1221	0.11	0.32	0.00938
Whiteind	24943	0.66	0.47	Whiteind	1221	0.74	0.44	0.07814
HS_Class Rank	13004	59.94	64.21	HS_Class Rank	734	52.35	55.56	−7.58649

Z Denominator	Z-statistic	Conc.	O. Sort	Effect Size	Effect Size Name	Effect size	Effect Size Name
0.009770451	2.93210592	SIG	76	0.087379739	Less than Small	0.033210605	Less than small
2.145061812	1.173473439	ns	77	0.033664832	Less than Small	0.004216257	Less than small
2.127359922	2.144547303	SIG	78	0.060435216	Less than Small	0.007920488	Less than small
0.01404221	1.158456854	ns	79	0.034127318	Less than Small	0.047730281	Less than small
0.178361885	0.536701473	ns	80	0.015692049	Less than Small	0.028306964	Less than small
0.009326528	1.005741479	ns	81	0.029984487	Less than Small	0.089096436	Less than small
0.012878489	6.067568188	SIG	82	0.171720341	Less than Small	0.117704796	Less than small
2.126606697	−3.567414288	SIG	52	−0.126685499	Less than Small	−0.12656652	Less than small

References

Achieve, Inc. 2008. *Closing the Expectations Gap: An Annual 50-State Progress Report on the Alignment of High School Policies with the Demands of College and Careers.* Washington, DC: The American Diploma Project.

Adelman, Clifford. 1999. *Answers in the Tool Box: Academic intensity, Attendance Patterns, and Bachelor's Degree Attainment.* Washington, DC: U.S. Department of Education. http://ed.gov/pubs/Toolbox/toolbox.html.

Babbie, Earl. 2004. *The Practice of Social Research,* 10th ed. Belmont, CA: Wadsworth.

Bailey, Thomas R., Katherine L. Hughes, and Melinda M. Karp. 2002 (Apr. 4). *What Role Can Dual Enrollment Programs Play in Easing the Transition Between High School and Post Secondary Education?* Paper prepared for the U.S. Department of Education, Office of Vocational and Adult Education. New York: Community College Research Center and Institute on Education and the Economy, Teachers College, Columbia Univ.

Bailey, Thomas R., and Melinda M. Karp. 2003. *Promoting College Access and Success: A Review of Credit-Based Transition Programs.* Washington, DC: U.S. Department of Education, Office of Adult and Vocational Education.

Bureau of Labor Statistics. 2010. Economic News Release. United States Department of Labor. http://www.bls.gov/news.release/emosit.t04.htm.

Cohen, Jacob. 1998. *Statistical Power Analysis for the Behavioral Sciences.* 2nd ed. Hillsdale, NJ: Lawrence Erlbaum Associates.

Duffy, William R. 2008. "Persistence and Performance: The Relationship between Dual Credit and Persistence and Performance at a Four-Year University." Doctoral diss., Univ. of Memphis.

Dutkowsky, Donald H., Jerry M. Evensky, and Gerald S. Edmonds. 2006. "Teaching College Economics in the High Schools: The Role of Concurrent Enrollment Programs." *Journal of Economic Education* 37(4): 477–82.

———. 2009. "Should Your High School Adopt Advanced Placement or a Concurrent Enrollment Program? An Expected Benefit Approach." *Education and Finance Policy* 4(3): 263–77.

Edmonds, Gerald S., and Sari Signorelli. 2009. *Our Courses Your Classroom: Research on Syracuse University Courses Taught in High School.* Syracuse, NY: Project Advance Press.

Hedrick, Terry E., Leonard Bickman, and Debra J. Rog. 1993. *Applied Research Design: A Practical Guide.* Los Angeles, CA: Sage.

Illinois Dual Credit Task Force. 2008 (Dec.). *Illinois Dual Credit Task Force Report to the General Assembly.* OCLC 298329055.

Karp, Melinda M., Juan Carlos Calcagno, Katherine L. Hughes, Dong Wook Jeong, and Thomas R. Bailey. 2007. *The Postsecondary Achievement of Participants in Dual Enrollment: An Analysis of Student Outcomes in Two States.* New York: Community College Research Center, Teachers College, Columbia Univ. ERIC ED498661.

Kim, JoHyun. 2008. "The Impact of Dual and Articulated Credit on College Readiness and Total College Credit Earned in Four Selected Community Colleges." *Career and Technical Education Research* 33(2): 133–58.

Klopfenstein, Kristin. 2003. "Recommendations for Maintaining the Quality of Advanced Placement Programs." *American Secondary Education* 32 (1): 39–48.

Klopfenstein, Kristin, and M. Kathleen Thomas. 2009. "The Link between Advanced Placement Experience and Early College Success." *Economics of Education Review* 23(2): 115–31.

Krueger, Carl. 2006. *Dual Enrollment: Policy Issues Confronting State Policymakers.* Denver, CO: Education Commission of the States.

Levin, Joel R. 1993. Statistical Significance Testing from Three Perspectives. *Journal of Experimental Education* 61(4): 378–82.

Marklein, Mary Beth. 2005. "College Gender Gap Widens: 57% Are Women." *USA Today*, Oct. 19. http://usatoday.com.

Pascarella, Ernest T. 1982. "Studying Student Attrition." In *New Directions for Institutional Research 36*, edited by M. W. Peterson. San Francisco: Jossey-Bass.

Pascarella, Ernest T., and Patrick T. Terenzini. 2005. *How College Affects Students: A Third Decade of Research, Vol. 2.* San Francisco: Jossey-Bass.

Sadler, Phillip M., and Robert H. Tai. 2007. "Advanced Placement Exam Scores as a Predictor of Performance in Introductory College Biology, Chemistry, and Physics Courses." *Science Educator* 16(1): 1–19.

Stillman, Matt. 2009. "Making the Case for the Importance of Student Retention." Dissertation, Southern Oregon Univ.

Swanson, Joni L. 2008. "An Analysis of the Impact of High School Dual Enrollment Course Participation on Postsecondary Academic Success, Persistence, and Degree Completion." Doctoral diss., Univ. of Iowa.

Thompson, Trina, and James O. Rust. 2007. "Follow-up of Advanced Placement Students in College." *College Student Journal* 41: 416–22.

Tinto, Vincent. 1987. *Leaving College: Rethinking the Causes and Cures of Student Attrition.* Chicago: Univ. of Chicago Press.

————. 1993. *Leaving College: Rethinking the Causes and Cures of Student Attrition* (2nd ed.). Chicago: Univ. of Chicago Press.

U.S. Department of Education. 2010. *ESE Blueprint for Reform*. Washington, DC: Office of Planning, Evaluation and Policy Development.

Venezia, Andrea, Patrick M. Callan, Joni E. Finney, Michael W. Kirst, and Michael D. Usdan. 2005. *The Governance Divide: A Report on a Four-State Study on Improving College Readiness and Success*. San Jose, CA: National Center for Public Policy and Higher Education.

Venezia, Andrea, Michael W. Kirst, and Anthony L. Antonio. 2006. *Betraying the College Dream: How Disconnected K–12 and Postsecondary Education Systems Undermine Student Aspirations*. Final policy report from the Stanford University Bridge Project. Palo Alto, CA: Stanford Institute for Higher Education Research.

Waits Tiffany, J. Carl Setzer, and Laurie Lewis. 2005. *Dual Credit and Exam-Based Courses in U.S. Public High School: 2002–03* (NCES 2005–009). Washington, DC: U.S. Department of Education, National Center for Education Statistics.

Windham, P., and Perkins, G. 2001. "Dual Enrollment as an Acceleration Mechanism: Are Students Prepared for Subsequent Courses?" Paper presented at the meeting of the Association for Institutional Research Forum, Long Beach, CA.

18

Dual Enrollment Course Participation and Effects upon Student Persistence in College

JONI L. SWANSON

Transitions between High School and Higher Education

In September 2006 the U.S. Department of Education, under Secretary Margaret Spellings, published a report on the future of higher education, which included recommendations for assessing college students' knowledge acquisition. Spellings' report drew attention to the national dilemma of low college retention and graduation rates. In response to the report—and to increasing college tuition costs as well as the knowledge that less than 35% of the National Education Longitudinal Study (NELS):88/2000 national data sample had earned a bachelor's degree within eight years of high school graduation (Adelman 2006, 106)—The Education Trust produced a website called College Results Online (www.collegeresults .org), where parents and students could evaluate college graduation rates, tuition costs, and a variety of student demographic information related to individual postsecondary institutions. Concerns have existed for quite some time over the structure of the K–16 education system. Particularly disconcerting is the "great divide" separating high school from college (Kirst and Venezia 2004; Venezia, Callan, Finney, Kirst, and Usdan 2005; Venezia, Kirst, and Antonio 2003). Current efforts to collect information from students as they progress through school toward postsecondary education are being assessed by organizations such as Achieve, Inc., the American Diploma Project, Education Commission of the States, and the Data Quality Campaign. States are beginning to organize data to track students from kindergarten to postsecondary education through longitudinal systems funding, supported in part by federal stimulus dollars.

Related literature and research clearly supports the premise that college persistence is affected by the skills and knowledge students bring to their initial matriculated postsecondary experience. Research conducted by the U.S. Department of Education, utilizing secondary data sets, has consistently suggested that high school curricula exhibit strong and positive impacts on college persistence and degree attainment (Adelman 1999, 2004, 2006). The quality and breadth of the high school course of study, according to Adelman (1999), produces the greatest influence upon students' future college persistence and degree attainment. Vincent Tinto's theory of individual departure from institutions of higher education has provided researchers with an explanatory model of students' departure from college (1975). However, in regard to student decisions to persist or depart, Tinto's revised 1993 theoretical model places less importance upon attributes preceding postsecondary entrance and more emphasis on academic and social experiences during the college years (see Figure 18.1). Tinto's theory has been tested in relation to the roles that academic and social integration play upon persistence decisions (Pascarella and Terenzini 1980; Nora 2001–2). According to Nora, the constructs of separation, transition, and integration affect incoming college students from the very first day on campus. Clearly, the transition to college has proven problematic for students seeking to enter and persist within academe. Recent concerns linking higher education's failure to improve diploma production to students' questionable knowledge gains have been publicized as detrimental to our national economic security (Casner-Lotto and Barrington 2006; College Board 2008). When considering the complexities of college matriculation and persistence to degree, students face a myriad of challenges as they contemplate persistence in the higher education system.

Considering that the overall theme for this volume surveys dual enrollment programming, I believe that Vincent Tinto's theory of individual departure has the potential to assist researchers in evaluating the possible effects of dual enrollment course participation on precollege events and on academic and social integration experiences gained from

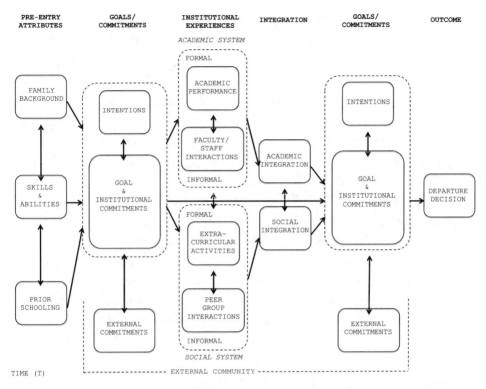

Figure 18.1. Longitudinal Model of Institutional Departure. Source: Tinto, V. 1993. *Leaving College: Rethinking the Causes and Cures of Student Attrition* (2nd ed.), Chicago: Univ. of Chicago Press, 114. Reprinted with permission.

the college environment. Dual enrollment courses, where students concurrently participate in both high school and college academic work, may also influence student academic performance within that portion of Tinto's longitudinal model labeled "institutional experiences" (Figure 18.1). Goals and commitments to college may be strengthened by experiences with dual enrollment courses. Attending college classes with familiar high school classmates may strengthen peer group interactions. According to Tinto's model, these interactions both directly and indirectly impact academic and social integration. If dual enrollment classes perform both a high school and a college-oriented function by promoting academic and social integration, then their impact on decisions to persist in college may be inferred by the structure of Tinto's explanatory model.

Leaving high school and entering college, according to Barefoot (2000), Lotkowski, Robbins, and Noeth (2004), and Napoli and Wortman (2005), involves more than minimum levels of academic course completion prior to matriculation. Students also must demonstrate both the willingness and ability to assume college behaviors and attitudes toward learning. Dual enrollment courses and programs facilitate successful high school to college transitions, improve academic and social preparations for college, and motivate students to choose more rigorous high school classes prior to graduation (Bailey, Hughes, and Karp 2002).

Not surprisingly, Tinto (1993) endorsed dual enrollment course participation by specifically mentioning Syracuse University's Project Advance as an acceleration program providing "firsthand insight into the character of academic life at an institution of higher education" (158). Academic preparation, in concert with accepting responsibility for increased academic rigor within less structured learning environments, may improve academic integration in postsecondary education for dual enrollment students.

By referencing Project Advance, Tinto supported the view that participation in college courses during the regular four-year high school regimen provided academic and socialization benefits to students transitioning to higher education. Therefore, the predominant premise of my research on dual enrollment program participation and possible impacts upon student achievement in postsecondary education looks to Tinto's theory of individual student departure for support. Clearly, Tinto's theoretical model considers the impact of precollege skills, in addition to those experiences affecting students after matriculation. Because dual enrollment courses occur at the cusp of high school and college, Tinto's words substantiate the premise that a theory of departure from higher education explains multiple impacts of these prematriculation courses on student persistence in the college setting.

This study stands apart from previous investigations of dual enrollment course participation in at least three respects. First, prior researchers have utilized samples of students obtained from individual institutions (Puyear 1998; Spurling and Gabriner 2002) or statewide data (Hanson 2005; Windham and Perkins 2001; Karp, Calcagno, Hughes, Jeong, and Bailey

2008), thereby limiting the ability to generalize the results to students across the nation. Selection bias, low survey return rates, and self-reported data decreased the power of previous studies' results. Therefore, the NELS:88/2000 transcript data—the only available set of nationally representative data to have isolated students who participated in dual enrollment—was utilized for this research. Second, statistical methods used in previous studies employed primarily census or frequency data, or utilized limited inferential statistics (Eimers and Mullen, 2003; Karp, Calcagno, Hughes, Jeong, and Bailey 2008; Menzel 2006). Third, previous research has not employed a causal model, linking theory to inferential statistical research methods to explore the effects of dual enrollment participation on outcome variables, while controlling for a wide range of pre-existing conditions.

Research Questions

At the genesis of this research project, a causal model was created to form the basis for targeted logistic regression equations. The resultant relationships between variables in the model sought to answer the following questions regarding postsecondary persistence and academic momentum:

1. Does dual enrollment participation affect the likelihood that students will enter college within seven months of high school graduation as compared to non–dual enrollment participants?

2. Does dual enrollment participation affect the likelihood that students will earn at least 20 credits during their first year in postsecondary education as compared to non–dual enrollment participants?

3. Does dual enrollment participation affect the likelihood that students will demonstrate higher rates of second-year college persistence as compared to non–dual enrollment participants?

4. Do students who have participated in dual enrollment programs experience positive effects upon college persistence after accounting for specific demographic attributes, when compared to non–dual enrollment participants after accounting for these same attributes?

The specific construction of the causal model describes the direct and total effects of the independent variable (dual/concurrent enrollment course participation) and control variables (demographic, high school and college attributes) on the dependent variables (postsecondary persistence) (see Figure 18.2). The model takes into consideration the following factors from Vincent Tinto's theory of individual departure from institutions of higher education: pre-entry attributes, goals/commitments, institutional experiences, integration, and outcomes (Figure 18.1).

Due to the complex relationship between dual enrollment program participation and high school and college experiences, the causal model assumes that several factors of Tinto's model act in tandem. Dual enrollment, occurring during high school but before college entry, interfaces with demographic variables existent during the high school experience. Likewise, dual enrollment courses generate college transcripts, which impact first-year grade point averages and college credits earned before high school graduation.

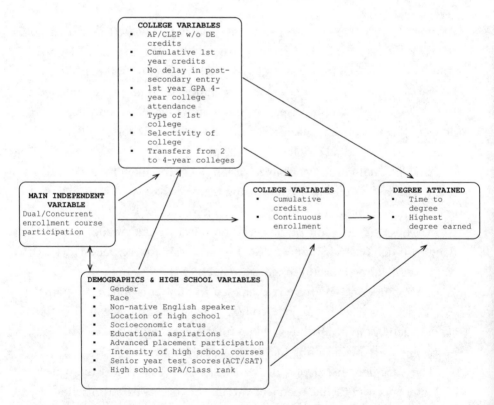

Figure 18.2. Causal Model—The Direct and Total Effects of Dual Enrollment Course Participation on College Persistence

Tinto's model highlights integration into and commitments to college as important factors in persistence. Experiences in dual enrollment courses provide students with their earliest college-level activities. When students successfully complete dual enrollment courses and gain credits, their experiences may be perceived as a positive indicator of future college activity. Likewise, students who immediately enter college after high school graduation produce increasing rates of college persistence (Adelman 2006). The model for this research study proposes to test the theory that dual enrollment courses offer similar integration and commitment characteristics as college classes taken in the initial year of postsecondary education.

Study Sample and Variables

In order to answer the research questions and create the appropriate analytical sample, two filters were utilized before any statistical methods were employed. The sample for this study identified and isolated NELS:88/2000 surveyed students who were members of the senior class of 1992 and who attended a postsecondary educational institution at any time before December 2000. Therefore, the first filter, identified as F4UNI2D, selected members of the second follow-up survey during the students' high school senior year. The second filter, also functioning as a panel weight for the study, was identified as F4F2P2WT. This variable selected all known NELS:88/2000 postsecondary participants who were 12th-grade students in 1992 and were participants in each of the follow-up surveys and transcript collections in 1992 (F2), 1994 (F3), and 2000 (F4).

The NELS:88/2000 postsecondary data, obtained two and six years after high school graduation, included variables describing transcript-related numeric values associated with college credits earned by students who were concurrently enrolled in high school. These data constitute the primary independent variable for this research study. To put into perspective the number of students involved in acquiring accelerated credits, the following statistics are offered for comparison. Of the total number of participants in the NELS:88/2000 study, 19% of the students who went on to earn postsecondary credits after high school graduation in 1992 earned college credits while still enrolled in high school (via dual enrollment courses) and/or by examination (via Advanced Placement, AP, or college level examination placement, CLEP) (Adelman 2004, vi). NELS:88/2000 12th-grade students who participated in AP courses entered postsecondary institutions at a rate that was 22% higher than those who did not complete any AP classes in high school (Adelman 2006, 37). After separating out those students who participated in dual enrollment programs, regardless of the configuration or delivery system by which student credits were earned, the NELS:88/2000 transcript data indicates that a weighted 213,000 students participated in dual enrollment courses (Adelman 2006, 99). This statistic represented approximately 18 of 1.19 million students in the 2006 analytic sample prepared by Adelman. Dual enrollment credits must be separated from AP and CLEP credits in order to suggest any independent value of dual enrollment program participation on persistence and degree attainment. This separation, through statistical analysis, has not been previously performed and represents the primary purpose of this research.

The original NELS-R:88/2000 (restricted) data sample allowed for the analysis of 19,893 students. After application of the filters, 4,514 student cases were available for analysis. The large reduction in the sample size was due to large numbers of missing cases among the transcript data, mainly supplied through the PETS (Postsecondary Education Transcript Study) data set. Specific information regarding all variables used in the research project is detailed in Table 18.1. The original NELS-R/PETS dual enrollment participation variable (TCREDD) included only 860 valid cases when dichotomously coded for participation. That number was further reduced to 425 cases once filters were applied. However, the valid percentages of the total possible participants for both the original and filtered samples were comparable: 9.7% of participants in the original 19,893 case sample and 9.4% of the 4514 case sample. These statistics resulted from the fact that 55.3% of the original cases were missing data on variables critical to the study. Compared to the national census of 2002–3, conducted by Kleiner and Lewis (2005), which yielded a 5% dual enrollment participation rate of high school students, the NELS:88/2000 data may have actually oversampled students involved in these programs.

TABLE 18.1

List of Original NELS/PETS Variables and Recoded Variable Labels

ORIGINAL VARIABLE	ORIGIN	RECODING LABELS
Independent Variable		
TCREDD	PETS	DEPARTIC
		Dual enrollment participant
Demographic Control Variables		
COMPSEX	PETS	MALE, FEMALE*
RACE4	PETS	HISPANIC, API, BLACK, NATAM**, WHITE*
F2S107	NELSR	ENGFRST
		English is first language
PHSURBURAN	PETS	URBANHS, RURALHS
		SUBURBHS*
		Urban, rural, suburban high school
FIRSTGEN	PETS SUPP	NOCOLEX
		First generation student
SESQUINT	PETS	SES1, SES2, SES3*, SES4, SES5
		Socioeconomic status in quintiles
High School Control Variables		
EDUANNEW	PETS SUPP	EDULBA, EDURBA, EDUBA*
		Educational expectations are lowered from a BA, raised to BA, are consistently to earn a BA
APTOTREV	PETS SUPP	APPART
		Participant in Advanced Placement class and/or Advanced Placement test
HSCURREV	PETS SUPP	HSRIGOR1, HSRIGOR2, HSRIGOR3*, HSRIGOR4, HSRIGOR5
		High School academic intensity quintiles
SRTSQUIN	PETS	SATACT1, SATACT2, SATACT3*, SATACT4, SATACT5
		Senior test quintiles (SAT or ACT)
CRANKREV	PETS SUPP	RANK1, RANK2, RANK3*, RANK4, RANK5
		Class rank/Grade point average quintiles

TABLE 18.1

List of Original NELS/PETS Variables and Recoded Variable Labels *(Continued)*

ORIGINAL VARIABLE	ORIGIN	RECODING LABELS
College Control Variables		
TCREDE	PETS	APCLEP
		Credits earned by examination (AP/CLEP w/out dual enrollment credits)
TCREDG	PETS	CREDMOM
		Earned 20 or more credits by the end of the first post-secondary year
DELAY	PETS	NODELAY
		No delay in entering postsecondary after high school within 7 months after graduation
GPA1	PETS	GPA1YR
		First-year grade point average of 2.88 or above
F4ATT4YR	NELSR	FOURYR
		Ever attended a four-year college
REFINST	PETS	FIRST4, FIRST2***, CERTIF***
		Type of first college of attendance
REFSELCT	PETS	SELCT1***, SELCT2***, NONSELCT*, OPENDR
		Selectivity of first postsecondary institution
Postsecondary Persistence Variables		
PSC1992-3 & PSC1993-4	PETS	CUMCRED (combined)
		Cumulative credits of 50 or more by the end of the second postsecondary year
CONTIN	PETS	NOSTOP
		Continuous enrollment with no more than one semester break
Weights and Filters		
F4UNI2D	NELSR	Second follow-up status in 1992
F4F2P2WT	PETS	Known postsecondary education participant and member of NELS: 88/2000 F2, F3, F4 follow-up; 12th grade student in 1992

   * Reference group
    ** Eliminated from final models
   *** Combined into new variable

Adelman's 1999, 2004, and 2006 studies emphasized the importance of an academically rigorous preparation in high school before entering into college. Dual enrollment courses produce transcripts detailing postsecondary credits for high school students prior to graduation. The variable TCREDD isolates, by way of transcript evaluation, those college credits earned by dual enrollment course participation. TCREDD likewise excludes credits earned by external examination programs such as CLEP and AP national examinations. As the primary independent variable for the causal model, the TCREDD variable was coded as a dummy variable (DEPARTIC), identifying students who participated in dual enrollment programs as compared to nonparticipants, regardless of the exact number of college credits actually earned. In each logistic regression equation, DEPARTIC was entered as the first block of the analysis.

Measuring college persistence requires researchers to evaluate the impact of credits earned through the end of the second postsecondary year. Variables PSC1992 and PSC1993, found within the NELS-R/PETS data, were combined into a new variable, CUMCRED, to identify all undergraduate credits earned by the end of the second academic year, and specifically flagged students with an accumulation of 50 or more credits. The CUMCRED variable was created to describe persistence outcomes related to acquiring credits, much like CREDMOM, developed from TCREDE, described credits earned in the first academic year. In terms of persistence to degree, the second academic year allows students the opportunity to regain any momentum they may have lost due to low credit production in the first year (Adelman 2006). Data generated by Adelman's "Toolbox Revisited" study revealed that students who were awarded bachelor's degrees also earned an average of 57.4 credits by the end of the second year, whereas students who earned fewer credits in the same amount of time were less likely to graduate (2006, 56). Of all students in Adelman's 2006 study, the average number of credits earned by the end of the second year was 49.5 (55). For purposes of this study, I used the rounded amount of 50 credits as a minimum number to represent second-year momentum toward degree attainment.

In the final logistic analysis of variables employed in his study, Adelman evaluated student persistence through the end of the second college year. He found that first-year college grades and continuous enrollment (no stop-outs) ranked as the highest positive indicators for earning the bachelor's degree. Continuous enrollment is defined as no more than one semester of time out of school. Continuous enrollment, including enrollment in summer school, increased the likelihood of degree completion for the NELS:88/2000 sample by 43.4% ($p < .001$) and produced the strongest effects of the "Toolbox Revisited" study (Adelman 2006, 74–75). Similarly, the Baccalaureate and Beyond 2000/2001 survey showed that 52.6% of college graduates with less than six months absence from school completed their degrees within four years after their first enrollment (Bradburn, Berger, Li, Peter, and Rooney 2003, 28). These previous research results seem to indicate that students who stop attending college for more than one semester at a time lose their momentum toward a degree. In this study, the variable CONTIN indicates the continuous enrollment of NELS:88/2000 participants to the end of the second year of college past high school graduation. CONTIN was recoded as a dichotomous variable, identified as NOSTOP.

Statistical Methods

Logistic regression analysis forms the basis of the research method, due to the dichotomous nature of the dependent variables in the theoretical model. Parameter estimates (unstandardized coefficients) indicate positive or negative strengths of each variable in the logistic equations. ExpB coefficients (odds ratio) signaled effect sizes of each of the variables in the model. Delta-p statistics, converted into percentages, determined the probability that participation, in the categories defined by either independent or control variables, impacts outcomes described by each dependent variable. A computed pseudo R^2 statistic suggested total variance explained by the final regression model, although in logistic regression pseudo R^2 commands less importance than the R^2 of linear regression. Ultimately, the statistical analysis sought to uncover the strength of dual enrollment course participation upon the criterion variables, as well as the relative strength of the various control variables.

A causal model was used to investigate direct and total effects of a wide range of control variables on dependent variables. As shown in

Figure 18.2, for each outcome variable a series of regressions were conducted following pathways indicated in the causal model. To ascertain the
direct and total effects of dual enrollment participation on each dependent
variable, logistic regression equations were developed, and corresponding charts of resultant data created as a result of statistical calculations
performed by SPSS and AM software. The basic model for the statistical
analysis is:

$$y_i = b_0 + b_1 DE_i + b_2 D_i + b_3 H_i + b_4 C_i + e_i$$

where y_i is the dependent variable; DE represents whether the student participated in dual enrollment classes in high school; D, H_i and C_i are vectors
that include demographic, high school and college variables, respectively;
e_i indicates random error; and b_0, b_1, b_2, b_3 and b_4 represent parameters to
be estimated by the logistic regression analysis. The main interest of this
study lies in $b_1 DE$, the parameter linked to dual enrollment participation
and its impact on students' postsecondary persistence.

Referring again to Figure 18.2, logistic regression analysis was used
to evaluate the effects of the primary independent variable—dual enrollment course participation (DEPARTIC). The main independent variable
(1) was regressed alone in the first statistical regression block against each
dependent variable describing postsecondary and degree attainment in
order to answer the initial three research questions. In each subsequent
regression step, the main independent variable was regressed, in concert
with all demographic and high school control variables (2), against the
dependent variable for that particular equation. Fourth layer variable
blocks included the college variables (3) and served as both control and
dependent variables. Postsecondary variables CUMCRED and NOSTOP
(4) performed as dependent variables.

In total, thirteen different models were utilized to ascertain the likelihood or probability that involvement in dual enrollment programs affects
various student persistence outcomes in postsecondary educational
endeavors. The strength of a causal model for logistic regression analysis
resides in the capacity of the instrument to analyze many different variables in varying combinations. The model itself was not designed to create
the strongest combination of effects, but rather to test the strength of dual

enrollment participation on a variety of outcome variables, while controlling for many different student attributes and circumstances. Therefore, the logistic models will not eliminate those variables failing to statistically contribute to the strength of the relationship, but will maintain all variables and watch their strength increase or decrease regardless of the statistical significance of their contribution to each model.

Results

Inferential statistics suggested that dual enrollment participation may play a significant role in persistence to degree, especially for students who entered college within seven months of high school graduation, those who acquired 20 or more college credits by the end of the first year of college, and those who continued their enrollment in postsecondary education without a break of more than one semester through the second year of college.

Research Question 1. Does dual enrollment participation affect the likelihood that students will enter college within seven months of high school graduation as compared to non–dual enrollment participants?

To answer the first research question, a logistic regression equation with dual enrollment participation (DEPARTIC) as the independent variable and NODELAY (no delay in entering postsecondary education after high school) as the dependent variable was created. Inferential statistics obtained from the direct effects model showed variables producing statistically significant effects. Regressed without controls, DEPARTIC demonstrated significant results, in that dual enrollment students were 11.7% more likely to enter postsecondary education within seven months of high school graduation than nonparticipants (p < .001). After controlling for demographic attributes, dual enrollment as an independent variable remains significant and suggests odds of participating students entering college after high school are 4.578 greater than those students who did not participate in dual enrollment classes. Adding high school academic attributes to the logistic model further improved the strength of DEPARTIC, with student participants 12.6% more likely to enter college immediately after high school. Although adding the high school controls decreased the likelihood of male as compared to female dual enrollment students entering college after high school, dual enrollment participation improved the odds of black students entering college after high school by 2.694 as compared to white students.

Dual enrollment participating students whose family incomes were in the highest two quintiles of the socioeconomic variable and those students whose ACT or SAT scores were in the highest quintiles benefitted most from dual enrollment participation when considering students who entered college without delay.

Research Question 2. Does dual enrollment participation affect the likelihood that students will earn at least 20 credits during their first year in postsecondary education as compared to non–dual enrollment participants?

The variable CREDMOM was created to evaluate the impact of first-year credits upon success in postsecondary education for dual enrollment participants. When regressed directly with DEPARTIC, CREDMOM created no statistically significant results. Therefore, dual enrollment program participation itself may not influence whether or not students earned 20 or more credits in the first year of college.

However, when used as a criterion variable rather than a dependent variable in an equation where continual enrollment through the second year in college with no more than one semester break (NOSTOP) serves as the dependent variable, the value of earning 20 credits or more in the first year of college created a strong and positive parameter estimate and corresponding delta-**p** statistic. These findings suggest that dual enrollment students who earned 20 or more first-year credits were 28.4% more likely to also be continuously enrolled in postsecondary education. Previous studies (Adelman 2004 and 2006) have indicated that students enrolled through the end of the sophomore year in college with no more than one semester off from school during that time are more likely to complete a college degree. Therefore, it appears that earning 20 or more credits in the first year of college has a strong impact on continuous enrollment for dual enrollment students. This study did not identify or further classify students by the number of credits earned from dual enrollment programming. Rather, students were included in the DEPARTIC variable even if they had enrolled in only one course or earn as few as one credit hour of postsecondary coursework in high school.

Research Question 3. Does dual enrollment participation affect the likelihood that students will demonstrate higher rates of second-year college persistence as compared to non–dual enrollment participants?

College persistence in the third research question is defined by both earning a particular amount of credit and by continuous enrollment in postsecondary education. Previous studies (Adelman 2004 and 2006) utilizing the NELS:88/2000 data have suggested that these two factors lead to higher likelihoods of college graduation.

In addition to CREDMOM, used in research question 2, another variable was created to describe earned credits. The new variable, CUMCRED, was created by joining together credits earned in the first and second year of college, and utilized 50 or more credits as a criterion marker. When DEPARTIC was regressed directly with CUMCRED, no statistically significant results were indicated for students participating in dual enrollment programs. This result was true for both direct and total effects models.

To evaluate the impact of continuous enrollment, NOSTOP was used as a dependent variable and regressed directly with DEPARTIC. The resultant statistics suggested quite a different result for dual enrollment participants. When regressed alone, dual enrollment students were 11.4% more likely to be continually enrolled through the end of the second year of college. Adding demographic and high school variables decreased that same likelihood to 10.6%. Further analysis suggests that dual enrollment students who continually enrolled in postsecondary education through the end of the second year were also 16.6% more likely to enter college within seven months of high school graduation.

Research Question 4. Do students who have participated in dual enrollment programs experience positive effects upon college persistence after accounting for specific demographic attributes, when compared to non–dual enrollment participants after accounting for these same attributes?

Demographic variables were entered in the second step of each of the regression equations in this research design. Considering entrance into college after high school (NODELAY), male participating students were 7% less likely to enter college within seven months of graduation compared to females, whereas black participants of dual enrollment programs were 9.5% more likely to continue on in college immediately after high school compared to white students. Earning 20 credits during the first academic year produced statistically significant results for male and Hispanic students, as compared to white and/or female dual enrollment participants, but showed an 11% to 17% decrease in the likelihood for students in these demographic groups to earn the minimum 20 credit hours.

Results of logistic regression equations for the variable CUMCRED (50 or more credits by the end of the second year in postsecondary education) show that first generation college students who participated in dual enrollment programming were between 15.5% and 23.2% less likely to earn 50 credits in the first two years of college compared to students whose parents had attended college in the past. Pacific Islander students showed a 12% greater likelihood of earning 50 credits by the end of the second year than white students.

Resulting data analysis of the variable NOSTOP shows that Hispanic students, as compared to white students, were between 11% and 13% less likely to continue in college through to the end of the second year. Black students were 12.9% less likely to enroll in college continuously than white students. Male dual enrollment participants were 8.9% less likely to remain enrolled in college than female students. Overall, control variables describing demographic attributes did not seem to positively impact dual enrollment college persistence. However, it should be noted that the NELS:88/2000 data contained only a small number of identified students within each demographic group. The small sample size may have impacted the validity of these results.

Conclusions

Results of logistic equations point decidedly to statistically significant positive estimates for dual enrollment participants who persist toward a degree. These results are a consequence of academic momentum in college to the end of the second year. Academic momentum describes students who enter postsecondary education immediately after high school, acquire at least 20 credits by the end of the first postsecondary year, and continuously enroll in college courses with no more than one semester break until the end of the second year. Students who participated in dual enrollment programs and who also exhibited these characteristics of academic momentum were more likely to complete Bachelor of Arts or advanced degrees. Interestingly, the acquisition of credits in the first year was more important to degree attainment than credit momentum by the end of the second year in college. Dual enrollment students reaped the benefits of earning initial year credits, some of which were a result of college classes successfully completed in high school and subsequent continuous enrollment in college. Although a greater percentage of dual enrollment participants had completed at least 50 hours of college credit by the end of their sophomore year in college than had nonparticipants (see Table 18.1), this fact did not translate into an increased likelihood of degree attainment. Earning college credits early in the postsecondary career positively impacted students' abilities to complete degrees through academic momentum. Credits earned in dual enrollment classes contributed positively to academic momentum.

More important, dual enrollment participation provides students with the momentum to persist, without which a degree is unlikely. No matter how many credits are earned by students in their collegiate careers, the strongest indicator of bachelor's and advanced degree completion was persistence to the second year in postsecondary education (NOSTOP). Dual enrollment participation, as a positive factor in persistence, also proved to be a stronger influence than was found utilizing the NODELAY (no delay in entering postsecondary education after high school) variable in Adelman's "Toolbox Revisited" (2006). Proponents of dual enrollment programming are encouraged to shift away from proclaiming that dual enrollment courses decrease the overall cost and time to complete college degrees toward suggesting that completion of a college credential is more possible when students participate in such programs. Completion of a credential is the most desired outcome of postsecondary attendance. Dual enrollment participation increases the likelihood of persistence toward that goal.

At least forty-two states have adopted policies, rules, regulations, funding schemes, or incentive programs pertaining to student participation in dual enrollment programs (Western Interstate Commission for Higher Education 2006). The financial consequences of dual enrollment courses loom large for community colleges. In some states, both local school districts and community colleges receive state funding for individual students dually enrolled in these educational institutions. Some may label this type of funding as "double dipping." In states where school districts pay tuition for dual enrollment students, however, programs have not grown because local school districts cannot afford the additional programmatic costs. Loss of revenue in association with dual enrollment programs may also occur when state aid payments follow high school students to the community college district. State laws have also allowed individual community colleges and four-year institutions to create their own rules governing tuition payments.

So, the questions remain: Is this investment worth the time, effort, and resources in the way of a payoff for student success? The answer, of course, has a lot to do with how success is measured. Were students adequately prepared to enter the degree or training programs? Do students persist long enough in postsecondary education to complete academic or training programs? Dual enrollment program participation, this research suggests, assists most obviously in the persistence phase of postsecondary education. As stewards of the public purse, educational institutions in concert with state legislative bodies should establish realistic guidelines to measure student outcomes of participation in dual enrollment and other forms of acceleration programs (AP/IB) with the same zeal and interest that went into the creation of the laws and regulations that helped establish these programs.

This research supports the contention that policy makers should insist that dual enrollment courses duplicate the content and academic expectations of college credit courses taught on campus by college instructors. Whether the course originates in a high school classroom, is viewed via satellite or cable hookup, or is taken online or as an Internet-based offering, dual enrollment courses generate college credits. Course credits are recorded on a transcript, backed by the reputation of an accredited institution of higher education and by a state-level higher education board of directors or department of education. The integrity of the credits earned through dual enrollment programs rests on the assurance that the fundamental requirements of college and university accreditation are acknowledged and duplicated.

High school reform has caught the attention of the media and of philanthropists, such as Bill and Melinda Gates. The Gates Foundation's efforts to establish early college high schools across the country has given further credence to the idea that students in high school may benefit from exposure to college courses before high school graduation. I believe this iteration of dual enrollment programming, if embraced more enthusiastically by school districts, community colleges, and universities, could provide a better alternative to early college entrance or credit bearing transition programs such as Advanced Placement. Although primarily aimed at troubled youth, early college high schools have the potential to benefit a broad spectrum of students and provide yet another way to build a better and smoother pathway between secondary and postsecondary education and workforce training.

Results of the logistic equations point decidedly to positive and statistically significant estimates for dual enrollment participation and persistence toward a degree by continuing enrollment in college through the end of the second year. Therefore, as dual enrollment participation positively impacted students' persistence, it likewise positively affected students' accomplishments in degree attainment at both the bachelor's and the advanced/graduate degree levels. These data lend credence to the idea that dual enrollment participation may create for students the "nest egg" effect: when students accumulate credits, it is harder to give them up. Furthermore, students who participate in dual enrollment may receive a psychological boost of confidence about their chances of college success while still within the safer confines of the high school.

The analytic sample taken from the NELS:88/2000 data provides a glimpse of the past; when dual enrollment participation was beginning to grow, but had not reached the coverage seen today. While there are definite differences in the types of program offerings labeled as dual credit courses, the results of this research support the premise that dual enrollment programming positively impacts students' abilities to persist toward the completion of postsecondary credentials. Options for students to participate in accelerated courses while remaining in high school appear to be advantageous for the long-term achievement of students in the postsecondary setting. Dual enrollment may provide a means to support students as they experiment with college and make decisions about enrollment and future academic endeavors. Dual enrollment course participation likely provides a catalyst for student success in postsecondary education.

References

Adelman, Clifford. 1999. *Answers in the Tool Box: Academic Intensity, Attendance Patterns, and Bachelor's Degree Attainment.* (PLLI1999-8021). Washington, DC: U.S. Department of Education, Office of Education Research and Improvement, National Institute on Postsecondary Education, Libraries, and Lifelong Learning.

———. 2004. *Principal Indicators of Student Academic Histories in Postsecondary Education 1972–2000.* Washington, DC: U.S. Department of Education, Office of Vocational and Adult Education.

———. 2006. *The Toolbox Revisited: Paths to Degree Completion from High School through College.* Washington, DC: U.S. Department of Education, Office of Vocational and Adult Education.

Bailey, Thomas, Katherine L. Hughes, and Melinda Mechur Karp. 2002. *What Role Can Dual Enrollment Programs Play in Easing the Transition between High School and Postsecondary Education?* New York: Teachers College, Columbia University, Community College Research Center.

Barefoot, Betsey O. 2000. "The First-Year Experience: Are We Making It Any Better?" *About Campus* 4(6): 12–18.

Bradburn, Ellen M., Rachael Berger, Xiaojie Li, Katharin Peter, and Kathryn Rooney. 2003. *A Descriptive Summary of 1999–2000 Bachelor's Degree Recipients 1 Year Later, with an Analysis of Time to Degree.* (NCES 2003-165). Washington, DC: U.S. Department of Education, National Center for Education Statistics, Institute of Education Sciences.

Casner-Lotto, Jill, and Linda Barrington. 2006. *Are They Really Ready to Work: Employer's Perspectives on the Basic Knowledge and Applied Skills of New Entrants to the 21st Century U.S. Workforce.* Washington, DC: Conference Board, Inc., Partnership for 21st Century Skills, Corporate Voices for Working Families and the Society for Human Resource Management.

College Board. 2008. *Winning the Skills Race and Strengthening America's Middle Class: An Action Agenda for Community Colleges, The Report of the National Commission on Community Colleges.*

Eimers, Mardy, and Robert Mullen. 2003. "Dual Credit and Advanced Placement: Do They Help Prepare Students for Success in College?" Paper presented at the meeting of the Association for Institutional Research, Tampa, FL.

Hanson, S. 2005. *Running Start: 2004–05 Annual Progress Report*. Olympia, WA: State of Washington, State Board for Community and Technical Colleges.

Karp, Melinda M., Juan Carlos Calcagno, Katherine L. Hughes, Dong Wook Jeong, and Thomas R. Bailey. 2008. *Dual Enrollment Students in Florida and New York City: Postsecondary Outcomes*. CCRC Brief No. 37. New York: Teachers College, Columbia University, Community College Research Center.

Kirst, Michael W., and Andrea Venezia. 2004. *From High School to College: Improving Opportunities for Success in Postsecondary Education*. San Francisco: Jossey-Bass.

Kleiner, Brian, and Laurie Lewis. 2005. *Dual Enrollment of High School Students at Postsecondary Institutions: 2002–03*. NCES 2005–008. Washington, DC: U.S. Department of Education, National Center for Education Statistics.

Lotkowski, Veronica A., Steven B. Robbins, and Richard J. Noeth. 2004. *The Role of Academic and Non-Academic Factors in Improving College Retention: ACT Policy Report*. Iowa City, IA: American College Testing, Inc.

Menzel, Mary Jean. 2006 (July). "Type III Concurrent Enrollment Program Participation Effect on Time and Cost to Baccalaureate Degree Completion." *Dissertation Abstracts International* 67(1) (UMI No. 3205232).

Napoli, Anthony R. and Paul Wortman. 2005. "A Meta-Analysis of the Impact of Academic and Social Integration on Persistence of Community College Students." Unpublished manuscript.

Nora, Amaury. 2001–2. "The Depiction of Significant Others in Tinto's 'Rites of Passage': A Reconceptualization of the Influence of Family and Community in the Persistence Process." *Journal of College Student Retention* 3(1): 41–56.

Pascarella, Ernest T., and Patrick T. Terenzini. 1980. "Predicting Freshman Persistence and Voluntary Dropout Decisions from a Theoretical Model." *Journal of Higher Education* 51(1): 60–75.

Puyear, Donald. 1998. *Concurrent and Dual Enrollment of High School Students in Arizona Community Colleges: A Status Report*. Phoenix, AZ: Arizona State Board of Directors for Community Colleges.

Spurling, Steven, and Robert Gabriner. 2002. *The Effect of Concurrent Enrollment Programs upon Student Success at City College of San Francisco*. San Francisco: City College of San Francisco, Office of Research, Planning and Grants.

Tinto, Vincent. 1975. "Dropout from Higher Education: A Theoretical Synthesis of Recent Research." *Review of Educational Research* 45(1): 89–125.

————. 1993. *Leaving College: Rethinking the Causes and Cures of Student Attrition* (2nd ed.). Chicago: Univ. of Chicago Press.

U.S. Department of Education. 2006. *A Test of Leadership: Charting the Future of U.S. Higher Education.* Washington, DC: Secretary of Education's Commission on the Future of Higher Education.

Venezia, Andrea, Patrick M. Callan, Joni E. Finney, Michael W. Kirst, and Michael D. Usdan. 2005. *The Governance Divide: A Report on a Four-State Study on Improving College Readiness and Success.* Washington, DC: National Center for Public Policy and Higher Education and Stanford Institute for Higher Education Research.

Venezia, Andrea, Michael W. Kirst, and Anthony L. Antonio. 2003. *Betraying the College Dream: How Disconnected K–12 and Postsecondary Education Systems Undermine Student Aspirations.* Palo Alto, CA: Bridge Project, Stanford Institute for Higher Education Research.

Western Interstate Commission for Higher Education (WICHE). 2006.

Accelerating Learning Options; Moving the Needle on Access and Success: A Study of State and Institutional Studies and Practices. Boulder, CO: WICHE Policy Analysis and Research Unit.

Windham, Patricia and George Perkins. 2001. "Dual Enrollment as an Acceleration Mechanism: Are Students Prepared for Subsequent Courses?" Paper presented at the meeting of the Association for Institutional Research Forum, Long Beach, CA.

Contributors | Index

Contributors

Brenda E. Abbott retired as Director of the Center for Secondary Students at Laramie County Community College in Cheyenne, Wyoming. Abbott has more than thirty-five years of experience teaching in secondary and postsecondary classrooms and managing postsecondary programs serving high school students.

Jason P. Alteri is a former doctoral student in Instructional Design, Development and Evaluation at Syracuse University. He was previously a graduate assistant for Syracuse University Project Advance.

E. J. Anderson, EdD, is Director of Community Partnerships for Rio Salado College, where she oversees the largest dual enrollment program in the state of Arizona. She also serves as the membership chair for the National Alliance of Concurrent Enrollment Partnerships (NACEP). Anderson completed her doctorate in Education Leadership at Northern Arizona University.

Brian A. Boecherer is Executive Director of the Office of Early College Programs and Director of Research and Development for UConn Early College Experience at the University of Connecticut. Boecherer is a doctoral candidate at the University of Connecticut with a focus on political trust in new democracies, law and society, and identity.

Donald H. Dutkowsky, PhD, has been Professor of Economics in the Maxwell School of Citizenship and Public Affairs at Syracuse University since 1985, and previously taught at Clarkson University. He has served as a faculty liaison in economics with Syracuse University Project Advance since 1993.

Gerald S. Edmonds, PhD, is Assistant Provost for Academic Programs at Syracuse University. He also serves as Executive Director of Project Advance and as an adjunct professor. Edmonds is the founding president of NACEP, where he served two terms. His publications include research on knowledge management, instructional design models, and change.

Jerry M. Evensky, PhD, is Professor of Economics and Laura J. and L. Douglas Meredith Professor for Teaching Excellence at Syracuse University. Evensky designed and developed the introductory economics course for Syracuse University. He has also taught economics at Hamilton College and secondary social studies in the Webster Groves (Missouri) School District.

Cynthia Grua has worked in higher education for twenty-six years. She began her career as Director of Distance Education at the University of Utah. Grua works in the Office of the Commissioner for Utah System of Higher Education coordinating the state's concurrent enrollment program, which involves over 28,500 students annually and 52% of Utah's public high school graduating class.

Susan Henderson, PhD, is past Director of Precollege Programs in the College of Continuing Education at the University of Minnesota. She led College in the Schools, the university's concurrent enrollment program from 1997 to 2013. Henderson has served on NACEP's Board of Directors and as the chair of its Research Committee.

Barbara D. Hodne, PhD, was a Senior Teaching Specialist in the Department of Postsecondary Teaching and Learning at the University of Minnesota until the department closed in 2016. She taught literature and writing in the First-Year Experience Program and served as a College in the Schools Faculty Coordinator from 2002 to 2012.

Daniel R. Judd, PhD, MPA, has a background in marketing research and evaluation. Owner of Judd Research, he is an expert in the development and implementation of monitoring systems through extensive experience designing and conducting customer satisfaction surveys for clients in both the private and public sectors.

Angela L. Kremers, EdD, is Senior Director of Corporate Strategy for a national nonprofit education technology organization. Kremers gained national attention in educational philanthropy by increasing support and collaboration for improvement in higher education college completion work and K–12 system reform.

Thomas E. Leahey began his work for the Advance College Project (ACP) at Indiana University Bloomington in 1986. Leahey has served ACP as Adjunct Instructor and English Coordinator/Site Visitor, and he retired as Associate Director in 2010. Currently Leahey is an adjunct instructor for speech at Indiana University East.

Adam I. Lowe, MPA, is Executive Director of NACEP. At the University of Indianapolis, he assisted in the launch of new high schools throughout Indiana. Lowe has previously served as an education policy consultant advising on education reform for a variety of universities, nonprofit organizations, and state and federal agencies.

Amanda L. Nolen, PhD, is Assistant Professor with Teacher Education and Educational Foundations at the University of Arkansas at Little Rock. She teaches a variety of education psychology courses and serves on the Governor's Commission to Close the Achievement Gap in Arkansas.

Carl A. Saltarelli, EdD, retired in 2013 as Assistant Professor of Radio/Television at Texas A&M University–Kingsville. For fourteen years he instructed students in television and radio courses while serving as station manager of the campus radio/television stations. Saltarelli is remembered for building a premiere hands-on learning environment for radio and television students. Saltarelli taught in higher education for twenty-eight years.

Richard Seils, PhD, is Coordinator of University Partnerships at the Educational Service Center of Central Ohio, and is a former staff member of three colleges and universities. He has also served as a public school teacher and administrator.

Tiffany M. Squires, PhD, is a specialist for Research, Evaluation, and Assessment with Syracuse University. She has fifteen years of experience in K–12 education as teacher, principal, and professional development facilitator. Squires completed her doctoral work at Syracuse University with a focus on curriculum, leadership, and standards-based reform.

Kalpana Srinivas, PhD, is Director of Retention at Syracuse University. Srinivas serves on NACEP's Research Committee and its Accreditation Review Committee. She received her doctorate from Syracuse University's School of Education in 2012.

Joni L. Swanson, PhD, is the Executive Director of Teaching and Learning for the Mount Vernon School District and chairs NACEP's Secondary Partners Committee. In 2009, Swanson was awarded the National Association of Secondary School Principals High School Dissertation Award for her research related to participation in dual enrollment programs.

George Tombaugh, EdD, is Assistant Superintendent and Client Services Representative for the Educational Service Center of Central Ohio. He is a former superintendent of the Springfield, Ohio, Schools and the Westerville Schools. Tombaugh also served as Executive Assistant for Education and Educational Policy Advisor to former Ohio Governor, Bob Taft.

Ted R. Ungricht, EdD, is Director of Concurrent Enrollment at Utah Valley University. He began his career as a school psychologist and served fourteen years in the United States Air Force. Ungricht is a founding member of both NACEP and the Utah Association of Concurrent Enrollment Partnerships.

Dennis R. Waller, EdD, is Academic Director of the Concurrent (enrollment) Credit Program and Professor of Communication Studies at Northwest Nazarene University. Waller has served as an educator or administrator for nearly thirty years with high school to university experience. He currently serves on NACEP's Board of Directors.

Julie Williams is Director of College in the Schools the University of Minnesota–Twin Cities. Williams served as Director of Communications and Evaluation for the program for seven years and led the development of educational programs in public and charter high schools for more than twenty years. Williams has also served on NACEP's Board of Directors and as chair of its Communications Committee.

Index

Italic page numbers denote illustrations and tables.